John Adams and the American Press

John Adams and the American Press

Politics and Journalism at the Birth of the Republic

by WALT BROWN

McFarland & Company, Inc., Publishers
Jefferson, North Carolina, and London

British Library Cataloguing-in-Publication data are available

Library of Congress Cataloguing-in-Publication Data

Brown, Walt.
    John Adams and the American press : politics and journalism
at the birth of the Republic / by Walt Brown.
      p. cm.
    Includes bibliographical references and index.
    ISBN 0-89950-998-3 (lib. bdg.: 50# alk. paper) ∞
    1. Adams, John, 1735–1826—Relations with journalists.
2. Press and politics—United States—History—18th century.
3. United States—Politics and government—1797–1801. I. Title.
E322.B83 1995
070.4'4997344—dc20   94-41569
                                             CIP

Manufactured in the United States of America

McFarland & Company, Inc., Publishers
  Box 611, Jefferson, North Carolina 28640

Dedicated to the memory of my parents,
Marjorie L. Brown and Walt Brown, Sr.,
and my aunt, Annie Brown

Table of Contents

Acknowledgments

The author would like to extend his heartfelt thanks to Drs. Robert F. Jones, Robert Kerby, Peter Lombardo, and Philip Gleason for their efforts and interest in this topic. A very sincere thank you belongs equally to the late Marshall Smelser.

A generic acknowledgment is also extended to the countless archivists and librarians who gave freely of their time to assist the author in finding arcane sources. This is especially true of the staffs at Duane Library at Fordham University, the Memorial Library of Notre Dame, the New York Public Library, the Library of Congress, and the National Archives.

Lastly, the words "thank you" fall well short of the author's purpose in recognizing the two Mrs. Browns in his life: the first, Marjorie L., who gave him life, and the second, Jill, who has sustained and enriched that life.

Preface

The purpose of this work is to study the interaction between John Adams and the American press during the four turbulent years of Adams's presidency. It begins with the supposition that Washington, by virtue of his "hero of the Revolution" status, was initially above press criticism as we know it today. The major question then is, "What would the press do, and how would editors react, when a person of lesser stature, physically as well as politically, became president when the 'hero' retired?" In answering that question, we shall be studying the causes, the nature, and the results of the confrontation between Adams and editors, and it is possible to see in that confrontation the underlying cause of the decline of Federalism as well as many precedents for future confrontations between the executive branch of government and the news media.

This book attempts to break fresh ground in several historical areas, while at the same time it either reinforces or challenges previously published concepts. Among new ideas, the study posits the theory that the untimely press attacks on George Washington during the latter stages of his presidency were but a prelude to genuine interaction between press and president. The years of Adams's presidency, 1797–1801, were the first full-scale, full-term confrontation between a president and the press.

Second, although Adams bore press attacks with a stoic and uncharacteristic taciturnity which was in sharp contrast to Washington, the second president was nevertheless very able to gauge public and editorial opinion and direct his policies accordingly. Whereas Washington expected continued popular adulation and held little respect for opposition viewpoints, Adams maintained a healthy suspicion of press elements on both sides of the political spectrum and tried to steer a middle course that would be acceptable to public opinion.

Third, this book will attempt to show that the transfer of the executive mansion and the control of the Congress from the Federalist party to the

Democratic-Republicans in 1801 was a direct result of the interaction between Adams and the press. The leaders of Jefferson's party and Democratic-Republican editors worked unceasingly to elect the sage of Monticello. The Sedition Act had forced Republican newspapers to fight for survival, and after 1798, a rejuvenated Republican press repeatedly presented unpopular Federalist policies to the electorate. But Republican editors did not oust Adams by themselves. They were ably abetted by a numerically weak yet surprisingly vocal minority of Federalist editors. Disgusted by Adams's 1799 peace initiative toward France and mindful of the president's independent character, "High-Federalist" editors worked as hard to unseat Adams as Republican editors worked to overturn Federalism in general. Despite attacks from both sides, Adams came within 214 popular votes of victory, a statistic which strongly suggests that Adams had, in fact, created policies acceptable to the voting public.

The last new theory presented consists of a reevaluation of Adams's character as president. From his inauguration as vice president in 1789, editors were quick to find fault with Adams's personality and mild idiosyncracies, and historians since then have for the most part accepted and reiterated contemporary editorial comment. That Adams had strong character defects cannot be doubted; yet those very traits may, in fact, have made John Adams the badly needed, middle-of-the-road leader indispensable to deal with the crises of his times. A Federalist lackey willing to follow the Hamilton-inspired party line could have had disastrous consequences for the fledgling republic, just as a Democratic-Republican, hewing to the Jefferson party platform and overly sympathetic to France, could have done equal if not worse damage to America's position. But Adams could not be bought by praise nor budged by intimidation from either Federalists or Republicans, and his strong stand in the face of the French threat aroused a martial spirit among the populace that caused militarily superior enemies to back down, thus preventing a war. In that way, Adams's much maligned character proved a valuable asset in the closing days of the eighteenth century.

Several previously published concepts helped to provide the building blocks for this book. One cannot but agree with historians who have seen the Federalist period as an extremely tumultuous age in which political passion and inflamed rhetoric were key factors. Agreement is also found with authors whose works mentioned, although usually only in passing, the significance of "gazettes" in the Federalist era. That significance, as an index of political and journalistic maturity of the infant nation, cannot be overlooked.

On the other hand, one must strongly disagree with published works which have consistently pictured the Founding Fathers as dignified aristocrats who, with the help of Providence, worked toward a more perfect union. At times, they were bitter, petty individuals operating solely on the principle of self-preservation.

Other historical conclusions inevitably must come under scrutiny. George Washington's most recent multivolume biographer, James Thomas Flexner, saw his subject as the president who suffered most from newspapers. Dumas Malone, in volume five of *Jefferson and His Time*, arrived at the same conclusion regarding his subject. This book does not claim that Adams suffered more than all other presidents. It does, however, make a strong case that Adams suffered at least as much, if not more, than his predecessor and successor, but his suffering was largely overlooked because of attention focused on the founders of the republic who bracketed him in the presidency. The point also needs to be made that many other presidents have received hostile, or worse, reviews from an unsympathetic press. Few presidents indeed have escaped scathing attack, and perhaps the brevity of William Henry Harrison's and James Garfield's terms, along with the political calm of at least some of James Monroe's and Calvin Coolidge's terms, makes them the exceptions. Only one president, however, could be the first to face the press for his full term. Washington's exalted status prevented him from filling that role, and Adams, his successor, inherited it and became the first president to meet the press.

This book also questions the widely accepted idea of the "Revolution of 1800." Although the Federalists were stripped of their power in Congress as a result of the election of 1800, the presidential contest was far too close to call it a revolution. Power did change hands, but only as a result of a very close election which was really decided by an ever-so-thin margin of 214 popular votes for Jefferson in New York City.

Essentially, this book deals with three eminent Americans and one nebulously defined interest group, each of which should command the reader's attention. The three Americans, along with their retinues, followers, and lackeys, left a marvelous roadmap of political tradition, the signposts of which they discovered only as they reached them on their respective journeys. The fourth entity, "the general public," followed those signposts and delivered the United States to where it is as a nation today.

The initial historical curiosity is, of course, George Washington, who performed enough presidential "firsts" in his two terms to monopolize a good chapter or two in any *Guinness Book of World Records*. First to be elected and reelected (the only president to be elected unanimously both times), first and only president to appoint an entire Supreme Court, first to give an inaugural address, first to sign or veto a law, first to create a cabinet; in sum, first to fill a position unique in the world of 1789. Most importantly, perhaps, Washington was the first of a half dozen or so American heroes, a few of whom were ultimately elected president.

The second historical curiosity is John Adams, the first man to discover how meaningless the job of vice president can be, except that as a vice president under a national hero, he quickly became the target for newspaper editors who wanted to audition their newly won First Amendment guarantees of free speech, which they took literally. Adams's firsts included his unintended participation in two hotly contested vice presidential elections, as well as his involvement in the first hard-fought presidential election. He was the first nonhero president, but he was given a journalistic honeymoon by the same editorial wolves who bayed under Washington's windows at the end of his term. Adams was the first president who had to agonize over a decision whether to engage America in a major foreign war, and he was the first to opt for a mutually profitable negotiated settlement rather than for bloody battlefields. For those efforts, he was the first president to be voted out of office, undone politically by an unlikely coalition of his enemies and his quondam friends.

The third and final individual who rounds out the portrait of the Federalist years is Thomas Jefferson, who was the first man in the modern era to wrest power away from a political opponent and to do so without violence before or during the act, and without recourse to a purge following the taking of power. He was also the first president to realize that not all the situations he had criticized as an outsider were necessarily solvable as an insider and that extremely unpopular decisions, like the embargo, must sometimes be made.

In sum, we have three talented individuals who served as president and therefore became the focus of journalistic praise or abuse: the first, a land-owning Virginia general of modest intelligence whose greatest pre-electoral claim to fame was that he kept his army in existence while the government controlling the opposing army lost its will to confront revolutionaries on the other side of a massive ocean. As president, he was relatively free from criticism until certain policies promulgated with a view to the greater good jeopardized certain interest groups, who let their displeasures find expression in the venom-heavy newspaper columns aimed directly at the well-meaning first president.

The second man, a brilliant yet thin-skinned lawyer from Massachusetts, had relatively modest political stature for attempting to take the place of his predecessor and found himself repeatedly in trouble with editors on both sides of the political spectrum when he had to choose between peace and war. He ultimately made the right choice, but he pleased nobody in the political or editorial community and was run out of town for his efforts.

The third individual was such a truly talented man that when President John F. Kennedy once entertained at dinner a gathering of some of America's greatest minds he joked that the only previous time that so much talent had been assembled around a table in the White House was "when President Jefferson dined alone." Jefferson, as we shall see, led in a gentlemanly way the political opposition to his two predecessors, and that shall be the concern here, as Jefferson's real problems began in a time frame which extends beyond the scope of this study.

The fourth historical curiosity, "the general public," requires considerably more brushstrokes to capture on historical canvas. They were the ultimate political arbiters on election day, as well as being the reading public whose choice of which newspaper to read and which to ignore ultimately spelled success or failure for the editors appearing in the text. We can perhaps generalize about John and Jane Colonist here, and not in the chapters that follow, because unfortunately they did not leave us enough of the source materials on which histories such as this are woven.

We do know a great deal about them, and what we do know will help us to understand the subtitle, *Politics and Journalism at the Birth of the Republic*. The editors provided the journalism, but it was citizens who elected the political luminaries.

First and foremost, those citizens were descendants of survivors: gritty, hard-working artisans, mechanics, farmers, preachers, and teachers to whom rote toil was a way of life and luxuries we take for granted were wholly unknown. Many of their ancestors had come to this land as refugees from the Crown's religious, fiscal, landholding, and judicial policies, and half of them died from starvation, the elements, or from the understandable hostility of the indigenous population. The survivors, however, persevered and, with precious little support from the mother country, turned the wilderness into a going concern within a few generations.

By the 1760s those descendants had grown to maturity, and "king and country" were dim memories to which they paid little more than lip service. At the end of England's great war for empire, they were told they would have to pay taxes, not lip service, and once again became servants to the collective laws known as the Navigation Acts. The colonists thus found themselves in the position of adults who have matured on their own but are now treated as disobedient children by a parent once again eager to control them.

And they would not hear of it. Their independent spirit and innate grit propelled them (not all, but enough of them) toward a rebellion which rid them of the king and his ministers, and good riddance. But that was only half the solution, as the void created by the American Revolution was filled by opportunistic souls who always seem to appear when the situation is characterized by chaos. Out of that void came the Constitution, a document less widely hailed by the citizenry than by its notable creators. In fact, it took a series of promises known to us as the Bill of Rights to pacify an

anxious population that they had not spilled their blood only to have one
bad government replace another one.

That anxiety came of age in the Federalist era. The common man and
the common woman saw one George replaced by another, and one
bicameral legislature replaced by something which looked quite similar.
The taxes that had originated in London and led to such unpleasantness
as the Boston Tea Party were now revisited upon the population, except
they emanated from New York, Philadelphia, and ultimately, the new
Federal City. Those hard-working folks that had secured independence
thought that they had won independence from taxation, laws, tariffs, and
politicians in general, and they were quite naturally disappointed when
their naïveté became obvious. That disappointment manifested itself in
the rage and editorial rhetoric which fill the pages that follow.

In this great experiment, nobody, not even the leaders, knew exactly
what the future held. And the common people were concerned about the
present. Very concerned. So they read much of the drivel that appeared
in contemporary newspapers and pamphlets and listened to the orators
that shouted the loudest. Ultimately, they voted to replace John Adams
with a president who would have just as many problems but twice as long
to solve them.

We are thus presented with three major concerns in the pages that
follow. First, the interaction between president and press will be scrutinized, beginning with the closing days of Washington's terms, but focusing
on, and culminating in, a microscopic scrutiny of the whole four years,
from day one to the last day of John Adams's term.

Second, it is the intent of this book to make reasonable inroads into
the dearth of worthwhile materials on John Adams. Few indeed are the
members of the American political tradition who have had less written
about them; Adams's shelf currently holds one definitive biography, a
handful of monographs on minutiae, and several edited collections of
writings and diaries. While this volume will not suddenly elevate Adams
to the biographical plane his talents merit, the author hopes it will provide
an incentive for others to pursue similar monographic studies and bring
a talented and overlooked president into the historical mainstream.

Finally, the author hopes that by providing a brief history of the
Federalist era and its journalism, necessary background material about
Washington and the press, information about the character and modus
operandi of John Adams, and a microscopic sectioning of Adams's presidency with regard to the press, he will encourage the general reader as well
as the scholar to discover the internal workings of the Federalist era, a truly
fascinating twelve years in which America perfected a heretofore very
shaky experiment.

The author must here add two cautions. First, given the huge corpus of source material concerning the cast of characters, it is ironic that objective historians are only now bringing into focus the complete works of some of the individuals who appear in the pages to follow. Others have had smaller collections edited and published, often by relatives with such subjectivity that lineage has tended to obscure accuracy. It has thus been the author's goal to separate historical justification from truth in the published collections.

Newspapers of the period are also in many cases equally unreliable as source material for the truth because that was not their purpose. Adams once commented to the effect that newspapers would be out of their element if they aimed at truth. Nevertheless, hundreds of newspapers will appear in the text, primarily because citizens who lived during the hectic conclusion of the eighteenth century took newspapers seriously as partisan politics developed, and what was believed may have equal or greater value to our investigation than what was true. It is not the author's intent that the reader should believe every snippet from America's inchoate journalistic corps.

Lastly, what of the author's bias? Is it possible to pore through thousands of documents and penetrate the psyche of a long-dead political leader with 100 percent objectivity? Probably not. The author confesses to an admiration for Adams's courage in doing what he thought was right, and I would think most people would at least grudgingly respect a man who takes such an action and says, "And to hell with politics!" Such an assessment is reflected by Leonard Baker, in his biography of John Marshall:

> If possible, John Adams would solve America's problems by peaceful means.... To an American that lived by the musket his position was not a popular one, and Adams' insistence on peace if at all possible destroyed him politically; he did not win re-election to the presidency and his reputation was tarnished for many years. Still, if he lost a moment's glory, he gained the satisfaction of knowing that no lands were ravaged by his command, no families destroyed, no young men killed to solve a problem that was solvable by other means. And also if he lost the adulation of the majority at that time, he gained a position in history as one who demonstrated—for those courageous enough to see beyond the pressures of the time—that the peacemakers are indeed blessed.

CHAPTER ONE

The Federal Era I:
Passion and Invective,
1789–1797

*The public and the papers have been much occupied
lately in placing us in a position of opposition to each
other. I trust with confidence that less of it has been felt
by ourselves personally.*
—Jefferson to Adams, December 28, 1796

George Washington saw the last ten years of his life as "an age of
Wonders." John Adams, less prone to being elliptical than his predecessor,
nevertheless relied on a double entendre in viewing the brief Federalist
ascendancy as "the Age of Paine."[1] Twentieth-century historians, echoing
Washington, Adams, and many of their contemporaries, have stressed the
hysteria and rhetoric of the times. Thus the years 1789 through 1801 have
been portrayed as "an Age of Passion," "an era of invective," and an "Age
of Rage."[2] In addition to being a "lusty, brawling age," it was also an "age
of precedent making," and passion, as a chemical agent in the precedent-
making process, became all the more volatile, thereby giving even greater
animation to the era.[3]

John C. Miller states that "Having been conceived in crisis, the
Federalist party depended for its continuance in power upon some com-
pelling public emergency."[4] Gaillard Hunt sees the friction between the
rival parties of the Federalist era as second in intensity only to the frictions
which consumed the nation in the years between 1850 and 1865. Richard
Hofstadter seems to dissent when he characterizes the issues of the day as
"overdramatized," yet he is merely proving the point at issue: that the relationship between Adams and the press stemmed directly from the passion,
rage, invective, and overdramatization of the times. When trivial molehills

9

were refracted through the prevailing temperaments of the era and became mountains, the infant American political establishment quaked.[5]

Add those kinds of situations to the common practices of name-calling, of seeing evil lurking behind Washington's willingness to follow Hamilton's lead, and of repeated yet petty threats of disunion when states or their political leaders did not get their every wish, and you have plumbed the nether regions of American politics in the Federalist era.

Name-calling certainly predates recorded history, so the first generation of American political leaders under the newly established Constitution cannot claim to have invented this practice, nor did it cease in the years after 1801. The practice, however, was so well developed during the Federalist years that Thomas Cooper at one time proposed putting a revenue duty on nicknames and political labels.[6]

Pennsylvania Republican representatives found levity in the proposal to give a title to President Washington and mockingly addressed each other as "Your Highness of the House." The tables were later turned when Federalist Uriah Tracy of Connecticut inquired of House Speaker Jonathan Dayton if it was in order to insult Pennsylvania Congressman Albert Gallatin. When the question was decided in the affirmative, Tracy and John Allen, also of Connecticut, opened fire on Gallatin.[7]

Each political faction found derogatory names for the other. The Federalists were labeled aristocrats, Tories, monocrats, or the British party. As Treasury Secretary Alexander Hamilton's British-oriented revenue policies became known, Patrick Henry wrote of Federalism: "It has an awful squinting! It squints at Monarchy!" Soon the "slaves of monarchy," having visited the president's house on Washington's birthday, were attacked in print for celebrating "the natal days of their tyrants."[8]

Hamilton's financial program gave the inchoate Republicans additional vocabulary with which to flay the Federalists, who were derided as "Paper-Hunters," "Hamilton's Rangers," "the order of the Leech," "their Rapacities," "the six per cent myrmidons," and, in a phrase attributed to Jefferson, "the corrupt squadron of paper dealers."[9] Later, John Adams's term as president was seen as "the reign of terror," and American naval tars were derided as "John Adams's jackasses."[10]

Federalists felt that their party was the exclusive preserve for anyone calling himself a gentleman, but they did not hesitate to lower their standards and abuse those they considered their inferiors.[11] The opposition were labeled Jacobins, to equate them with French sans-culottes. The gentlemen Federalists then outdid themselves to invent derogatory phrases to refer to Jacobins: "frog-eating, man-eating, blood drinking cannibals," "gallic jackals," "demons of sedition," or "refuse of nations." Even the staid Martha Washington, finding a grease spot on the wallpaper, noted that it probably implied "the presence of a 'filthy Democrat.'"[12] John Rutledge, Jr., commenting on a Democratic-Republican dinner, noted: "Here you saw an American disorganiser & there a blundering Irishman—in one corner a banished Genevan [Gallatin] & in another a French Spye."[13] Lacking specifics, the Federalists never hesitated to invoke the help of the clergy, the "black regiment," because "one of the most effective ways of running down a democrat was to call him an atheist."[14] Jacobins in general were stigmatized as "modern Goths" whose aim was "the overthrow of whatever good exists."[15]

Individuals fared as badly as parties. The prime target among non-presidential Federalists was Alexander Hamilton. He was constantly referred to as an "adulterer" following the Reynolds affair, and he was called a "creole" because of his West Indian birth. Republican editor Philip Freneau commented openly on Hamilton's "bastardy."[16] Modern historians have called the first treasury secretary "Remote Controller Hamilton" and noted that "He was born of an irregular relation, without the intervention of the clergy."[17] John Adams, writing to friends, called Hamilton "a bastard brat of a Scotch pedlar" and "that Scottish Creole," and he passed along a rumor that Hamilton used opium.[18]

Timothy Pickering, a cabinet member under Washington and Adams, was suspected of being a devotee of Hamilton. He was referred to as "the man Timothy" and "the fanatic of the Federalist party," and he was considered a reasonable candidate to be sent to a "mad house." Tom Paine wrote, "Of all the clowns that ever were intrusted to write public dispatches, he is the worst."[19]

Republican Senator Maclay saw Federalist Gouverneur Morris as "half pimp, half envoy," while Harrison Gray Otis was "the man with more than one shirt," a reference to Otis's caustic comment about Albert Gallatin having come to America with only the shirt on his back. Gallatin in turn called Abigail Adams "Mrs. President not of the United States, but of a faction." Jefferson believed Attorney General Edmund Randolph to be a political chameleon who changed colors to please Washington. Secretary of War Knox and his wife, Brobdingnagian in size, were the constant butt of fat jokes, while an unnamed Federalist pamphleteer's work was written off as "The Brayings of Hamilton's Young JACK-ASS!"[20]

Democratic-Republicans received equal abuse. Jefferson was the constant target, and his detractors seemed to grow even larger in number whenever they sniffed ballots or the gratis liquor which announced an election. As to general traits, Jefferson was attacked on the grounds of selfishness and was seen as the puppeteer behind much of the Democratic-Republican litany of falsehoods and calumnies. He was also accused of turning blacks into "tertium quids," with a status in the limbo between man and "Oran-outangs."[21]

Treasury Secretary Oliver Wolcott believed Pennsylvania Republicans McKean and Dallas "to be as vile as Porcupine [editor William Cobbett] represents them." George Logan was hailed with derision as "Jefferson's Envoy," "America's Jacobin Minister to France," and a "poor addled cat's paw."[22]

John Randolph, "the scourge of Federalism," suffered for his high-pitched voice and baby face which convinced Federalists that he was a physical neuter. John Beckley, "an indefatigable scandalmonger," lost his job for his politics, but repaid the Federalists in later years. Apart from the abuse Jefferson suffered, the man most often targeted was Matthew Lyon, Republican congressman from New England. Cobbett, alias "Porcupine," called him "This infamous and beastly wretch." Later, seeking Lyon's expulsion from Congress, the Federalists asked: "Was he not a coarse-grained half educated Irish clown?"[23]

Finally, name-calling knew no bounds. Gouverneur Morris in Paris saw the Girondins as a "set of damned rascals," and a Federalist pamphlet compared revolutionary France to a host of mythological demons.[24] These statements were but typical examples of political thinking of the times; many others, equally biting, could be cited.

The second key theme which had a great bearing on the politics of the Federalist era was the political affinity between Washington and Hamilton, and that relationship brought Washington into a political arena already characterized by name-calling. It was further exacerbated by Hamilton's willingness to attempt to manipulate Washington for his own purposes, and the practice continued until December 1799, when Washington's death severed the link and had deleterious overall effects on the weakening Federalist party.

There is a historiographical consensus that Hamilton, considering himself "prime minister" under Washington, combined a disdain for public opinion with an occasional monopoly on Washington's attention to push through measures dealing with the Treasury Department as well as the War and State departments.[25] Hugh Henry Brackenridge, a classmate of Madison's and Freneau's at Princeton and a Whiskey Rebellion moderate, asserted: "The excise law is a branch of the funding system, which is a child of the secretary of the treasury; who is considered as the minister of the President."[26]

When Hamilton left his post as secretary of the treasury to return to his law practice, he left office but not power. He continued to exert a vast influence over Washington, the cabinet, and legislative leaders, and would continue to exert this influence when Washington retired. Primarily, Hamilton and his minions were quick to exploit Washington's name for political mileage. "At the outset [of party factionalism] the charisma of Washington was a key ingredient, . . . [and Washington's foreign policy] was Hamilton's foreign policy. . . . But Washington was essential to the system."[27] The always acerbic Senator Maclay wrote in his journal that he wished Washington were in heaven, because "We would not then have him brought forward as the constant cover to every unconstitutional and ir-republican act."[28]

The issue of the pro–British Jay's Treaty showed the Washington-Hamilton connection in its most brilliant hues. The issue became focused in 1794, when Washington's mind, according to biographer James Flexner, was weakening, and therefore he placed additional trust in Hamilton. The standard interpretation of the Jay mission is that Hamilton was passed over because the nation at large and certain political interest groups lacked confidence in him. Alexander DeConde believes, however, that Hamilton was kept at home because the Federalists badly needed his influence in dealing with Washington.[29] Once Jay's Treaty came up for ratification, Washington's name and reputation were the primary Federalist arguments in favor of ratification, but as James Callender noted, Washington's weakening state of mind made Hamilton "the real president."[30]

After Washington's retirement, Callender's contemporaries continued to note Hamilton's past and present influence. Benjamin Rush congratulated Jefferson on his election to the vice presidency, and his escape from "the New York administration of our government." One newspaper noted a confession of adultery by Hamilton and called him "this Ex–Prime Minister of America." Wolcott wrote to Hamilton for advice to give Adams on the first three-man mission to France, concluding "either nothing will be done or your opinion will prevail." George Gibbs, editor of the Wolcott papers, has high praise for Hamilton's fine work in constructing the 1798 army. On the other hand, John Adams, upset because his appointments to the general staff were rejected, wrote, "But I was only viceroy under Washington, and he was only viceroy under Hamilton, and Hamilton was viceroy under the Tories as you call them, and Peter Muhlenburg was not appointed."[31]

Finally, the threat of disunion provided another common denominator, as it clearly demonstrated the tenuous, parochial nature of the infant union and served as the last potential resort for inflamed tempers, which were often contained within small political minds.

Disunion existed, in fact, when Washington was sworn in as president because Rhode Island and North Carolina had not yet joined the union. In addition, geography in the western regions of some states and territories dictated a different way of life which made separatist tendencies a de facto reality that was easier to consider.[32]

The first crisis which threatened disunion was Washington's serious illness in early 1790. Abigail Adams, in noting this in a letter to her sister, wrote that her husband sought no promotion and that the union might dissolve if Washington was suddenly removed from the helm.[33] When Washington's health improved, disunion rhetoric was set aside. It was reconsidered soon after, however, when Hamilton sought a cure for the nation's financial ills. Secessionist talk again appeared when Hamilton's plan for the assumption of state debts was threatened by Southern intransigence. Assumption passed, but a similar North-South split (South Carolina favoring the North) developed over proposed commercial retaliation against Great Britain in 1794. Jay's Treaty again exacerbated existing tensions. Washington feared that the moment of choice had arrived between "order and good government" or "anarchy and confusion." The *Aurora* reported that Virginia would depart from the Union with the ratification of Jay's Treaty and asked, "If this detestable instrument is enforced, may we not anticipate the speedy dissolution of the Union?" Wolcott, writing to Hamilton, indicated he believed these threats of southern secession.[35]

William Loughton Smith, a staunch Federalist, recoiled at the possibility that Jefferson would be elected in 1796. Smith warned that "Disunion would not long lag behind." Other Federalists feared that the French were trying to divide America, and as the Federalists supported the creation of a navy to protect American commerce, they created an agrarian backlash which was willing to consider disunion. "Pelham," an unknown polemicist writing on slavery, spoke of disunion as the only way to preserve the sacred principles embedded in the Constitution.[36]

"Centinel," writing in Bache's *Aurora*, feared "discord, disunion, and ruin" after Adams's message about the XYZ affair. That prompted comment from Abigail Adams predicting a civil war if editor Bache was not suppressed. George Clinton also predicted civil war at about the same time.[37]

In 1799, William B. Giles of Virginia was quoted as being in favor of disunion. "Porcupine" urged speedy enlistment of army regiments, or else "a *civil war,* or a *Surrender of Independence,* is not at more than a twelve month's distance."[38] With the election of Jefferson in 1800, New England spinsters were cautioned to hide their Bibles, but the Bible, like the union, was guaranteed a lasting permanence.

During both of Washington's terms, passion and invective were woven into the vast majority of the important issues as well as into some incredibly trivial incidents that showcase the leaders of the age in their most rhetorical moments. These occasional excesses frequently involved "statesmen" in actions which included hysteria, paranoia, mobism, and vigilantism. There is in fact a surfeit in each category.

Washington was feted and hailed by an admiring populace on his journey from Mount Vernon to New York, the first national capital, and this patriotic symbolism tended to mask the economic problems which lingered from the days of the Articles of Confederation. Although Washington's triumphant procession seemed a national outpouring, it occurred at an hour of low ebb in American economics: each state had its own currency, and each state discounted other states' notes. It was also a time when few citizens bothered to vote, even for a Washington.[39]

Upon arriving in New York City, Washington delivered an inaugural address noted for its "solemnity." At the same time, uncertain of his own abilities and desiring advice, he created the institution of the cabinet.[40]

The issue of titles for elected leaders distracted Congress in its first session and did little more than produce a few petty nicknames and generate some doggerel. Jefferson correctly concluded that "Washington needed no title that he did not already have."[41]

But while the titles issue was etched in comic relief, Hamilton's economic program was looked upon as harsh economic reality. Because the location of the permanent national capital had not yet been decided, several states were willing to exert themselves to house the proposed federal city. Some states were even willing to provide votes for Hamilton's economic program in return for some logrolling regarding the national capital. Philadelphians were rumored to be ready to offer their beds, wives, and daughters to congressmen if they would locate the capital there permanently. A bargain was eventually struck between Hamilton and Jefferson, to the latter's regret, and the seat of government was moved adjacent to Virginia while it was in its final building stages in 1800. Hamilton's national bank proposal faced rough sledding; an agrarian spokesman "declared that he would no more be seen entering a bank than a house of ill-fame."[42] The bank was disliked simply for what it was, but also for what it could represent. It was attacked as an engine of "*Consolidation*, that many headed monster of power."[43]

Political factions were relatively weak at the outset of Washington's first term, but events guaranteed the growth of those factions. When Washington began to consider retirement after one term, Jefferson implored him: "The confidence of the whole union is centered in you. . . . North & South will hang together, if they have you to hang on."[44] Despite this pledge from the seeming opposition leader, there was trouble brewing beneath the surface, much of it directed at Adams, a dissenter from American enthusiasm for the French Revolution. This marked the beginning of Adams's reign as executive scapegoat for editors who continued to consider Washington sacrosanct.

To do his part in promoting factionalism, Hamilton wrote as "Metellus" in Fenno's *Gazette* to attack Jefferson, and press attacks on Jefferson were certainly strong reasons for his resignation from the State Department. Hamilton, in turn, was by no means spared by Philip Freneau, and it was eventually suggested that Freneau change the name of his sheet from the *National Gazette* to the *Anti-National Gazette*.[45]

Hamilton was attacked for the excise law, seemingly the work of "an aristocratic junto," as economics and the spreading stain of the French Revolution seemed to divide the developing factions. Freneau bitterly lamented: "Can those, who are attached to Monarch and Aristocracy, be, in their hearts, friends to such a republican constitution?" Hamilton fought back with such vigor that Jefferson complained to Washington, concluding, in defense of an opposition press: "No government ought to be without censors; and where the press is free, no one ever will."[46]

In the midst of the developing newspaper war, the election of 1792 began to loom large, increasing the existing press scurrility. Hamilton wrote under a series of aliases and singled out Jefferson as the leader of the opposition. Gibbs's *Memoirs* shows how Wolcott and some contemporaries believed Jefferson to be everything Hamilton said, while in fact Jefferson merely attempted to channel a moderate program through Madison in the House of Representatives. Nevertheless, "The greatest pleasure of all, for both Jefferson and Hamilton, consisted in censuring the other."[47]

Washington regretted that his name was used for electioneering purposes, but Adams, in retrospect, caught the flavor of the 1792 canvass more accurately: "Cabal, intrigue, manouvre [sic], as bad as any species of corruption, we have already seen in our elections; and when and where will they stop?"[48] Ballot box stuffing entered the American political scene at least as early as the 1792 election; one newspaper suggested an efficiency award for citizens of Mifflin County, Pennsylvania, where Federalists garnered 2,065 votes in a district of 1,100 qualified voters.[49]

Organization of the government and economic recovery had been the key features of Washington's first term, but the comparative calm of those four years, certainly the most quiet of the twelve years of the Federalist ascendancy, was shattered quite early in Washington's second term by events in Europe.

Many of the excesses of democracy generated by the French Revolution seemed stamped "for export to America," the only port where they would even be considered without the threat of French armies. Americans adopted the terms *Citizen* and *Citizeness* to address each other, and when liberty caps appeared and were not saluted, it led to "instant unpleasantness."[50] But the most menacing new household word, at least in Federalist households, was *guillotine*. Newspaper accounts told of lurid scenes in which Francophiles made very ghoulish yet effective use of miniature guillotines at fraternal feasts, dropping the tiny blades as contemptuous hints to Federalists that aristocratic American heads would soon roll. Federalists reacted as if they had become an endangered species.[51]

When Americans learned that Louis XVI had been sent to the guillotine, Hugh Henry Brackenridge wrote "LOUIS CAPET has lost his Caput." Freneau printed the article, and it was copied widely by Democratic-Republican sheets unsympathetic to royalty. Since Americans had missed the event, Louis XVI was guillotined in effigy several times daily for months in Philadelphia and elsewhere. To commemorate the monarch's passing, a Philadelphia theater company revived *Cato* and the actors sang "La Marseillaise" before the curtain nightly.[52]

France went to war with England in 1793 and in the same year exported a most combustible commodity to America in the person of Edmund Charles Genet, first minister to America from the Republic of France. Genet arrived aboard *L'Embuscade* at Charleston on April 8. However, as one editorial wag noted, "Fishes being unable to cheer or vote," Genet continued his journey to Philadelphia overland, accepting ovations all the way. His dilatory traveling had a high price, however, as between Genet's arrivals in Charleston and Philadelphia, President Washington issued the Proclamation of Neutrality, transforming the crowds along Genet's path from ready allies to sympathetic neutrals.

Genet's trip north has been described as "roses all the way," and his reception in Philadelphia exhibited much the same enthusiasm. The size of the crowd depended on the observer's politics: Hamilton estimated 600; Jefferson guessed 1,000; Genet boasted of 6,000. Sympathetic newspapers led by Freneau's *National Gazette* poured out encomiums. The main gala was held at Oeller's Hotel in Philadelphia on June 1, where Genet proposed toasts, acted the part of the parvenu diplomat, and sang songs, all in the same hall where Federalist John Marshall would be feted five years later in an anti–French outburst.[53]

Suspicious Federalists thought that Genet's arrival marked the beginnings of a "pro–French conspiracy" bent upon subverting America. The Federalists viewed the Jacobin societies, the Whiskey Rebellion, the influx of foreigners, and the growth of atheism as all woven from the same cloth, imprinted "Made in France." As a later American president commented on the Federalists' view of the Jacobin frenzy, "A spectre of tyranny stalked always somewhere in their forecasts of the future and in all their uneasy criticism of the present."[54]

Genet's arrival in America and his subsequent behavior, combined with public and editorial reaction, created a situation best diagnosed as hysteria. *L'Embuscade* challenged the British frigate *Boston* off Sandy Hook, New Jersey, on August 1, 1793. Businesses closed, a volume of cash was bet, and spectators sat in the tops of ships and on the beach to observe the spectacle. Bostonians celebrating the French Revolution raised a fund to free all prisoners in the town jail. In Philadelphia, "Bands of half-drunken Republicans paraded the streets, denounced neutrality, damned Washington, and threatened to make the Government declare war on England."[55] John Adams later wrote that Genet's "terrorism," abetted by Republican editors, caused rioting and created mobs of 10,000 which threatened to drag Washington from his house and effect a revolution.

Only the appearance of yellow fever, a regular event in Philadelphia in hot weather, Adams concluded, kept Washington safe and America out of war.[56]

Passion and hysteria proved Genet's undoing. Madison, a seeming ally, saw him as "a madman" and termed his behavior "dreadful." Jefferson wrote of "the addle-brained diplomat who has become raving mad." With his former friends turned against him, Genet became the French resident gadfly in America. After petitioning Congress for cannon and being told that he would not be given a pistol, Genet conceived a desperate plan to appeal for help over Washington's head to the American people. While the appeal itself might well have been a Federalist scam, it was believed at the time and was instrumental in Genet's recall.[57]

Once Genet's future was decided, two maladies stalked America. The first was yellow fever, "a more fearful enemy than monarchy or revolution." Hundreds of Philadelphians died at home, in the streets, and in hospitals. Looting of empty houses was commonplace, and nurses were so scarce that prostitutes were pressed into service in a Philadelphia charity hospital, a measure that quickly transformed the wards into a bordello.[58]

The second malady was Anglophobia and was more national in scope. English sailors in port became the target of French sailors or American mobs, while New England Federalists busied themselves trying to divert attention from the anti–British animosity by printing a rumor that Washington had been assassinated. Adams, commenting on the growing agitation, wrote of the "intemperate ardor of the people out of doors." Congress passed the subsequent winter in futility. Federalists feared that anti–British feeling would spark a war, so they provided an outlet for militarism by reporting a bill allowing privateering against the Algerine pirates, who had virtually no seagoing commerce. This led to a suggestion that a glass dome be put on the congressional meeting place, to "throw a better light on their proceedings."[59] Beyond this, Anglophobia manifested itself in congressional resolutions aimed at commerce with Britain that were proposed by Madison and opposed by William Loughton Smith, speaking for Hamilton. Smith was burned in effigy for his efforts. The infant navy also came under attack, with Madison going so far as to propose that America hire the Portuguese navy rather than construct its own navy. His colleague Giles saw navies as "very foolish things."[60]

While Congress was debating naval armament, tempers flared in the interior of the country over the issue of taxation of whiskey. Not only were alcoholic potables present at every social event from elections to funerals, they were the circulating medium in many areas of the backcountry, especially western Pennsylvania. The federal government, short of both revenue and ideas about how to obtain it, laid an excise tax on whiskey, causing a minor rebellion in several western counties of Pennsylvania.

Those who paid the tax found their stills or barns destroyed. The mails were pilfered, government officials were stripped, seared with hot irons, or tarred and feathered. Strangers were suspected as government spies. Nativist rhetoric, plus use of terms like "disunion" and "guillotine," spiced the conversation of the region.[61]

The Federal government, mindful of Shays's Rebellion, overreacted and dispatched several thousand troops under the command of Henry Lee to the inflamed frontier. Alexander Hamilton, the personification of the excise, unwisely accompanied the army. The troops managed to consume many of the spirits in question, committed acts of "thievery and wanton destruction," and rounded up 150 insurgents who were paraded through Philadelphia in shackles. After several months in jail, two of that number were convicted, but they were subsequently pardoned by Washington. The number of arrested insurgents would have been higher, but many young ladies of the backcountry padded their midsections to appear pregnant in an attempt to mitigate the charges against their lovers.[62]

Washington's leniency toward the convicted rebels is in sharp contrast to his outburst against the "Democratic Societies," which he saw behind the conspiracy. Washington wrote to Henry Lee, "I consider this insurrection as the first *formidable* fruit of the Democratic Societies."[63]

Those societies began in March 1793 in Philadelphia and grew to a total of 41 societies during the next 18 months. Some societies were involved in the Whiskey affair, while others answered the government call for troops. All of them were subject, however, to the vicious Federalist counterattack touched off in Washington's letters and in his "self-created Societies" message to Congress. Federalists boycotted Democratic-Republican merchants, formed countersocieties, and looked the other way or participated when unfriendly editors were beaten.[64]

Hamilton's successor in the Treasury, Oliver Wolcott, believed stronger measures were needed. Washington fumed against the societies, under "their diabolical leader Gt [Genet]," for their ignorance of the government's effort in behalf of the people "or from a wish to bring it, as much as they are able, into discredit."[65] Federalists again suspected "Made in France," but they refused to realize or believe that ongoing collaboration between the British and Native Americans on the frontier was part of the overall tension of backcountry Pennsylvania. In any case, Jay's Treaty, Pinckney's Treaty, and the French "reign of terror" did more to kill the Democratic Societies than Washington's rhetoric and Federalist chicanery. The societies left little behind, save a collection of pious declamations and a system for dating all correspondence from the Declaration of Independence, in true French fashion.[66]

Before the issue of John Jay and his treaty arose, all outbursts of passion "were by comparison mere musketry skirmishing. The fire directed upon John Jay was heavy cannonading."[67] As soon as Jay's nomination was announced, he was guillotined and burned in effigy in Lexington, Kentucky. The effigy, oddly enough, held a copy of Adams's *Defence of the American Constitutions*. Adams thought he knew why: "You cannot imagine what horror some persons are in, lest peace should continue. The prospect of peace throws them into distress."[68]

Jay's Treaty received Democratic-Republican villification, as well as a host of alternate names. Jeffersonians called it the "Grenville Treaty," while Jefferson himself called it an "execrable thing." Historians are willing to call it "Hamilton's Treaty," and Jefferson agreed, painting Hamilton as "a rogue of a pilot" who steered America "into an enemy's port." Other historians are content to call Jay's results "the most humiliating treaty" or "the most detestable treaty that America had ever signed."[69]

When the treaty arrived in America, Washington kept it secret and Adams refused to discuss it, even with Abigail.[70] Benjamin Franklin Bache, however, procured a copy from Senator Stevens Thomson Mason, of Virginia, in what may well be America's first political leak. Bache was only too eager to share his discovery and rage with the public, printing the treaty and barnstorming through cities distributing it. "Jay became in a day the most unpopular man of America." Insulting Jay and Britain now became Republican dogma, primarily because the treaty had the potential to clear up the Anglo-American problems which French sympathizers counted on as a *casus belli*.[71]

John Jay, to use a twentieth-century phrase, wound up standing in front of the fan. A toast proclaimed, "John Jay, may he enjoy all the benefits of purgatory." Punsters satisfied themselves with allusions to "Jay-birds" and "King-birds," playing on the names of Jay and Rufus King, American minister to Britain. An antitreaty Republican mob routed light-horse cavalry sent to put them down, in an event that has come down to us as "Morell's defeat." Morell's sword was mockingly sold for four cents. The treaty was burned on Jay's steps and on British minister George Hammond's steps; the latter's windows were also smashed. Hamilton was pelted with stones in New York while defending the treaty; Jay was hanged in effigy by a Philadelphia mob that was exhorted by Blair McClenachan to "kick this damn treaty to hell!"[72]

Jay was even accused of having written George III's 1794 speech from the throne, but Federalists looked on the accusers as an "ignorant mob." Boston citizens, nominally Federalist, voted down the treaty by a vote of 1500 to 0 and shortly thereafter, burned a British merchantman to the waterline as a suspected privateer. Jay was burned in effigy in Boston on July 4, even though, as one biased editor admits, "It was certainly an awkward task to oppose a treaty without knowing a word it contained."[73]

Some citizens actually read Bache's reprints of the treaty, while others acted on rumor and suspicion. In Boston, Robert Treat Paine's fence was treated to a spirited coat of graffiti: "Damn John Jay! Damn everyone that won't damn John Jay! Damn everyone that won't put lights in his windows and sit up all night damning John Jay!!!" A Boston newspaper likened America's shift from sympathy for the French to Jay's Treaty by concluding: "We are taken from the embraces of a loving wife, and find ourselves in the arms of a detestable and abandoned whore, covered with crimes, rottenness and corruption."[74]

In Virginia, there was "mobism and vigilantism" on both sides of the political fence, but antitreaty poetry took the prize for coarseness:

> I think J-y's treaty is truly a farce,
> Fit only to wipe the national ----.[75]

Further south, a South Carolina assembly lamented the absence of the guillotine as a remedy for Jay.[76]

Despite the antitreaty demonstrations, which Washington saw "as useless as they are *at all times*, improper and dangerous," the president expected ratification. Toward that end, Fisher Ames contributed a bit of "superlative demagogy" (which probably changed no votes) when he passionately warned of the dangers of rejecting the treaty: "You are a father: the blood of your sons shall fatten your corn field! You are a mother: the war-whoop shall wake the sleep of the cradle! . . . It is a spectacle of horror which cannot be overdrawn." John Adams gauged the immediate reaction of the listeners: "Not a dry eye, I believe, in the House, except some of the jackasses who had occasioned the necessity of the oratory."[77]

One Republican, William Findley, left the Senate chamber as the ratification vote was taken, explaining that he had to ship a trunk. When the vote passed 20–10, the barest possible two-thirds majority, one editor wished aloud that the trunk had been Findley's casket. Delaware citizens divided; some wanted to burn Jay and the 20 ratifiers in effigy, others wanted to do it in person. One Democratic Society eschewed an effigy burning but added, "If the original were here---!"[78]

The seeds of the Jay's Treaty hysteria produced a bitter harvest. Edmund Randolph, "of all high-ranking officers of government . . . [the] most severely damaged by the passions of the age," resigned in an unmerited disgrace.[79] John Rutledge, nominated as chief justice of the Supreme Court, made a strong antitreaty speech in which he reportedly hoped Washington would die rather than sign the treaty. Federalists accused him of insanity, and his nomination was rejected.[80] Republicans got a measure of revenge when they blocked an adjournment vote in the House on February 22 to allow members to call on Washington on his birthday. Federalists bolted and went anyhow.[81]

The ratification of Jay's Treaty, which should have lessened the decibel level of rhetoric when it became a fait accompli, only led to renewed outbursts of passion. For some, it was the perfect pretext to return to the days of flaying Hamiltonian finance. Fisher Ames saw much of the noise as Republican efforts to scratch Jay as a future presidential candidate or simply "to disorganize." Virginians circulated four resolves to limit governmental power, but there was little reaction.[82] Adams and the elder Wolcott each happily believed that the treaty furor would keep Washington as president for a third term, but that was not to be. Jay believed that neither calumny nor eloquence "can make it [the treaty] worse or better than it is." The treaty, however, did help the American economy. Between 1795 and 1801, imports from Britain rose from $23,313,000 to $39,519,000 and exports to Britain rose from $6,324,000 to a whopping $30,931,000. The Republicans mistakenly tried to ride the treaty into the presidency, yet "Perhaps John Adams was only speaking the truth when he described his inauguration as Washington's triumph rather than his own."[83]

The hysteria generated by Jay's Treaty never spent itself completely, as many of the issues generated became factors in the 1796 canvass. Gilbert Chinard has written: "In violence and scurrility the campaign of 1796–1797 has hardly been surpassed in the history of American politics."[84] It was, in fact, far surpassed four years later. The Jeffersonians tried to make political gains at Washington's expense during the controversies regarding ratification and appropriations for Jay's Treaty. Their assaults on Washington, conceived by John Beckley and put into operation by Edward Livingston, led to a backlash of public opinion which the Federalists exploited with counterpetitions.[85]

Federalists had, in fact, lost some Southern support due to the Yazoo frauds in Georgia. Washington was also unable to keep a Southerner in his cabinet because Southern political ideology became suspect as Washington leaned more toward purely Federalist policies. Philadelphia editor Bache wrote in early 1796 that the patriotic Jefferson was the obvious choice to succeed Washington, but this was not the beginning of the campaign, because back then, with limited suffrage, backwoods apathy, and issues badly clouded by the intensity of the competing rhetoric, it was only a real election campaign to a handful of deeply involved participants.[86]

The Republicans spent much of 1796 skirmishing for support with their Jay's Treaty strategy, yet lost much time waiting to make sure that Washington was not planning to stand for reelection. Adams noted a sudden lull in abuse from Bache, adding that he, Adams, knew of Washington's plans to retire as early as March of 1796. Yet Adams remained unconvinced, believing that the Jay crisis might prevent Washington's departure, and Federalists tried to convince Washington of the crisis to keep him in office.[87]

The key document in the 1796 campaign was Washington's Farewell Address, which was withheld until mid–September, either because of the crisis atmosphere or in an attempt to prevent campaigning until just before the electors met. The document itself was strikingly partisan.[88]

The main issue in the fall of 1796 was the Anglo-French war, and party lines could clearly be drawn around the personalities of Adams and Jefferson on that issue. The personal popularity of the candidates also proved to be a very important factor, and polemics were aimed at personalities. Neither candidate campaigned, although both were strongly abused. Federalists feared the lodging of power in the majority, while Jefferson feared it lodged anywhere else. Both candidates were attacked on differing religious grounds, while Adams was attacked for some of the high costs of his predecessor.[89]

The French, through their minister, Pierre Adet, tried to influence public opinion and regional voting habits. "Washington must go" was the theme of French meddling, which had some minor short-term successes, but proved, in the long view, a catastrophic failure. Nathaniel Ames noted in November 1796, "The Prigarchy straining every nerve to carry election," although the primary Federalist goal was to keep Jefferson out. A few Federalists, certainly with Hamilton's blessing, were willing to keep Adams as vice president under Thomas Pinckney. Others supported Adams, fearing a president elected by "a negro representation only."[91]

Adams was barely elected, with Jefferson finishing a close second, making him vice president. Jefferson then made conciliatory gestures to Adams, reminding him of old times when the two men worked as close friends and emphasizing that he was not aware of public gossip: "Pamphlets I see never: papers but a few, and the fewer the happier." Jefferson also tried to warn Adams of New York (Hamiltonian) intrigues concerning the election. The vice president–elect also sent letters to non–Federalist confidants which tend to prove that he was genuinely glad he escaped the presidency because he expected the bubble to burst.[92]

What can be said of the partisan passions, rhetoric, and frenzy that occurred during the two presidential terms of George Washington? Primarily, the passionate outbursts of Washington's terms were ad hoc and developed slowly at first, only gaining intensity after 1793, when it seemed inevitable that a successor would be found for Washington. That they were pretty, bitter, vindictive, and slanderous and that Washington was for the most part undeserving of them are two truths that emerge from all the rhetorical rubble. Most importantly, however, it must be kept in mind that these outbursts of passion were but a prelude to the real "age of passion," John Adams's four years as president.

CHAPTER TWO

The Federal Era II:
Passion and Invective,
1797–1801

*At Philadelphia, A Frenchman has been apprehended,
and is now in prison, for uttering treasonable expres-
sions. His words were "that in six months Adams's head
would be off, and Jefferson would be President."*
—*Farmer's Weekly Museum* (Walpole, N.H., July 10,
  1798)

Washington's first inauguration had occurred at a time when the national temperament was reasonably serene. Passions and rhetoric were
generated slowly at first, in reaction to specific domestic and foreign policies. They continued and intensified throughout Washington's second term.

In contrast to Washington's first inauguration, John Adams was
sworn in during a crisis. For one thing, Adams was not Washington, so
some individuals immediately feared for the safety of the union. Second,
Adams was sworn in at the same time that Americans learned that France
had refused to receive Charles Cotesworth Pinckney as minister plenipotentiary. Third, the election of 1796 had been an impetus to the growth
of parties, which began to take on lives of their own, and the growth of
those parties and the outbursts of rhetoric of individuals and newspaper
editors became a fixture of American political life.

This chapter will illustrate the nature and volume of the frenzy and
invective of Adams's presidency. Subsequent chapters will also study
Adams's term, but the focus there will be limited to the political analysis
of the interplay between Adams and the press, while the focus here will be
on the crisis atmosphere of Adams's term as it laid the groundwork for the
confrontation between president and press.

Shortly after the inauguration, Wolcott strongly warned Adams of "a dangerous French influence." Still seeing himself as prime minister, Hamilton provided Adams a list of legislative suggestions, but the president was horrified: "I read it very deliberately, and really thought the man was in delerium [sic]." Once the calm of Adams's political honeymoon was ended, he was given the name "President by *three votes*" by the enraged Bache, who also accused Adams of trying to "*gasconade* like a bully, and to swagger as if he were the emperor of all the Russias." Federalists rushed to defend their newly found militaristic president, while Bache was fuming that the cost of three weeks of congressional debate to answer Adams's May 16 message to Congress cost $21,000. In Boston, the admonition was printed: "Fellow citizens! Fear a WASHINGTON, an ADAMS, or a HAMILTON, but never be afraid of ... THE PEOPLE."[1]

Passions heated by the whiskey excise, Jay's Treaty, the election of 1796, and other events discussed above slowly came to a boil in 1797 and continued to boil for four years. Jefferson noted how old friends crossed the street to avoid meeting each other, and towns began to divide: "There were Republican taverns and Federalist taverns; Republicans salons and Federalist salons." In addition, "The very ties of blood were sundered by the bitterness of the strife."[2]

James Monroe, recently returned from his diplomatic station in Paris, was the target of heavy Federalist fire at this time. Adams called Monroe's house in Paris "a school for scandal." An editorial wag provided "A PUN *for* Politicians — *not for the Ladies*" when he claimed Monroe's successes in France resulted from his "readiness to kiss their *Bar-as*!!" [a reference to French diplomat Barras]. Monroe was also accused of embezzling funds and then faking a robbery to cover it. He was charged as well with "inconstancy, infidelity, and ingratitude." Much of this attack developed because Monroe had weakened Jay's position in England and because he had been feted by Republicans at Oeller's Hotel in Philadelphia when he returned to America. Monroe wrote to vindicate his conduct, which prompted sharp, negative comment regarding that conduct from Washington. James Callender earned a measure of revenge for the attacks upon Monroe by printing a pamphlet detailing Hamilton's sordid infidelities with the Reynolds family.[3]

The remainder of 1797 featured a wait-and-see attitude, as Adams had sent John Marshall and Elbridge Gerry to join the repudiated Charles Cotesworth Pinckney in Europe. Federalist newspapers and politicians, now joined by ex-president Washington, lambasted the French, their sympathizers, and their allegedly subservient American editors. Bache, in particular, was threatened with imprisonment as early as September 1797 to show him that the government was not lacking energy.[4]

On the other hand, 1798 was the year of hysteria in early American history. It began with one political and one diplomatic charade and concluded with character assassination, armament, and overall shabby politics previously unknown in America.

The incident of the "spitting Lyon" had elements of the comic and the tragic. Very early in 1798, Congressman Roger Griswold made some untoward remarks about Matthew Lyon's "wooden sword," a reference to a period in Lyon's military career when his self-preservation instincts overrode his customary courage. Lyon overreacted to Griswold's abuse and spat in his face. Griswold later snuck up behind Lyon in Congress and caned him; the two then tussled on the floor of Congress. Spectators enjoyed the combat briefly, then separated the combatants, who later made for each other out-of-doors. Federalists then had an oratorical field day at Lyon's expense. Otis exclaimed that Lyon's behavior "would not be suffered in a brothel or in a den of robbers." It was suffered in Congress, however, as a vote to expel Lyon failed. Otis also suggested that Lyon be made ambassador to Kamchatka, "where he would be at home among the furred tribes." Abigail Adams wrote of "the beastly transported Lyon" and "the spitting animal." Newspapers referred to Lyon as "the knight of the wooden sword" and demanded his ouster.[5]

Subsequent to the passage of the Alien and Sedition Acts, Lyon was arrested, given a trial which included a one-hour jury deliberation, and was convicted of sedition against the president. He was then jailed in a dungeon 40 miles from his trial site, where he conducted his campaign for reelection to Congress, which he won by a vote of 4,576 to 2,444. As soon as he was released from jail, he announced that he was on his way to Philadelphia to take his seat in Congress, which provided immunity from further legal entanglements. The procession that followed him to Philadelphia at one time reached a length of 12 miles. Federalists, who should have learned from the example of John Wilkes, an English political martyr reelected to the House of Commons while in jail, were forced to content themselves with needling Lyon with the taunt that he needed the $6 per day congressional salary to pay his fine. Lyon's friends exacted a measure of revenge by girdling the apple trees of those who had testified against Lyon.[6]

Prior to and during the time that Lyon and his Federalist foes were making news, the American commissioners in Paris were being treated to a bit of commonplace, old-world diplomacy, as the French Directory played into Federalist hands by putting a price tag on French friendship. America, however, was too far removed, both physically and philosophically, to be interested in the purchase.[7] French foreign minister Charles Talleyrand, having no fear of a nation which took three years to debate three frigates, authorized three male agents, later coded by Americans as X, Y, and Z, and a female intermediary, W, later described as "undoubtedly the organ of the Executive Directory," to seek a bribe and a loan from the American commissioners prior to negotiations. Marshall and Pinckney refused, asked for their passports, and departed. Elbridge Gerry remained behind long enough to gauge Talleyrand's temper and to enrage many a Federalist temper.[8]

The coded dispatches of Marshall, Pinckney, and Gerry began arriving in America in early 1798, but they were withheld pending translation and the departure of the envoys from France. Rumors of the contents, however, were leaked exclusively to Federalists: Hamilton, a private citizen, knew the contents of the papers, while Vice President Jefferson did not. Democratic-Republicans rashly led a call for the publication of the papers and were happily seconded by better-informed Federalists who knew that publication would produce an uproar. They were not disappointed, as "The publication by congress of all the [XYZ] papers was like the falling of a spark into a powder magazine."[9]

Adams may have desired war after reading the dispatches of the disgraceful French opéra bouffe, but he hesitated at a time when Wolcott wanted only "firmness, consistency, and temper in the Executive." Northern Federalists, like Wolcott, had always wanted war with France, but the XYZ affair awakened lethargic southern Federalists. Primarily, the twice-humbled Pinckney was a Southerner. Second, the threat of war created a panic in the defenseless South, and this panic was compounded by the growing fear among Southerners that their slaves might behave in an untoward manner in the event of war. Commercial areas also reacted strongly, as "Marine insurance jumped 10 per cent overnight."[10]

Republican editors tried to divorce X, Y, and Z from Talleyrand, picturing the envoys as dupes, but Federalists were in control of the situation. Washington castigated contumacious editors, and his words were far more influential than the yelpings of biased journalists.[11]

John Marshall returned home aboard the ship *Alexander Hamilton* in June 1798. Traveling overland to Philadelphia, he was met by a throng six miles away from the city and was feted at Oeller's, where Federalists drank a toast to each of the 16 states. The thirteenth toast, which was soon translated into more flamboyant rhetoric, became Federalist dogma: "Millions for defense, but not one cent for tribute." The Jeffersonians, however, saw it as "Millions to Pitt, but not a cent to Talleyrand!" In truth, Americans up to that time had been tighter with their defense dollars than with their tribute. Republicans quickly cited the Algerine tribute as proof of that. In any case, Marshall's welcome proved that correctness in politics was better than success in diplomacy.[12]

Elbridge Gerry had remained in Paris, under threats of war by Talleyrand, and at this point Gerry replaced Lyon as the Federalists' enfant terrible. They sent anonymous letters to Mrs. Gerry suggesting that a mistress, not Talleyrand, was keeping Gerry in Paris. Effigies, obscenities, bonfires, and a blood-smeared guillotine near Gerry's house reinforced the poison-pen campaign. Pickering hoped the French would guillotine Gerry as a favor to the United States because an act that dastardly perpetrated against an American minister would surely launch the war against France that the Federalists craved. But Gerry was spared, and upon his return, he was ostracized by the Federalists (except Adams), his movements were watched, and his mail was tampered with. Pickering accused him of "*duplicity* and *treachery*," Washington accused him of being "led astray by his own vanity and self-importance," and subsequent historians accused him of being "received with open arms by the opposition."[13]

The XYZ affair had its effects. It was made into a play, "The Politicians; or, A State of Things." More importantly, it marked the beginning of the climax of the age of rage and served to cripple opposition and stifle criticism because "it produced an explosion which almost blew away the First Amendment."[14]

The year 1798 has been styled the "reign of terror in the United States," but even that is a vast oversimplification. First, the crisis had been building for several years. Ordinary anxieties, fed by mutual suspicion, conjured up intrigues and conspiracies everywhere: "It became almost normal to consider opposition as seditious and, in extraordinary cases, as treasonable."[15] Second, Federalism began sliding toward senility at a tender age. Federalists identified France with their opposition party and considered French democracy "merely a way station on the way to the Inferno." The Federalists saw themselves as the "only true American party," and their latent nativism blossomed in hysterical xenophobia. Harrison Gray Otis exclaimed: "I do not wish to invite hordes of wild Irishmen, nor the turbulent and disorderly of all parts of the world, to come here with a view to disturb our tranquility, after having succeeded in the overthrow of their own governments." Washington had expressed these sentiments earlier, and contemporary pamphleteers echoed them.[16]

As events fed the hysteria, they created "social paranoia," and "repressive legislation seemed the only sure defense." The Naturalization Act extended American citizenship requirements, but failed to prevent immigrants from becoming state citizens, as even Talleyrand had done in Pennsylvania earlier in the decade. Thus newly arrived aliens voted Republican despite Federalist legislative roadblocks. In addition, "The Alien Act was expected to do much toward working a reformation in the press" because foreigners seemed to get one whiff of printers' ink and become loyal Jeffersonians.[17]

Federalists believed they needed the Alien Friends Act. Washington wrote of treasonable letters passing between congressmen and the Directory and feared "confusion and anarchy," while Adams believed "French spies swarmed in our Cities." The law "established the concept of guilt by suspicion," and although it was never used, boatloads of Frenchmen left America contemporaneously with the passage of the act, "indicating that their consciences at least, were guilty."[18] An Alien Enemies Act was also enacted, but this was a Republican bill, and inoperative except in war, which explains its lack of use.[19]

Before examining the Federalist legislative outburst that resulted in the Sedition Act, it is worth taking the pulse of an anti–French political malady called "black cockade fever." (The black cockade was a legal insignia, at times associated with army uniforms, so it lent itself easily to the program of Federalist patriotism.) At Harvard, "cockade fever" caused the cancellation of a French oration at commencement, and it spread southward with rumors of French Negro agents stirring up a slave revolt. In Philadelphia, children played the game of Frenchmen and Americans, while newspapers warned "ARM! or STARVE!"[20] Adams's visits to the theater now occasioned more excitement than the plays, and the French revolutionary song "Ça Ira" was replaced by "Adams and Liberty" and "Hail Columbia!" Talleyrand replaced Jay and Gerry in burning effigies, and the clergy, fearing French deism, lined up with the Federalists. A New Hampshire chaplain lost his job by praying for the success of French armies, and Ebenezer Bradford was denied a pulpit in Essex County, Connecticut, for favoring Jefferson and democracy.[21]

Subsequent events kept the cauldron boiling. Adams received enthusiastic petitions of support and answered them in the strongest language of patriotism. A paper wrote of "PUBLIC SPIRIT," describing a procession of 1,200 young men who called on Adams. Threats were sent that Philadelphia would be torched on May 9, 1798, a day of fasting proclaimed by Adams. Bache's *Aurora* did not mark the fast day because Adams allegedly had no constitutional authority to proclaim it. One wag who did not mark the fast noted: "I am not of the opinion that in *Adams' fall*, we sinned all."[22]

The president's family, with Abigail in the vanguard, looked to a law to suppress criticism of the president. It was the press, however, which clamored the longest and loudest about internal foes. One sheet bluntly reported: "He that is not for us, is against us," while another claimed, "It is *Patriotism* to write in favour of our government—it is Sedition to write against it." What was needed was "a bill for punishing DISORGANIZERS, whether aliens or citizens."[23]

Adams asserted, "This country never appeared to me to be in greater danger than at this moment." Federalist editor William Cobbett warned Philadelphians to "Take care; or, when your blood runs down the gutters, don't say you were not forewarned of the danger." A New England sheet warned: "LOOK OUT! French white-men and Negroes creeping into our

seaports!" One paper claimed that an "internal faction" of "horrid, out-
landish sans-culotte Frenchmen" was aiming at "discord and confusion";
another feared that virtuous daughters would become "the concubines of
the Illuminati."[24]

Americans were told of the civilian murders and other atrocities in-
flicted by a French army in Suabia. French intrigue and agents were a constant theme, as was slave rebellion: "Take care, take care, you sleepy
southern fools. Your negroes will probably be your masters this day twelve
month." Artisans were warned that "The noisy hum of industry will no
more be heard among us—the hammer rests on the anvil, and the axe lies
rusting in the earth." A soldier, writing a letter signed "INVASION," gave
military tips in case a French army showed up.[25]

Jefferson was musically greeted with "The Rogue's March" beneath
his windows, while excitable Federalists predicted bonfires for the writings
of Paine, Bache, and others. Bache, although spared the bonfire, was frequently assaulted. Other wary Federalists discovered a "tailor plot," where
80 people were making French military uniforms ordered by Toussaint
L'Overture in Haiti. Federalists swore the French would create a directory
of Jefferson, Madison, Monroe, and Burr and were equally sure that the
South was gravely threatened by elements of this plot. It was reported in
Philadelphia that a Frenchman had been jailed for saying that "in six
months Adams's head would be off, and Jefferson would be President."[26]

In the summer of 1798, Jefferson went home to Monticello, a retreat
that indicated a temporary Republican demoralization almost bordering
on an eclipse.[27] Jefferson's departure was timely, however, as it was again
fever season in Philadelphia, where "The streets of the city stank with
refuse and litter, fish offal, rotting vegetables, and animal excrement."
Thieves again held sway, robbing houses, shops, and the Bank of Pennsylvania, while convicts in the local prison attempted several escapes.
Adams's action in donating $500 anonymously to alleviate the fever-
induced suffering was in sharp contrast to the image that Republican editors were presenting of him.[28]

But even deadly yellow fever could not match political cockade fever.
The black cockade, now public domain as well as a legal insignia, was "a
badge by which the friends of government & of their country man to distinguish themselves." Thirty French cockades were burned, but a New
York paper offered a $50 reward for the capture of the "assassin-like crea-
tures" who were mugging the wearers of the American cockade. Frenchmen had their cockades torn off in Boston, while in Norwich, Connecticut,
a group of brazen Jacobins received "Federal discipline." One Jacobin
wore a cockade fashioned with cow dung and Federalists urged other
Jacobins to follow suit. One Federalist newspaper happily noted: "In
Georgia and South Carolina, scarce a Jacobin can be found."[29]

The best that Republicans could hope to do was muster levity and hope to ride out the storm with their party intact. "Cockaderophobia" was lampooned by Republican editors, who also spread the rumor that a Frenchman was jailed in Philadelphia "for mentioning the *president's head* and *guillotine* in the same sentence!" It was further passed around that a man was arrested "for calling the President's dog a son of a b---h, but for want of sufficient proof was discharged!" Republicans fearfully construed treason under the Sedition Act as laughing at the cut of a legislator's coat or giving board to Frenchmen, a worse sin. Bache, in an "ADVERTISE-MENT EXTRAORDINARY" announced the formation of a "THINK-ING CLUB" to meet at "the sign of the *Muzzle in Gag* Street ... N.B. No member will be permitted to think longer than fifteen minutes." The *Aurora* also conceded that "opposition to a good government was deplorable," but "so was support of a bad one."[30]

Federalists joyfully awaited Bache's arrest. Republicans looked to the same treatment for William "Porcupine" Cobbett and saw treason as a willingness to violate the Constitution and punish free speech. Bache, after his arrest, which predated the Sedition Act, wrote: "In Turkey, the voice of the government is the law, and there it is called *despotism*. Here the voice of government is likewise the law and here it is called *liberty*." "Liberty poles" echoed these sentiments. The Sedition Act became law on July 14, 1798, and William and Mary students reacted by burning President Adams in effigy. Congress adjourned and fled the fever, while an editor boasted "WHAT CONGRESS HAVE DONE: They have checked Sedition by providing punishment of Slander: And, they have said to the rebellious alien, depart ye cursed."[31] The reign of terror was nearing its peak.

Republican demoralization, evidenced by Jefferson's semiretirement at Monticello, had given the Federalists the legislative clout they needed to put through the Alien and Sedition Acts. The passage of those legislative measures convinced the Federalists that they could go ahead with what amounted to a strengthen-America campaign, and the provisional army was the most immediate result of that thinking. The army had been created on paper in the weeks after the XYZ affair, but it was not until after the Sedition Act was passed that America learned "General WASHING-TON commands!! HARK! the DRUM beats to arms!" Although he would be little more than a figurehead in an army actually commanded by Hamilton, Washington devoted much time and ink to convincing friends and subordinates that officers must be sound in their politics and "proper and fit men."[32] Adams shared this suspicion of politically misguided generals, although he did try to nomimate some Democratic-Republicans.[33] Despite differing philosophies on appointing Republicans, Adams and Washington agreed that southern Federalists should play an important role in the new army. Washington seemed to draw heavily on members of the Order of the Cincinnati in the South, demonstrating that the army existed for influence-peddling as well as for defense.[34]

The army was voted and staffing and manning begun, all in the absence of any genuine French threat. The lack of danger, plus the "Federalist only" stamp on the officer corps, made the army an instant object of attack from several quarters. One newspaper was founded by Philadelphia Republicans specifically to make public the atrocities committed by the troops. John Randolph called the army a set of "ragamuffins" and was attacked in the theater for his rhetoric. Even Federalist John Allen referred to the army as "so miserable a looking set of men" in the midst of an attack on the *Aurora* on the floor of Congress. Charles Holt, editor of the New London *Bee*, was arrested under the Sedition Act for anti–Hamilton remarks tied to the army because he had expressed the fear that the youth of America would learn to "eat, drink, and play with girls" in the army of "the adulterous Commander." George Clinton saw armies as "not only expensive but dangerous to the liberties of the state."[35] With an army in being and no French enemy to face, Hamilton had thoughts about annexing parts of South America or reforming recalcitrant southern states along lines of Federalism. Washington drew the line at allowing those plans, while Adams dismissed them as being as visionary as "an excursion to the moon in a car drawn by geese."[36]

Washington wanted no show of strength in South America, although he did look to strong measures at home, particularly regarding "all secret enemies to the peace and happiness of this country." So, with Washington's blessing, the Federalists put the army on hold and began to use the enforcement machinery of the Sedition Act. Although neither Adams nor Hamilton had pushed for the measure, their often intemperate rhetoric created the atmosphere in which the law was passed and enforced, and although the High-Federalists cried "self-preservation," the enforcement "almost amount[ed] to a massacre of saints by saints."[37]

If we accept the postulate of constitutional law scholar Leonard Levy that "Freedom of the press, like chastity, was either 'absolute' or did not exist," then it did not exist in America from 1798 to 1801. A handful of arrests was made, either under the vaguely defined common law or the Sedition Act itself. The trials, "political medicine shows," featured partial judges and juries so packed that James Callender faced a twelve-man Federalist jury during his trial in Virginia.[38]

Because the Republican press had become less active during the XYZ backlash and because the Sedition Act covered the president, but not his vice president, it meant that Jefferson's abusers were not subject to prosecution. Therefore the number of arrests actually made under the Sedition Act was small. Although small numbers were involved, the ludicrous nature of the trials, the reasons behind the arrests, and the severity of some of the penalties blew the issue all out of proportion. Anthony Haswell served two months and was fined $200 for advertising a lottery to pay Matthew Lyon's fine and for suggesting that Adams appointed Tories. David Frothingham, an $8 per week printer in New York, was sentenced to four months, fined $100, and required to post $2,000 bond. His conviction stemmed from an article accusing Hamilton of trying to buy the *Aurora* to silence it. Jedediah Peck, founder of the New York public school system, was arrested for circulating a petition to repeal the Sedition Act, although his case was dropped. The *Boston Independent Chronicle* defended the Virginia and Kentucky Resolutions, and its printer was jailed. William Durell was arrested two years after his paper went bankrupt and was convicted, but he was pardoned. David Brown erected a liberty pole, an "emblem of sedition," in Dedham, Massachusetts, and was jailed for two years. Two requests for a pardon from Adams were ignored. Brown's codefendant spent six hours in jail and was fined $15.50. The proceedings were such that "The gullet of Gargantua was not wide enough to swallow such hideous absurdities."[39]

The Republicans countered with the Virignia and Kentucky Resolutions, fully as extreme as the legislation they attempted to counter. Madison and Jefferson were among the prime movers in the attempt, but it was the lodging of authority, and to a lesser extent the substance of law, that they questioned.

Several issues arise here. First, there was no clearly established consensus about the exact nature of the guarantees of liberty provided by either the First Amendment or by any of the other nine. Leonard Levy, calling the Bill of Rights "a lucky political accident," has argued that "One searches in vain for a definition of any of the First Amendment freedoms in the rhetorical effusions of George Clinton, Elbridge Gerry, Patrick Henry, Thomas Jefferson, Richard Henry Lee, Luther Martin, George Mason, Spencer Roane, Melancton Smith, and other advocates of a Bill of Rights." Levy concludes: "We do not know what the First Amendment's freedom of speech-and-press clause meant to the men who drafted and ratified it at the time they did so."[40]

Second, both Jefferson and Madison saw the Sedition Act as a frontal assault on the doctrine of states' rights. Walter Berns, in "Freedom of the Press and the Alien and Sedition Laws: A Reappraisal," contends that Jefferson, as well as Edward Livingston, Nathaniel Macon, and other Republicans who opposed the Sedition Act, based their opposition not on "a broad 'libertarian' understanding of the principle of freedom of expression," but rather on "the doctrine of states' rights." Berns adds: "They [Republicans] were not contending for free speech and press; they were contending for states' rights, for the right of the states to punish seditious libel." There is a wealth of evidence that Jefferson, Madison, and other

Republicans did not object to the principle of state laws dealing with seditious libel, and Leonard Levy has argued that Jefferson was later willing to use federal machinery to punish sedition in the name of the common law in areas where Federalists controlled the state machinery. Madison, sharing Jefferson's states' rights orientation, was also inclined to a strong freedom of the press stand on the basis of the First Amendment. According to his biographer, Irving Brant, Madison wrote under the nom de plume "Republican" in Freneau's *National Gazette*, concluding "Liberty disdains to persecute." Brant adds that "the constitutional mandate engineered by him [Madison]" had made freedom of opinion absolute. Yet even Madison admitted that calumny "might receive its punishment in the State courts." Similarly, Jefferson, according to Levy, "never protested against the substantive law of seditious libel, not even during the Sedition Act controversy."[41]

Irving Brant, reflecting upon the failure of the Virginia and Kentucky Resolutions, sees them as "propaganda." A Federalist editor dissented, however, and wrote of the resolutions as "Fruits of French Diplomatic Skill." Jefferson was disheartened by the failure of the resolutions because he feared the Alien and Sedition Acts were the thin edge of an unconstitutional wedge which would redirect state power into federal hands. Jefferson summarized this belief in a letter to Stevens Thomson Mason: "For my own part, I consider those [Alien and Sedition] laws as merely an experiment on the American mind, to see how far it will bear an avowed violation of the Constitution." Madison also did yeoman service in the cause of the resolutions by his ability to tone down the rhetoric of Jefferson's original protest, which pointed toward the subsequent theory of nullification.[42]

Just as the Federalist legislative juggernaut seemed to be slowing down, George Logan, Philadelphia Republican and pacifist, gave the Federalists yet another dead horse to flay. Logan, "unwilling that peace should be forfeited for want of the efforts of a man of good will," sailed for France on a do-it-yourself peace junket on June 13, 1798. In August, Washington questioned the wisdom of the effort, and Adams expressed similar doubts in November. By December, Robert Goodloe Harper was calling the mission an attempt to lay plans for a French invasion, but Logan did manage to talk with French leaders and did learn of their newly found willingness to negotiate with America.[43] When Logan returned home, he found that it had been easier to obtain an audience with French leaders than it would be to get a fair hearing from ruling Federalists. Washington treated him with contempt, while editor Cobbett lamented the scarcity of "addled eggs" to greet Logan's return. Nathaniel Ames, Republican brother of Federalist Fisher Ames, correctly gauged the situation when he wrote that the real problem was that this particular diplomatic initiative redounded to the credit of Jefferson, Logan, and Republicans, not "the President with all his tiptoe envoys." Logan did make a small contribution to peace and a larger one to the legislation of the period. On January 17, 1799, the "Logan Act" passed in the House of Representatives by a vote of 58 to 36, and it was signed by President Adams on January 30. The law, which is still on the books, makes it illegal for private citizens to engage in diplomacy. In effect, they could not work for peace, although they could continue to work for war.[44] While Washington had little further comment on Logan or his act, his letters of late 1798 were continued endorsements of the Alien and Sedition Acts.[45]

After the numerous contretemps of 1798, 1799 was a year of comic relief. Aside from Adams's nomination of yet another set of envoys, it seemed for a time as if national figures were either no longer taking things seriously or were taking them too seriously. In February, a riot termed "SHOCKING OUTRAGE" typical of "ALIEN ENORMITIES" occurred in a Philadelphia churchyard when several Irishmen petitioned for repeal of the Alien Act while services were in progress.[46] In the same month, Adams nominated William Vans Murray to go to France, and Federalists made the ludicrous suggestion that Rufus King, then minister to Great Britain, be sent instead of Murray. Adams threatened to resign if the Federalists blocked the nomination of Murray, and in truth, the Federalists would have been happy had the episode ended "in failure or disgrace."[47]

In the winter of 1798-1799, Adams found himself in yet another role-reversal when his renewed peace efforts caused him to be abused by the same mobs which menaced Washington in the time of Genet, a group which had been, by and large, silent, amenable, or stifled during the height of the 1798 reign of terror.

Rumors concerning Adams during this period varied from the sublime to the ridiculous. Following congressional adjournment, Adams headed for Braintree, but it was said that he had emptied the treasury and was on his way to Canada. It was also whispered about that Adams intended to marry his son to the daughter of George III but that this was prevented when Washington threatened Adams with murder.[48]

The most ludicrous example of Federalist suspicion found its expression in the "tubs plot" of early 1799. Federalists were convinced that foreign agents were arriving at Charleston with secret papers containing plans for an insurrection, and they were even sure that the papers in question were concealed in the bottom of tubs. Federalist newspapers indicted and convicted the alleged plotters before the truth became known. Republicans answered with rumors that the secret papers were billets-doux, brought over by a woman bearing a newborn child, who, it was hinted, was the only tangible result of the first three-man mission to France. In general, Republicans were content to laugh aloud that the whole rhubarb was founded on a "false bottom." As Alexander DeConde has shown, Federalists' suspicions were totally unfounded because the accused individuals were in fact enemies of the French Directory en route to Santo Domingo to aid the anti–French uprising in progress there.[49] The tubs plot was followed by another small upheaval in Pennsylvania, as German hausfrauen poured hot water on tax collectors sizing up windows and houses for the purposes of taxation. The women's alleged ringleader, John Fries, was arrested and convicted of treason. He was sentenced to death but was pardoned by Adams.[50]

Adams received a letter in May 1799 containing an anonymous assassination threat, and he noted that if it was incumbent upon him to satisfy all parties hurt by the French, "I believe Mr. Assassin may do his work."[51] At the same time, the Federalist Sedition Act show-trials continued, with Holt, Peck, and John Daly Burk of the New York *Time Piece* providing the Republicans with political martyrs each worth their weight in ballots. The final and most hapless victim of this legislative paranoia, however, was Luther Baldwin of Newark, New Jersey. When cannons were fired to honor the passage of Adams through that city on his way to Braintree, the inebriated Baldwin expressed the vain hope that cannon wadding would lodge itself in the posterior of Adams's breeches. "Then, exclaims the dramseller, that is sedition."[52]

The last prominent actor on the 1799 stage was Jonathan Robbins, a sailor who was adjudged to be a British mutineer and given over to the British, who executed him. Newspapers shouted of "this new martyr to liberty" and luridly speculated on the disposition of the disfigured corpse. Adams was described as "that man whose hands are reeking with the blood of the poor friendless Connecticut sailor!"[53] Although the Federalists did well in the 1799 elections, the eclectic group of martyrs they created would shortly return to haunt them.[54]

The year 1800 was a presidential election year, so the crisis atmosphere of 1798 returned, with occasional touches of 1799 levity. Adams saw the period from 1760 to 1800 as "one uniform state of doubt, uncertainty, and danger." Another certitude in Adams's mind was the need for cabinet changes. Washington and Wolcott agreed on Secretary of War James McHenry's unfitness for office as early as 1798. Adams tolerated him until May 1800, when the president requested and received McHenry's resignation. Secretary of State Pickering refused to resign and was curtly fired. Republicans were inwardly ecstatic about the removals, but this was an election year, so Adams was flayed for his choice of replacements: "Mr. Dexter [secretary of war designate] very candidly confesses that he is as well qualified for the office of feeder of the Chinese Emperor's Crocodiles as for that of Secretary at War."[55]

Republican Nathaniel Ames continued to fume about the high taxes because his levy for one year came to $7.03. Republican writers suggested the Sedition Act was an antidote to Pickering's comments about Adams and then accused Adams of avoiding a Baltimore church service because the clergyman was a Republican. Federalists countered with news of a gunpowder plot to blow up Congress.[56]

Jefferson was attacked in print with rhetoric reminiscent of Fisher Ames's "war whoop" speech about Jay's Treaty. "Burleigh" wrote of the horrors that would attend the election of the man from Monticello: "Murder, robbery, rape, adultery, and incest, will be openly taught and practised." It was later asked, "Are you prepared to see your dwellings in flames, hoary hairs bathed in blood, female chastity violated, or children writhing on the pike and the halbert? . . . Look at every Jacobin, as at a ravening wolf." Jefferson's biographer, Dumas Malone, characterizes the attacks on Jefferson as "the most vicious in any presidential campaign on record." Federalists offered the voters a choice: "GOD AND A RELIGIOUS PRESIDENT or JEFFERSON AND NO GOD." The Republicans saw the choice as "between Adams, war, and beggary, and Jefferson, peace, and competency!"[57] Federalists pulled out all the stops because a loophole in New Jersey voting qualifications allowed female suffrage, which the Federalists made use of to carry the state. Federalists were even dilatory in conducting the census of 1800, which would have given more electoral votes to non–Federalist areas.[58] For the superstitious, a hen near Winchester, Virginia, supposedly laid an egg which read: "Thomas Jefferson shall be the SAVIOUR of his Country." In New York, fortune smiled on Republicanism. A British warship escorting several captured American vessels arrived in port on the eve of the election.

The national capital was transferred to the Federal City at Washington in 1800. As the government was transferred, a couple of suspicious fires occurred in the War Office and the Treasury Department. Republicans saw this as a cover for frauds, but the truth remains unknown.[59]

Effigies, epithets, taxation, repressive legislation, the army, plots, counterplots, suspicion, rumor, and arrogance, which formed the essential Federalist political arsenal in 1800, gave the Republicans, the political "outs," sufficient ammunition to turn the tables on the Federalists in 1800. Federalists were said to be so upset with the results that barbers were charging extra to shave such long faces.[60]

From Washington's inauguration to Adams's swearing in, there was a gradually mounting clamor on both sides of the political fence that involved situations ranging from humor to rage. These were the beginnings of the brief skirmishes between Washington and the press, which led, after the election of 1796, to the full-scale, four-year confrontation between Adams and the press. In reviewing the many events, from the trivial tubs to the far more serious Jay's Treaty, it might be well to conclude by borrowing from the late Professor Marshall Smelser: "The Federalist period of American history can thus be presented as a span of twelve years in which every great public decision, every national political act, was somehow governed by fierce passions, by hatred, fear and anger."[61]

CHAPTER THREE

The Federal Era III:
Scissors, Paste, and Ink

A Free press would soon destroy the most gloomy despotism.
—George Clinton, *An Oration, Delivered on the Fourth of July, 1798*

Morton Borden, writing on the differences between America in the revolutionary period and America under the Federalists, has commented: "the age of blood had passed, [and was] replaced by that of ink." But the ink of the 1790s, like much of the revolutionary ardor, was generated primarily in Philadelphia and was exported, in an era of tediously slow communications, to the remainder of the country. Philadelphia newspapers amounted to a wire service "in an era of scissors and paste journalism" because editors in the outlying states were satisfied to reprint recently arrived news from Philadelphia. Frank L. Mott has depicted the first quarter of the nineteenth century as "a kind of Dark Ages of Journalism"; if 1801–1825 was indeed the Dark Ages, then Federalist and Republican editors were the Vandals and Huns whose editorial barbarism brought on the journalistic darkness.[1]

Having viewed in the two previous chapters the frenzy of the era, we need now to delineate what newspapers were and what they were not, as well as to explain how they were subject to and contributors toward the passions of the era. In addition, brief sketches of the careers of some of the more influential editors will be provided.

A consensus was established by the leading figures of the Federalist age that the contemporary press was extremely licentious and lacking in ability to provide accurate information to the general public; modern historians have opted to accept that consensus wholeheartedly. In 1793,

Washington wrote to a friend: "Sequestered you say you are, from the World, and know little of what is transacting in it but from newspapers. I regret this exceedingly."[2] John Jay later wrote Pickering, "Many of our presses are licentious in the extreme, and there is little reason to presume that regard to propriety will restrain *such* parties." Federalist editor John Ward Fenno wrote that "The newspapers of America are admirably calculated to keep the country in a continual state of insurrection and revolution."[3] Fenno also offered the strongest overall indictment of journals and editors when he complained: "The American newspapers are the most base, false, servile, and venal publications that ever polluted the fountains of society—their editors are the most ignorant, mercenary automatons that ever were moved by the continually rustling wires of sordid mercantile avarice."[4]

Historians have concurred on the low intrinsic value of the press of the Federalist years. Allan Nevins, agreeing with Henry Adams, viewed "the infant press of the country, about 1800, as simply a storehouse of political calumny." Other historians have found the press to be "a mass of crimination and recrimination," "lively and intensely personal," and "the most violent and vituperative that was to appear in a century and a half of American history."[5] There is a historiographical debate whether Federalist polemics were more or less dignified than those of their opponents, but the partisanship, the political propaganda, and the electioneering of many (but not all) of the sheets of both parties of the Federalist period are common historical themes.[6] Another theme is the willingness of editors to use violent abuse and to indulge in personalities and name-calling. Marshall Smelser has shown that the early Republican attacks on "Publicola" prove that abuse of leading figures became commonplace early in the era. Even though one author saw the period as the "Golden Age of American political writing," it is more accurate to say that "The invective displayed in this newspaper war certainly debased the standards of journalism."[8]

It is time to consider what the "standards of journalism" were during this period. Primarily, what we consider a newspaper did not exist in the Federalist period, except for a few trade-oriented mercantile sheets which bear a very slight resemblance in form to today's *Wall Street Journal*. The politically oriented Federalist-era newspapers were generally one sheet, folded in half to create a four-page effect. They contained foreign news, domestic events, local gossip, abusive columns resembling editorials, letters to the editor, and "entertaining scraps" (which included everything from bad jokes to obituaries to marriages). Finally, advertisements took up a greater or lesser amount of room, depending on the volume of commerce in the area or the amount of politics the printer wished to include in a given issue. The newspapers lacked features we take for granted today—banner headlines, photos, comics, television listings, and horoscopes—and they also lacked objectivity and decorum. Trade journals such as the *Pennsylvania Packet* featured more objective reporting than the political sheets, but politics became a factor in trade as the Anglo-French war cut deeply into American commerce. Other newspapers, such as the Philadelphia *Minerva*, printed literary tidbits, lonely hearts columns, anecdotes, amours, and some incredibly soporific vignettes. This style of publication had little to fear either from the Anglo-French war or from the Sedition Act.[9]

Journalism in the 1790s depended on scissors and paste. In the absence of news-gathering services, rural editors reprinted news from the capital or from a nearby urban center, which undoubtedly had gotten its news from Philadelphia. This technique virtually guaranteed a uniformity in the political news printed by each faction. It also had the tremendous advantage of repetition, because when editors printed the same scandal or canard repeatedly, it became easier to believe. One sheet noted: "JACOBIN INFAMY . . . Every slander that is published in one Jacobin paper is republished in all the rest, and nine tenths of them go uncontradicted." Occasionally, there was no news to report in Philadelphia, as Bache once admitted, "not even so much as a piece of private abuse to grace a paper." But lack of news in Philadelphia meant that other editors also lacked news; one Vermont editor printed an apology for the lack of news in the past week because no papers had arrived from New York or Boston.[10]

As tenuous as this practice of reprinting Philadelphia reportage was, the situation only worsened when rural editors went out on their own because they frequently mistook bombast for rhetoric and mistook doggerel for poetry. Poetry, at least, improved in the 1790s; Federalists were willing to print Freneau's poetry—it was only the man and his politics they detested.[11]

Newspapers kept the public's attention for several reasons. National politics and local gossip had an intrinsic entertainment value, then as now. In addition, a population that was 95 percent rural required some workable form of communication, and newspapers were the only medium then. Sunday papers or papers oriented toward science had not yet appeared. In the meantime, politics, commercial information, and literary pieces were able to answer the public's need for information and grew in sophistication as time passed.[12]

Newspaper titles were as widely copied as were their contents. Between 1704 and 1820, "Gazette" (by definition, "a kind of official record") appeared in the titles of 488 newspapers. "Advertiser" appeared in 440, "Herald" in 115, "Journal" in 114, "Intelligencer" in 104, "Register" in 86, "Republican" in 77, "Chronicle," in 75, "Patriot" in 57, "Centinel" or "Sentinel" in 56, and "Courier" in 45.[13]

One issue of a newspaper was printed in 1690, but the paper was suppressed for reasons best known to the English Crown at the time. The *Boston News-Letter*, begun in 1704, was the first regular sheet to appear. By 1760, the press had taken the form it would maintain for the next five decades and became hotly involved in the revolutionary agitation. Between the Treaty of Paris in 1783 and Jefferson's inauguration in 1801, 450 newspapers and 75 magazines were founded. Some newspapers existed only briefly, but at least a few had some significance. Magazines, on the other hand, were not in sufficient demand to make them an economic success. Among newspapers in 1790, there were 70 weeklies, 10 semiweeklies, three triweeklies, and eight dailies, a daily being a Monday to Saturday press run. Ten years later, there were 178 weeklies, 29 semiweeklies, three triweeklies, and 24 dailies. In 1810, there were 302 weeklies, and there were 422 in 1820. Philadelphia had 12 newspapers as early as mid–1791, but only Fenno's *Gazette of the United States* had any national influence. The spread of newspapers was due in large measure to the extraordinary freedom enjoyed by the press in the years immediately following the American Revolution and also to the extreme unwillingness of government, at least at the outset, to interfere with an obvious First Amendment guarantee, even when it was suspected that such guarantee was being used as a cover for slander. The growth in newspaper circulation was also a direct response to the ongoing inland march of the population.[14] For a complete breakdown of the newspapers as they existed during the presidency of John Adams, refer to the table on page 43.

In terms of circulation, the *Boston Columbian Centinel* led all rivals with 4,000. *Porcupine's Gazette* averaged about 2,000 per issue, the equal of any British daily, and was matched by the Walpole, New Hampshire, *Farmer's Weekly Museum*, the finest country newspaper of its era. The *Aurora* was close behind with 1,700 copies per press run. A subscription to a daily cost $6 to $10 per year, while a weekly or semiweekly cost between $1.50 and $5 yearly. Frontier sheets ran about $4 to $5 per year. Average newspaper circulation in the decade 1790–1800 was between 600 and 700 and determined cost and wages. A journeyman printer usually earned about $6 per week, plus $.25 for each 1,000 ems of composition, in a job noted for long hours, hard work, and grime.[15] Advertising was the chief source of revenue, and ads drew the readers' attention to newly published books, ship arrivals and departures, lotteries, rewards for runaway slaves, rooms to let, and jobs for hire. A large amount of advertising space was devoted to medicines claimed to be capable of curing everything from coughs to social diseases.[16] Editors frequently had trouble collecting the subscription fees and were willing to take goods or food in lieu of cash. One editor, evidently addicted to politics, issued an urgent appeal in 1800: "Never did Mr. ADAMS want to hold his seat—Nor did ever the Republicans want to turn him out of it, than at this crisis, the editor

NEWSPAPERS IN THE UNITED STATES
BY STATE AND POLITICAL AFFILIATION
1797–1801

State	Total	F	I-F	N	I-D	D	LP	JA
Connecticut	23	11	5	3	3	1	2	4
Delaware	4	1	1	0	1	1	0	0
District of Columbia	8	2	0	3	2	1	0	0
Georgia	6	1	4	0	1	0	2	1
Kentucky	6	0	0	1	1	4	0	0
Maine (part of Mass.)	9	7	2	0	0	0	1	0
Maryland	14	1	5	3	3	2	2	1
Massachusetts	34	19	4	4	3	4	3	0
Mississippi (terr.)	1	1	0	0	0	0	0	0
New Hampshire	20	14	4	1	0	1	3	0
New Jersey	11	6	1	1	0	3	0	3
New York	53	19	6	13	4	11	10	1
North Carolina	14	6	3	3	1	1	2	0
Ohio (terr.)	3	0	0	2	0	1	0	0
Pennsylvania	50	16	6	11	3	14	4	1
Rhode Island	8	4	2	0	0	2	0	0
South Carolina	9	2	1	4	2	0	0	0
Tennessee	5	1	1	2	1	0	0	0
Vermont	12	2	5	2	1	2	2	0
Virginia	24	6	1	4	3	10	0	0
West Virginia (part of Va.)	4	0	1	1	1	1	0	0
Total	318	119	52	58	30	59	31	11

Sources: Donald H. Stewart, *The Opposition Press of the Federalist Period* (Albany: State University of New York Press, 1969), pp. 867–93; Clarence L. Brigham, *History and Bibliography of American Newspapers, 1690–1820,* 2 vols. (Worcester, Mass., American Antiquarian Society, 1947); findings confirmed where possible by the author's research.

Total—The number of newspapers in the state, published for any part of the period from late 1796 to mid–1801

F—Federalist

I-F—Independently-Federalist

N—Neutral, doubtful, or of a literary nature

I-D—Independently Democratic-Republican

D—Democratic-Republican

LP—Devoted little space to politics

JA—Believed to have existed for the duration of John Adams's term, March 1797 to March 1801 of the *AMERICAN* wants the payment of the monies due to him." Lastly, although papers were passed around "until dog-eared" and each copy was often read by several people, it is still an open question whether readers took political news as seriously as did the editors who wrote it. While the average citizen did not eat, sleep, and drink politics, as did Bache or Fenno, the early journals nevertheless provided information and opinion of value to citizens in their daily pursuits and at election time.[17]

Franklin printed the first cartoon in 1754, but cartoons were still scarce as late as the Federalist years. In their absence, woodcuts of horses, ships, and slaves, as well as patriotic symbols such as flags, eagles, drums, or anchors occasionally broke the monotony of words. Citizens wrote letters to the editor, but Philip Freneau is credited with the introduction of "the extract of a letter" technique, a device which allowed him to print a letter he had written to himself, while giving the reader the impression that it came from a concerned citizen.[18] Printers usually operated bookstores along with their newspapers because the running of a newspaper could become a lonely and profitless business if the anticipated ship did not arrive from Philadelphia. The position of editor began to emerge in the 1790s, although some newspapers remained one-person operations. In the latter cases, the editor also sold ads and subscriptions and served as typesetter and delivery boy. Editorials in the pure form as we know them rarely appeared as such because opinion was essentially propagandized directly into the news. Styles changed with editors: "Bache criticized men rather than measures, while to Duane the policy rather than the man was the object of attack." There were several women editors at this time because women sometimes took over the printing business at the death of their husbands. Margaret Bache and Ann Greenleaf edited two of the most prominent sheets.[19]

There were a few foreign language journals which lasted briefly. French sheets, such as the daily Philadelphia *Courier Français* were reserved, but German language papers in Pennsylvania were so strongly Jeffersonian that the Federalists were forced to respond in kind with the *Deutsche Porcupein* in 1797.[20]

Rumors were stock-in-trade. The heading "Important-If-True" was commonplace, while the *Massachusetts Mercury* ran a regular column entitled "Rumors from Europe." Once a rumor was printed in one paper, however, it became public domain and spread through reprints as if it were true. In this way, six New England newspapers printed the "news" of Napoleon's death (supposedly in December 1798) between March 6 and 13, 1799.[21]

Newspapers faced several problems. The first was limited to Democratic-Republican sheets and arose from Federalist control of the Post Office. Federalist sheets were often politically franked, while opposition papers were secretly suppressed by Federalist postmasters. The second problem was nonpartisan: editors of both factions were forced to abandon shop in Philadelphia during fever outbreaks, and when Philadelphia was not turning out news, the remainder of the nation's editors were left to survive on their aforementioned limited talents. A third problem was the time lag in reporting news. The delay in printing foreign news, such as Napoleon's alleged passing, could run into months, as noted above. Domestic news, more easily routed yet still slow, was hampered by bad roads and inclement weather. John Adams's inaugural address was printed under the date March 4, 1797, in Philadelphia and was printed as late as March 28 in New Hampshire. Adams's message to the special session of Congress in May 1797 was printed between May 17 and 29, depending on the distance between source and press.[22]

Government printing contracts were sought by editors, and that explains at least some of the partisanship of the press, which apparently even extended to disease. Federalist editors blamed the yellow fever on a French ship, the *Marseilles*, while the opposition blamed a British bottom, the *Arethusa*. Fisher Ames, in a eulogy on John Fenno, commented, "No printer was ever so *correct* in his politics." One German language paper, the *Readinger Adler*, claimed to be "unpartisan," but it was an empty claim.[23]

Perhaps the best index to partisanship is the reportage on commerce raiding. Federalist newspapers were conspicuous for columns which noted "French Fraternity," "French Depredations," or, in the candor of Cobbett, "French Piracies." Bache showed the way to Democratic-Republican editors by printing a regular column sarcastically titled "EVIDENCES OF BRITISH AMITY," which was usually copied verbatim by sympathetic printers.[24]

Charles Warren has written: "It was with the newspaper editors . . . on both sides, that a climax of rancorous and venomous abuse was reached."[25] Before noting this abuse, however, an introduction of the more noteworthy editors is in order. Many were foreign in origin, as were many of the plain folk for whom they wrote. Federalists were quick to lament the foreign origins of some editors, although Cobbett was as much an alien as any of the editors the Federalists disliked. Modern historians have echoed Federalist sentiments on the alien urge to become a journalist. Harold Weisberger portrays the editors as "gentlemen," although he cites Adams's comments that editors were "vagabonds, fugitives from a bailiff, a pillory, or a halter in Europe."[26]

On April 15, 1789, before Washington left Mount Vernon to be inaugurated, John Fenno launched the *Gazette of the United States* "to hold up the people's own government, in a favorable point of light—and . . . by every exertion, to endear the GENERAL GOVERNMENT TO THE

PEOPLE." Fenno ironically shared a birthday with his opposite number, Benjamin Franklin Bache, and the two men died four days apart from the fever in Philadelphia in 1798. Fenno received badly needed financial help from Federalists, which caused him to think of himself as the editor of a "court journal." Philip Freneau, in a satire on Adams and Fenno entitled "Pomposo and his Printer," accused Adams of being the moving force behind Fenno, and a few historians have agreed with Freneau. Adams later strongly denied aiding Fenno in any way. Fenno's death was mourned by Federalists, who hoped for a continuance of his policies from his son, John Ward Fenno.[27]

Benjamin Franklin Bache, "gadfly to the Federalist party," began the *Aurora* on October 1, 1790. In the following eight years, he established himself as a master of journalistic scurrility. Despite a mild beginning, his peak years were distinguished for frequent strong calumnies, biting invective, and occasional weak judgment. He must also have been very dedicated, because he lacked the kind of financial support that Fenno could draw upon and he lost an estimated $14,700 in eight years as an editor. After Bache's death, his widow continued the paper briefly on her own. She then turned the editorship over to her second husband, William Duane, whose publishing talents made him the defendant in 60 libel suits by 1806.[28]

Bache was ably abetted and forwarded in his career by Philip Freneau, once described as "more Jeffersonian than Jefferson." Freneau had been Madison's roommate at Princeton and had invested in a ship (ironically, the *Aurora*) to fight Britain during the American Revolution, but he spent much of the Revolution aboard a British prison ship, watching many of his comrades die. While those circumstances explain his Anglophobia, his position as a Philadelphia journalist was made possible by an offer of a clerkship in Jefferson's State Department, which provided a $250 yearly salary and sufficient free time to do as he pleased. Jefferson's precise role in Freneau's decision to become an editor is still unresolved. Nevertheless, Freneau began the *National Gazette* on October 21, 1791, and slowly but surely began to attack Federalist canons and leaders one by one or en masse. Although the paper did have a literary merit equal to Freneau's widely recognized prose talent, it was more oriented toward vituperation: "All of Freneau's formidable literary talent was devoted to the cause of destroying Hamilton's good name." Freneau's *National Gazette* ceased publication in 1793, a victim of the fever and subscriber apathy. Freneau then went on to found the *Jersey Chronicle*, which lasted from May 2, 1795, to April 30, 1796; in 1797 he served as editor of the New York *Time Piece*.[29]

Freneau's hatred of all things British was matched by William Cobbett's "ultra and uncompromising Toryism," which ultimately damaged the Federalist cause as much as it helped it. Having left Europe behind,

Cobbett established himself in America as a pamphleteer without peer, turning out ream after ream of rancor. A New Jersey newspaper noted the launching of *Porcupine's Gazette* in March 1797 with the warning: "Ye Democrats now beware, and hasten to gird on your armour and shield, that you may render yourselves invulnerable to the piercing quills of that groveling animal, the Porcupine." A student of Cobbett has written: "Cobbett needed enemies: he was happiest when he felt that the 'miscreants' of the moment were mobilizing all their forces in order to grind him into dust." Federalists as well as Republicans felt his venom, and Cobbett thought Adams had marked him for deportation. Eventually, libel suits brought against Cobbett by Benjamin Rush greatly diminished Porcupine's operating capital, and he returned to England in June of 1800. Cobbett remained a well-known literary figure and later published parliamentary debates. In the 1830s, the man of the quill realized his lifelong ambition to sit in the House of Commons.[30]

Other editors require less attention. Noah Webster demonstrated sound Federalism throughout the period, and his later works on the language went into countless editions. Among Republican editors, "James Thomson Callender was a Scotchman of whom nothing good is known." Callender was nevertheless widely read, and Jefferson aided him financially. As Donald Stewart concluded: "That Jefferson sent him money in ignorance of his scurrility defies belief."[31] Benjamin Russell of the *Columbian Centinel* imbibed his Federalism as a member of the guard which hanged the British spy, Major John André; he grew to idolize Washington and later coined the term *gerrymander*.[32]

Politicians made greater or lesser contributions to the polemic literature. Timothy Dwight, John Trumbull, Lemuel Hopkins, and Richard Alsop saw themselves as the "Hartford Wits." Hamilton wrote under numerous pseudonyms. Madison used "Helvidius" and other names, and Benjamin Austin, Jr., was "Honestus" and "Old South." Monroe was "Agricola," and John Marshall was "Gracchus" and "Aristides." John Beckley may have been "Valerius," "A Calm Observer," "Pittachus," and "Belisarius."[33]

To the same degree that they abused political figures, editors abused each other in print, and occasionally in person. A Republican newspaper complained of the Federalist editors' "base prostitution to their stepmother Britain." Callender lamented, "The newspapers printed under the presidential banner, breathe nothing but irritation, calumny, and every imaginable ingredient of civil discord." Republican editors were castigated as "those wet nurses of a French faction in the bowels of our country."[34]

The individual who received the worst treatment short of a Sedition Act jail term was Benjamin Franklin Bache. At one point he printed a pamphlet titled *Truth Will Out*, detailing some of the attacks against him.

After its publication, his enemies provided material for another volume. He was called "Talleyrand Bache," "Infamous Bache," and, sarcastically, "Patriotic Bache." His paper, the *Aurora*, was seen as "a daily libel on our government," and "the pestilential retailer of sedition."[35] In an article entitled "Contempt," Bache was told that he was not considered the grandson of a philosopher (Benjamin Franklin), but rather "Ben Bache, the newsman." Wolcott wrote to Bache accusing him of a myriad of sins, and Bache was pictured in Congress as an agent of the French Directory. Porcupine, less concerned with diplomatic intrigues, wrote "Bache's Bow Wow" and dismissed his target as a fawning spaniel. Bache's veracity was also questioned: "*BACHE'S OATH* Resembles the case of a footpad, talking at the gallows of the honesty of his life and conversation, or a whore, shrieking to a bawd that her *virtue* is in danger."[36]

Becoming even more personal, Porcupine advised that Bache be treated "as we would A TURK, A JEW, A JACOBIN, OR A DOG," and Federalist ruffians answered the call. Bache was attacked by Fenno in the street, and by organized vigilantes at his office. One self-appointed censor, Abel Humphries, was fined $50 and then given a government job. Federalist newspapers could not conceal their joy when Bache succumbed to yellow fever on September 10, 1798.[37] William Duane replaced Bache as the *Aurora*'s editor and as consort to the widow Bache; Porcupine quickly labeled him "*Duane*, Mother Bache's Editor." Duane, following another Bache tradition, was attacked and beaten in the *Aurora* office on May 15, 1799, shortly after he began his editorial duties.[38]

Other editors received at least an equal amount of printed abuse. Porcupine was chastised as a "libel upon republicanism" and derided as a spaniel. Punsters mocked Cobbett as "Mr. Hedge Hog" and "The Pork Patriot," and he was more seriously attacked as an "arch-liberal and assassin of reputation."[39]

Freneau was upbraided in verse for his connection to Jefferson:

> SINBAT, the smutty link boy of the muse,
> who blacks himself to clean his master's shoes.

Fenno also noted the connection between Freneau and Jefferson and the "scurrility against the general government" that was Freneau's stock-in-trade. When Freneau began to turn the New York *Time Piece* from a literary sheet into a political organ, Noah Webster commented acidly, "The dog returns to his vomit."[40]

An anti–Callender group was formed in Richmond, with plans to treat the Scotch editor to the tar brush and feathers, but the plan evidently miscarried. A Massachusetts newspaper had good tidings for Federalists, as it noted one of Callender's many transgressions: "On the second of

August, a little dirty toper, with shaved head and greasy jacket, nankeen pantaloons, and worsted stockings, was arrested at a whiskey distillery, near Leesburgh, in Virginia, under the vagrant act."[41]

Holt, the editor of the *Bee*, was mocked for the survival of one year of "his INSECT," while John Daly Burk of the New York *Time Piece* was dismissed as "this wretch, who is composed of that stuff of which the spy, the assassin, and the sycophant are formed." Fenno received little space, save Callender's statement that Fenno's yearly lie output must be "some hundreds per annum." All of these epithets help to explain why "duelling pistols were essential equipment for members of the newspaper profession."[42]

Pens, however, were the most essential equipment, and a pen in the wrong hand could be as dangerous as a dueling pistol.

CHAPTER FOUR

George Washington
and the American Press

The publications in Freneau's and Bache's papers are
outrages on common decency.
—Washington to Henry Lee, July 21, 1793

Washington's two unanimous victories in the electoral college demonstrated three facts about the first two elections under the Constitution: first, that Washington was universally respected by that amorphous political interest group known as "the people"; second, that Washington was equally respected by the less numerous body of citizens who exercised the franchise and by the electors they chose; and third, that newspaper editors were not in the electoral college. For if newspaper editors had been polled, Washington's first election might still have been unchallenged, but the 1792 election would have been a contest, if not a donnybrook.

On the date of Washington's first inauguration, April 30, 1789, no editor in America would have questioned the sagacity inherent in the choice of Washington as president. Slightly less than eight years later, several editors used their newspapers to express rejoicing at the departure of Washington. Thus the events between April 1789 and March 1797 detail the gradual evolutionary development of the practice of abusing the president in print.

It is worth a paragraph or two to digress here and venture ever so briefly into the hypothetical, or the "what-if?" approach to history. The fundamental question is, Was there any other name that could be substituted for George Washington in the two paragraphs above? The answer, it would seem, would be a resounding no. Would a Jefferson, a Madison, or an Adams have been elected unanimously in 1789 and again in 1792? Certainly not, and for numerous reasons too detailed to list here. But the point is made, at least hypothetically, that Washington, in 1789, was the closest thing to perfection on the American political horizon. That fact would be gradually forgotten over the next eight years as Washington, adhering as closely as possible to constitutional dictates, made appointments, created policies, and set precedents. Some of those actions made newspaper editors unhappy, and they let Washington know it. They hurt him personally in the process because he seemed to be trying, with some sincerity, to remain the closest thing to perfection on the American political horizon. The last thought we should consider here is that had the first president been Jefferson, Madison, Adams, or anyone else, the timing, the nature, and the volume of the press attacks would have been quite different. If Washington had ever considered those possibilities, perhaps he would have derived at least a bit of comfort. We can thus conclude our hypothesizing by suggesting the possibility that Washington, and only Washington, could have taken the oath as president in the absence of newspaper abuse and that whoever that next oath-taker was would feel the full brunt of what Washington missed.

James Thomas Flexner, Washington's most recent multivolume biographer, has pictured the first president as the greatest American sufferer of newspaper libels. Flexner believes that the abuse heaped on Washington "has no parallel in modern America except in those fly-by-night sheets in which extreme crackpots shout at each other."[1]

The abuse directed by Washington, although perhaps not as extreme as pictured by Flexner, was certainly the most important precedent established by the press during Washington's terms. It should be stressed, however, that the editorial complaints addressed to Washington were partisan and limited almost exclusively to Democratic-Republican editors. They were also limited to what amounted to free-speech journalistic replies to policies or appointments that some editors, who believed they had the right to say what they thought, found objectionable. For every Republican attack, there was a defense printed by a Federalist sheet, and some of those replies made the Republican charges of idolatry believable. Federalist sheets even reprinted the *Aurora*'s charges, but only to question their wisdom or openly attack them.[2] Remember again, however, that the problem was slowly developing, partisan, and often so ludicrous that it was, in turn, aggravated by Washington's reactions, which seem to indicate that he believed that as president he should have been editorially sacrosanct. If we contrast the relatively small volume of abuse and Washington's reactions with the constant four-year attack on Adams and his relative lack of reaction, it is possible to see Washington and Adams from perspectives they are not usually accorded in history texts. Washington's outbursts and Adams's silence are both somewhat uncharacteristic. Such comparison will certainly call into question the conclusions of James

Thomas Flexner and other historians who have overdramatized the press's interaction with George Washington.

Washington always took a keen interest in the press. Before he became president, he wrote to Jay to complain that newspapers were not receiving fair treatment in the mails, while a subsequent letter to Hamilton had warm praise for the good political effects of *The Federalist*. As president, Washington considered proposing that newspapers go through the mails free. He also made a point of reading several papers, ranging from Fenno's *Gazette of the United States* to Bache's *Aurora*, as well as other papers which included moderate shades of opinion between the extremists. Bache's biographer has written that Washington, when embarrassed about the state of public opinion, read the newspapers. The reverse was also true: when Washington read the sheets, he was frequently embarrassed by them.[3]

Washington's first term saw nothing more than mild skirmishing, with an occasional challenge for a given action or policy. Washington's tour of New England looked to some like a state procession and had an air of monarchism about it. Individuals such as Senator Maclay of Pennsylvania saw Washington as a cloak to Federalist measures, and the "Washington as cloak" idea eventually brought Washington a good deal of negative press comment. Hamilton's fiscal policies were questioned, and this involved Washington at least indirectly. Abigail Adams noted that attacks against her husband were letting up in early 1792, as editors bore down on other targets: "the Minister at War, & the Secretary of the Treasury have been their Game. The Secretary of State & even the President [Washington, not Adams] has not escaped." Ironically, this early opposition came from Washington's home state, Virginia, just as one group of Adams's later enemies, the High Federalists, would be centered in or around Massachusetts.[4]

Other mild criticisms of Washington concerned his aloofness and the birthday celebrations. A more serious charge was a journalistic indictment against Washington for taking advances on his salary; his conduct during both the French and Indian War and the American Revolution was also questioned in the press. Washington reacted strongly against the accusatory polemics: "The latter are *sur*charged, and *some of them* indecently communicative of *charges* that stand in need of evidence for their support."[5]

The leading opposition propagandist at this stage was Philip Freneau, whose attacks increased in vehemence against Hamilton, the president, and even Martha Washington. Jefferson considered taking action against Freneau, nominally a State Department clerk, but decided against it, believing that "No government ought to be without censors." Jefferson later felt that Freneau had saved America from monarchy. Historian John

Bach McMaster has lashed Jefferson in the strongest language for remaining in the cabinet and keeping Freneau on his payroll to abuse Washington.[6]

Douglas Southall Freeman, viewing the overall newspaper situation of Washington's first term, believes the president was supported by most of the influential newspapers of the country. One John Adams biographer, Page Smith, sharply dissents because he believes Washington was treated "with savage contempt" by editors as early as 1792. The truth lies somewhere between these two positions. First, it should be noted that Washington was praised by some antifederal sheets during the first term. Second, although Washington suffered indirectly as a result of attacks against government, rather than attacks against himself, he thought that "these kind of representations is an evil wch. must be placed in opposition to the infinite benefits resulting from a free Press."[7] Finally, when Washington considered retirement in 1792, press attacks provided one of his motivations. Even Abigail Adams, never a worshipper at Washington's shrine, was upset about the abuse Washington was receiving in the closing days of his first term.[8]

Although press attacks did not drive Washington into retirement in 1792, Republican editors had material to work with in the second term which made Washington regret his continuance at the helm. From the coming of Genet through the Whiskey Rebellion and the ratification and implementation of Jay's Treaty, Washington was the constant target of Republican attack. Friendly Republican editors dwindled in numbers as Washington oriented his policies more toward Federalism. Adams noted in early 1793: "The hell-hounds are now in full cry in the newspapers against the President, whom they treat as ill as ever they did me." In May, Freneau printed an attack claiming that Washington signed the Neutrality Proclamation to save his head. Adams suggested that Washington might not bear the abuse, as "his skin is thinner than mine."[9]

Genet arrived in the spring of 1793, and his coming released passions among Francophiles that led to attacks on Washington in the press. Jefferson noted in June: "The President is not well. . . . He is also extremely affected by the attacks made & kept up on him in the public papers." A month later, Washington, realizing there would always be dissent, asked: "But in what will this abuse terminate? . . . The publications in Freneau's and Bache's papers are outrages on common decency." In a cabinet meeting of August 2, 1793, Washington lashed out against "that Rascal Freneau," noting that Freneau sent him three unsolicited copies of each edition of his paper. In the fall, Washington wrote that Genet was in league with the opposition press, and Jefferson confided to his "Anas" (a personal diary) that Washington "felt the venom of Genet's pen."[10] At least two historians also believe that some attacks against Washington may have been written by Federalists and sent to Republican sheets, in an effort to Federalize Washington. William Irvine, a Treasury clerk, is suspected of being "Veritas," who questioned Washington's right to proclaim neutrality. This suspicion was noted at the time by Tobias Lear, Washington's secretary, who passed his thoughts on to his chief; Jefferson agreed with Lear.[11]

Following Genet's denouement, the volume of abuse slackened temporarily. Washington, commenting on "the insidious attempts to poison" the public mind by French-inspired editors, warned a friend not to believe everything he read in print, which was probably just as well, as it was at about this time that the Federalists used the press to circulate the rumor that Washington had been assassinated.[12]

On January 1, 1794, Thomas Jefferson left the cabinet. This meant more abuse for Washington because Jefferson was now less vulnerable to the venomed darts. On January 2, Adams noted that Washington had superseded him as "libelee-general," and he cited a number of attacks against the president in Bache's paper, "which is nearly as bad as Freneau's." A week later Adams noted further abuse of Washington, but thought the worst was being withheld: "The Jacobins would make a sortie upon him in all the force they could muster, if they dared." For the rest of the year, Washington was attacked for his connection to the Order of the Cincinnati and for his participation in suppressing the Whiskey Rebellion. In the latter instance, Washington lowered himself slightly to answer "the impertinence of Mr. Bache" and his correspondents, who stressed "that I cannot, constitutionally, command the Army whilst Congress are in Session." By the end of 1794, Adams feared Washington would resign, but cautioned Abigail that this was only a rumor.[13]

Faced with the decision to ratify or reject Jay's Treaty, Washington, with little real choice from the point of view of policy, chose to ratify, losing whatever remaining immunity he had with opposition editors. The *Aurora* printed a pamphlet "to destroy undue impressions in favor of Mr. Washington," and the president was attacked in the *Aurora* by "Hancock," "Valerius," "Belisarius," "Portius," "Sydney," "Atticus," "Z," "Tully," and "Pittachus" with unkind barbs that were widely reprinted. Republican editors showed great zeal in their poison-pen campaign because they hoped to force Washington to retire in 1797 (he had in fact decided years earlier to retire after his second term).[14]

Jay's Treaty, with its seeming extension of executive power, was indeed the proper poison for Republican pens. Jay noted charges of idolatry and the indictment that politics had assumed the tone of Potsdam, not Philadelphia. James Callender proposed a toast: "A speedy death to General Washington," which, in its context, meant Callender wished an end to the title "General," not the man Washington. Yet Washington had made the right decision, as one John Marshall biographer has succinctly concluded: "One must admire Washington's courage [in agreeing to Jay's Treaty]. He was willing to risk personal criticism and his place in history to secure the peace he considered necessary for the nation he had fathered to grow and prosper."[15]

Republicans, distressed because Washington continued to possess the affection of much of the populace, redoubled their efforts. Freneau transformed his *Jersey Chronicle* from a literary medium to an anti–Jay's Treaty debate platform. Nathaniel Ames regretted Washington's signing of the treaty, lamenting, "Better his hand had been cut off when his glory was at its height, before he blasted all his laurels." The August 15, 1795, *Aurora* used large type to emblazon its incredulity: "We are assured that the President has signed the Treaty, but cannot yet believe it."[16]

Washington's handling of the incident in which cabinet member Randolph compromised himself seemed to confirm the suspicion of editors that Washington had been completely Federalized. Washington was accused of picturing himself as "the omnipotent director of a seraglio," who was "violating the constitution." "Valerius" warned: "The American People, Sir, will look to death, the man who assumes the character of an usurper." "Belisarius" catalogued the six-year loss of American virtue for reasons ranging from monarchism to funding and concluded with an accusation that Hamilton, "that ambitious Cataline," had pulled all the strings and "the name of Washington will descend with his to oblivion." "Atticus" wrote of Washington as "political pope" and looked to impeachment. "Pittachus" likened the president to Benedict Arnold and attempted to pierce the Federalists' cloak: "Even the name of Washington has lost its magic." Washington was also accused of political degeneracy, of being in his dotage, and of being "a pretended Man of the People." It was asked: "Will not the world be led to conclude that the mask of political hypocrisy has been alike worn by a CESAR [sic], a CROMWELL, and a WASHINGTON?"[17]

William Duane, writing as "Jasper Dwight, of Vermont," saw British gold behind Washington's policies, while a New England paper saw America "most clandestinely married to Great Britain." Federalists lamely countered with hints of French gold behind Republican editors' policies.[18] Addresses to the president in 1795 spoke of impeachment, while "Franklin," writing in the *Independent Gazeteer*, penned 14 impeachment letters between March 11 and June 10, 1795. Fisher Ames dismissed the impeachment rhetoric as further Jacobin efforts to disorganize public opinion. The year ended with John Adams writing his wife that Washington was in better spirits, a comment that may indicate the latter was becoming immune to Bache's abuse.[19]

Early 1796 featured attacks on Washington by the *Aurora* for withholding the papers relevant to Jay's negotiations; the *Aurora* also made the accusation that the decision was "moulded by the opinion of an ex–Secretary."[20] This attack served as the prelude to the final push to convince Washington to retire.

From the Farewell Address until the day he left office, abuse of Washington continued, although the subject of his retirement was the only remaining item on the Republicans' agenda. The remainder of the abuse was either repetition of past calumny or fabrication for the sake of filling columns. This scurrilous campaign caused Washington personal suffering, but did not bring about his decision to retire. Earlier abuse had convinced Washington of the rectitude of that course. By the same token, the misguided zeal demonstrated in the Republican poison-pen campaign planted the idea among Federalists that a licentious press should be controlled.

Adams noted in a letter to Abigail that Washington was set on retirement: "the turpitude of the Jacobins touches him more nearly than he owns in words. All the studied efforts of the Federalists to counterbalance abuse by compliment don't answer the end." Wolcott, perhaps not as aware of Washington's feelings as was Adams, wrote: "who, except the President, has not been assailed with success?"[21]

The truth of the matter was that Washington had been assailed with success. A week after Wolcott's letter, Washington mentioned Bache's abuse in a letter to Hamilton. In July, Washington wrote Wolcott, suggesting that Bache's abuse would have deleterious effects on government, "for drops of water will impress (in time) the hardest marble." The same day, Washington penned a letter to Jefferson, exonerating him for Bache's offenses, but lamenting the twisting of his every act. He characterized Bache in as "indecent terms as could scarcely be applied to a Nero; a notorious defaulter; or even to a common pickpocket." Washington later wished that French policies were scrutinized as carefully as Bache and his minions scrutinized his, and he also lashed out against the attacks against himself: "indecent and they are void of truth and fairness."[22]

Prior to the Farewell Address, an article condemning Jay's Treaty blasted Washington for criticizing "self-created SOCIETIES," while Washington was also abused in a "Republican Prayer":

> Our President which art in office, illustrious be thy name; thy election come, our will be done, resign for none on earth, until thou art called to heaven . . . lead Jay not into temptation and deliver us from the evil which we suffer under the British Treaty, for in thee is vested all constitutional power and glory. Amen.[23]

The Farewell Address marked the watershed of Washington's last year in office. A partisan document, it was based on recent experience and was practical rather than idealistic. One purpose was clearly to castigate French meddling in American affairs.[24] An original draft that was found, oddly enough, in Hamilton's papers contained strong antiparty remarks. One passage addressed itself to vituperation: "It might be expected at the parting scene of my public life that I should take some notice of such violent abuse. But, as heretofore, I shall pass over them in utter silence."[25]

Although the Farewell Address as given was more reserved, it still came under strong attack, led by William Duane. In a pamphlet occasioned by the address, Duane fumed: "Your Address in my mind is fraught with incalculable evils to your country!" Washington was accused of "extraordinary decadence," of being the object of "PERSONAL IDOLATRY," and was told, "Posterity will in vain search for the monuments of wisdom in your administration." Washington was further admonished: "You are lost, Sir, in the treacherous mazes of passion" and he was warned that because he had withheld the Jay papers, his name and reputation would sink to the "insignificance of a *Venetian Doge* or a *Dutch Stadtholder!*"[26]

George Gibbs partially misread events when he wrote that the Farewell Address steered criticism away from Washington. If anything, the abuse became shabbier, as it amounted to parting shots at a seemingly fallen idol. Before noting the parting shots, it is well to reflect on the historical consensus which sees press abuse, well before the Farewell Address, as a strong factor in Washington's decision to retire in 1797.[27] Although Samuel Eliot Morison listed character traits in the young Washington that might have later made him impervious to criticism, the evidence presented should make it clear that at least some criticism penetrated Washington's armor.[28] Washington at one point wrote that the abuse had not bothered him, other than "to increase the anxious desire which has long possessed my breast, to enjoy . . . retirement." Rush wrote to Adams that Jefferson had once seen Washington slam the *Aurora* on the floor and "damn" the author for an article picturing Washington as a criminal for having slaves. Rush also believed that the *Aurora* caused Washington "to retire from the President's chair."[29]

Washington's ownership of slaves was the subject of an attack in Duane's pamphlet. The *Aurora* of December 21, 1796, warming to its brief détente with Adams while still lashing Washington, noted "that ADAMS holds none of his fellowmen in slavery, but that WASHINGTON does." That particular issue of the *Aurora* also noted the House's rejection of an amendment to compliment Washington, and it added that it would have been easy to make Adams president and Washington vice president, but Washington chose retirement in the face of that possibility.[30] Adams regretted that his name was used against Washington and that Washington was accused of such absurdities as murder and attempting to betray the Continental Army. Other charges were equally nonsensical. Washington's back bothered him, so he rode in a coach. The *Aurora* saw this as anti-republican and likened Washington to George III. Adams's star continued to rise, as Washington was reminded that his Revolutionary War greatness must be shared with Gates, Greene, Franklin, and Adams. The president was accused of suggesting to Adams that his policies be continued when Adams followed him into office.[31]

The final humiliation Washington faced as president was an odious collection of abuse in the form of a letter from Thomas Paine. Paine, an American citizen, had been jailed in France, and Washington had not troubled himself to attempt to secure Paine's release. Paine published his revenge: "And as for you sir, treacherous in private friendship . . . and a hypocrite in public life, the world will be puzzled to decide whether you are an apostate or an imposter; whether you have abandoned good principles or ever had any." Washington noted the attack, while Adams wrote his wife that Washington had told him Paine's letter was "the most insulting letter he ever received."[32]

As Washington left office, his Federalism increased, and he was no longer above party. Washington's swing to Federalism made him a leader of the party, and as such he was at least an accessory to the Federalist press. Because of this partisan identification, the remaining interaction between Washington and the press must be considered from the Federalist as well as the Republican side.

Noah Webster's New York *Minerva* had high praise for Washington on the occasion of his leave-taking, while the Hartford *American Mercury* concluded a poem of adulation by lamenting: "And ah! 'his like we ne'er shall see again.'" The same paper printed many letters favorable to the ex-president from well-wishers. Many other sheets printed reports of Washington's birthday celebrations around the country and additional reports of galas held as Washington left office.[33] Bache, however, dissented from the adulation, preferring to offer "a valedictory compounded of acid, gall, and wormwood":

> If there ever was a period of rejoicing this is the moment—every heart in unison with the freedom and happiness of the people ought to beat high with exultation, that the name of WASHINGTON from this day ceases to give a currency to political iniquity; and to legalize corruption— A new aera is now opening upon us, an aera which promises much to the people . . . nefarious projects can no longer be supported by a name.

Bache later viewed Washington's retirement as a result of his failure as a president, "having brought our country to the verge of ruin." Bache also criticized what historians now refer to as the cult of personality.[34]

But Bache's bile was contravened by Federalist efforts that defended Washington against all past charges and pointed to a swift canonization.

The Hartford *American Mercury* reserved page one of every issue from Adams's inauguration to June 5, 1797, for Washington's official letters, with no slight intended for Adams. The Boston *Federal Gazette*, in reviewing 1797, saw the biggest event of the year as the retirement of the *"first Magistrate*, the *illustrious* Washington."[35]

After mid–1797, Washington relaxed into his natural Federalism in his private correspondence, joining with other Federalist leaders in execrating Monroe's attempt at self-vindication. Washington also saw evil doings in the workings of the spurious "John Langhorne," possibly Jefferson's nephew, Peter Carr, who requested information about Washington's feelings concerning press abuse.[36]

By 1798, the abuse heaped on Washington and his fears for the safety of the union put him in a position to agree with the Federalist legislative program of that year. Marshall Smelser has emphasized Washington's lively correspondence with Alexander White, James Lloyd, cabinet members Pickering and McHenry, and their master, Hamilton, during the debates on the Alien and Sedition Acts. Smelser has also emphasized the former president's hearty approval and applause of the subsequent legislation, and although James Thomas Flexner has noted that Washington did nothing to curtail free speech while in power, that begs the essential question of 1798. Flexner does note that Washington wanted Duane investigated and perhaps prosecuted.[37]

Attacks against Washington continued throughout 1798. Callender called the former president the "monarch of Mount Vernon" when he left his retirement to command the 1798 provisional army. Washington, now accustomed to abuse, treated it with the triviality it deserved, as he wrote to Pickering, "Truth and information is not their object." In late 1799, with another election a year away, Republican editors attacked Washington along with Adams. One toast proclaimed: "To the memory of Gen. Washington; may his illustrious actions and services be faithfully recorded down to the year 1787, but no farther!" Cobbett libeled Dr. Rush for the unnecessary death of Washington in December 1799, and even eulogies assumed a partisan tone. Republicans joined in the sorrow at first, but drew back when the eulogies went too far. Nathaniel Ames noted laconically that Washington had seemed to replace Christ in New Jersey.[38]

Thus the years between 1789 and 1797 marked the beginnings of the process by which the press questioned presidential actions and personalities. This initial opposition was limited, partisan, ad hoc, weak, and largely inconsequential during most of Washington's first term. In the second term, the opposition became stronger, although its partisan flavor and occasional resort to ludicrous issues meant that Washington paid less attention to it as a determining factor in policy decisions. In short, although Washington was abused and occasionally fought back, the full scope of the president-press relationship prior to 1797 was not fully developed and awaited the election of a man other than George Washington. In seeking to understand the nature of the full-scale clash between executive and press we must answer a question asked by Stephen Kurtz, in discussing America at the time of Washington's retirement: "What would be the result should a man of less popularity undertake the presidency, an office which by 1796 had become the first fruits of violent partisanship rather than unanimity?"[39]

John Adams was clearly "a man of less popularity."

CHAPTER FIVE

John Adams:
Character and Public Career

*Vapors avaunt! I will do my duty, and leave the event. If
I have the approbation of my own mind, whether ap-
plauded or censured, blessed or cursed by the world, I
will not be unhappy.*
—**John Adams to Abigail Adams, c. 1774**

A nineteenth-century biographer wrote that it was difficult "to sketch
the administration of John Adams with correct lines and in truthful colors."
That assertion remains an understatement a century later.[1]

In essence, the four years of Adams's presidency seem little more than
a crisis-filled interlude between the terms of America's early giants—the
heroic Washington and the scholarly Jefferson. Far more has been written
about either Washington or Jefferson than about Adams, as a well-stocked
Adams library can be purchased on a modest budget. American folklore
and usage have also reflected the adulation of the first and third presidents
to the neglect of the second. Federal holidays mark both the anniversary
of Washington's birth in February and the adoption of a Jeffersonian document (to which Adams contributed heavily) in July, and both founding
giants appear on paper money and coins. Adams was not completely
overlooked, however, as his profile graced a two-cent postage stamp in
1938, sandwiched between Martha Washington on the penny-and-a-half
issue and Jefferson on the three-cent stamp, all in a philatelic issue which
also included the likes of Grant and Harding. Lastly, it is possible to sit
near the Jefferson Memorial in the city of Washington and look up at the
Washington Monument without having the horizon interrupted by a
single concrete reminder of an overlooked Founding Father, John Adams.

Adams's failure to become a national hero is understandable for two
reasons. First, his character contained genuine flaws which are more clearly

61

visible than the shortcomings of many of his contemporaries. Second, and more significant, Adams was not fully understood by his contemporaries, and their misunderstandings, passed down and sanctified as "primary sources," have become history. This book will not make Adams a national hero, but it will certainly attempt to make Adams more understandable by probing his character, his strengths, his faults, and some of the events prior to 1797 which have a bearing on the subsequent relationship between president and press. By studying the "whats" and the "whys" of Adams's life, rather than the "wheres" and the "whens," we can better understand the psyche of the man. Important events are admittedly passed over because this is not a biography, but an all-too-brief character study. Adams's thoughts on the press will be stressed, while his political thought, his reputation as a scholar, and his commentaries on the works of others, all well treated by previous historians, will be less emphasized.[2]

No work on Adams is complete without the citation of a handful of adjectives, pro and con, which authors relied on to explain Adams. Page Smith has correctly called him "paradoxical" but has wrongly concluded, "since it did not worry [Adams] unduly, it should not worry historians."

Paradoxical, another way of saying unpredictable, is probably the key word in describing Adams. L.H. Butterfield sees Adams as "no 'type' at all, but a unique human being, individualistic to the point of eccentricity ... he was a 'character.'"[3] Once called "the last Puritan in American politics," Adams has had his character painted with a litany of negative brushstrokes, as numerous historians have pictured Adams as jealous, squeamish, unsocial, priggish, tactless, self-important, impetuous, pugnacious, stubborn, vain, suspicious, eccentric, naive, irascible, impulsive, dogmatic, thin-skinned, distressingly blunt, and peevish. These traits tend to explain his lack of friends and hence his "bad reviews" from the primary sources of the era; they also provide much subject matter for the press coverage of his presidency. On the positive side, he has been pictured as honest, scholarly, patriotic, deeply affectionate, warm-hearted, humorous, courageous, conscientious, learned, and sober. These attributes demonstrate why subsequent newspaper attacks hammered away at his weaknesses and resorted to name-calling rather than concentrating on scandal, of which Adams was as free as any American president since. On paper, his strengths seem to ameliorate some of his shortcomings, but Adams let his faults get the best of him: "John Adams never learned to govern his tongue or his pen.... Reading his diary is like watching a display of fireworks." A friendly biographer concluded that Adams was neither more ambitious nor more vain than the next person, but rather less successful in curbing his ambition and vanity.[4] Yet another biographer noted, and there is little evidence to the contrary, that Adams had the ability to control his temper, even under the sharpest attacks.[5]

The most telling diagnosis of Adams's behavioral traits to filter down to the twentieth century was penned in 1783 by Franklin, who wrote, "I am persuaded that he means well for his his Country, is always an honest Man, often a wise one, but sometimes, and in some things, absolutely out of his senses."[6] Writers who have seen in Franklin's thought a trace of madness in Adams have missed the point, as he was not crazy, but rather unpredictable. As Adams's unpredictable nature was the basis of several key decisions in his presidency, it was a significant factor in the events and the outcome of the executive-press relationship.[7]

Page Smith, Adams's sole definitive biographer, clinically summarizes Adams's character rather succinctly. He views Adams as paranoid and possessed of an inferiority complex which made him overachieve to compensate. Smith considers Adams schizoid, with a split in personality between farmer and philosopher-attorney-politician. He also describes Adams as manic-depressive, ranging from exultation to despair, and irrational and antisocial under stress. Smith also pictures Adams as a "mesomorph," an individual with a small, compact body and high energy, and further sees Adams as self-destructive and a hypochondriac. He concludes, "Abigail insured his sanity."[8]

That Adams was "overly suspicious of others" was undeniable. At times, Adams's tendency to overreact does almost lead one to a characterization of paranoia. Overreaction runs through Adams's life from his early years up to his failure as president to consult "suspected" cabinet members about the nomination of William Vans Murray. Adams thought he was the victim of a whisper campaign for his bold stand on independence in 1776, and he believed that his nomination of Washington to command made lifelong enemies out of John Hancock and Sam Adams. He dated his later weak position in Pennsylvania politics to his problems in 1774-1775 with John Dickinson and Charles Thomson. Adams also believed that his preference for Gates over Schuyler in 1776 caused Hamilton to oppose him steadily thereafter. Beliefs such as this led Adams to overreact in certain circumstances with regard to the individuals mentioned above, as well as others, and the trait remained with him for life. As late as 1790, Adams felt "There has been more little malignity to me, than to Jonathan Sewal, Silas Deane, or Benedict Arnold."[9] These beliefs of persecution and overreaction did not disappear after 1790.

Adams became very ambitious early in life and did not stop until he left the capital on March 4, 1801, when retirement was forced upon him by the volume of Republican ballots. One thing he had to compensate for was size. He wanted to be big, but turned out short and plump, so fame would have to compensate for physique. In 1759, the 23-year-old Adams wrote: "Reputation ought to be the perpetual subject of my Thoughts, and aim of my Behavior. How shall I gain a Reputation!" Years later, writing on his labors in the Continental Congress in 1775 and 1776, he concluded that he "unquestionably did more business than any other Member of that house."[10] Adams's weak position in Europe in the 1780s was undoubtedly behind his push for titles for American dignitaries in 1789, yet Jefferson, not privy to Adams's frustrations in Europe, saw in the question of titles proof of Franklin's assertion that Adams had taken leave of his senses.[11] Yet while Adams seemingly favored aristocracy in the titles issue, he strongly censured the Order of the Cincinnati for its ceremonies and titles.[12] Adams's notes on his pronavy efforts of 1775 and 1798–1800 combine overreaction and overachievement, although one historian agrees with Adams's own evaluation by calling him the "Father of the American Navy."[13] By the end of Adams's first term as vice president, time and abuse had at least moderated his ambitions, as he confided to Abigail, "I cannot say that my desire of fame increases. It has been strong in some parts of my life, but never so strong as my love of honesty."[14]

Adams has been described as being very jealous of others, particularly Washington, whom he believed to be his own creation, and Franklin, who he thought was concentrating more energy on dissipation than on diplomacy. He was jealous because they received the attention and because they were doing what he would have liked to do. He also undoubtedly felt a slight superiority to both, which made their respective fame and positions galling in the extreme.[15] Adams should have listened to his own rhetoric when he wrote: "The examples of Washington, Franklin and Jefferson are enough to show that silence and reserve in public are more Efficacious than Argumentation or Oratory."[16]

The schizoid traits which Page Smith mentions briefly can be expanded to cover two themes. First, wherever Adams was prior to 1801, he probably preferred to be somewhere else. Second, whatever he was doing before 1801, he would have been happier doing something else. When away from home, he longed for Braintree. Once there, he was ready to go forth to renewed battles. If in Congress, he wished to be a general; if abroad, he wished to be in domestic service; as vice president he wished to be on the floor of the Senate to debate. Of all these trends, the desire to get away from politics and return home would have the greatest effects on his tenure as president. As early as 1771, he wrote: "I feel myself weary of the wandering life. My heart is at home." Edmund Morgan, in a rather nonclinical diagnosis which seeks to explain the lure of Braintree to Adams, concludes, "He had almost an obsession with manure."[17] Adams happily retired from the Second Continental Congress on November 11, 1777, but was appointed to go to France 22 days later. Although he did not want the appointment, his vanity would not allow him to refuse it. In 1782, Braintree called again: "This is the Anniversary of my quitting home. Three years are compleated. Oh when shall I return?" He was still writing on the same theme in 1785.[18] As vice president, Adams found his station "as pleasing as any on earth, excepting Braintree," and he later considered running for the House of Representatives if Jefferson were elected in 1796.[19]

In considering the antisocial aspects of John Adams, it is well to reflect upon the conclusion of the late Clinton Rossiter: "One does not embrace lightly the man who wore the scratchiest hair shirt over the thinnest skin in American history."[20] As early as 1770, Adams wrote: "There are Persons whom in my Heart I despise; others I abhor," and he noted in August 1776 that there were few people he could bring himself to talk to. "This has made me a Recluse, and will one day, make me an Hermit."[21] He could have added "ex-president" to the list.

Later letters showed that Adams disliked much of day-to-day politics: levees, drawing rooms, Philadelphia in summer, speeches, messages, addresses and replies, and proclamations. Volumes could be written about Adams's dislike of all things Catholic.[22] Adams's unsocial nature, combined with other factors, tended to make him less than the complete Federalist that some authors have seen. Several writers have stressed, in fact, that Adams had a tendency to put himself above parties, especially when party action would violate conscience. Adams had the same tendency with regard to public opinion, which he respected, but he would never make it "the rule of action against conscience."[23]

Adams was also ambitious in his studies, and it affected his health. Like Madison and John Quincy Adams, the senior Adams overworked himself during his student period. For months afterward, he existed on a "milk diet." Adams's real anxiety, however, was a preoccupation with old age. His works teem with references to being "too old" very early in life.[24]

Beyond this clinical analysis, Adams had a few other foibles worth noting before reviewing his life. He was a passionate bibliophile, collecting 3,019 volumes, a very sizable library for the period. He was also a passionate lover of wine. In addition, his reading of Ovid's *Ars Amoris* to a married woman, plus some of his more risqué allegories, places him beyond the stereotypical New England Puritan. Adams, like his son, was strongly antislavery.[25]

So far, no cause for monument to Adams has been found. A man of talents and faults, Adams has nevertheless been characterized by historians as "the most able of Federalist constitutional historians" and "the leading political theorist of his generation." Harold Laski once commented to Zoltan Haraszti: "John Adams was the greatest political thinker whom America has yet produced."[26]

Adams's first 25 years contained at least some of his characteristic enigma, and the unpredictable nature of his future was discernible even in those early years. Born in 1735, Adams was a strong, fiercely competitive youth who was bored with education and preferred sports, shooting, or farm work to studying. Between the ages of eight and 11, Adams tried tobacco, which he would soon consume "in a very criminal degree." He also became enchanted with females, even finding their glances distracting in church. He also consumed a great deal of tea and was a late riser.[27] At his father's urging, he returned to his studies, this time under a tutor he enjoyed, and entered Harvard in 1751 with the intention of being educated for the ministry. Adams turned to law, however, because he did not want to involve himself in constant theological dispute. He graduated from Harvard in 1755 and in the same year developed a cyclical theory of empire which saw America as a successor to Rome and England. He taught at Worcester from 1755 to 1758 while studying law at the office of a Mr. Putnam. Sponsored at the bar in 1758, Adams was advised to pursue the law itself, "rather than the gain of it," and not to marry early. Adams at least followed the first bit of advice.[28]

The admission of Adams to the bar was as much a watershed in his own life and career as the years after 1758 would be a watershed in American history. Adams's law practice prospered, and he became a newspaper polemicist quite early in the revolutionary agitation. In May 1761, in a letter to the *Boston Gazette*, Adams strongly defended a free press. He concluded that he expected ridicule of wrong conduct and believed in the sanctity of such ridicule, "even altho I am myself the object." Shortly thereafter, he reflected: "I begin to feel the Passions of the World. Ambition, Avarice, Intrigue, Party, all must be guarded." His writings against the Stamp Act were published widely, and he used the name "Clarendon" in the *Boston Gazette* to answer the charges of "Pym" in the London *Evening Post*.[29]

Adams was married to Abigail Smith on October 25, 1764, and the pair spent the next few years generating heirs. From the time of his marriage until the Declaration of Independence, Adams kept a careful eye on the pulse of public opinion and even dared to challenge public sentiment in his defense of Captain Preston and the soldiers involved in the misnamed "Boston Massacre" (Adams was not paid for his defense).[30] But Adams's major concern at this time was in forming or gauging public opinion. Adams wrote to Jefferson in 1815 to remind him that it was pamphlets and newspapers which enlightened public opinion between 1760 and 1775, and he saw that ideological enlightenment as the real revolution. Adams himself contributed to this enlightenment because his "Novanglus" letters, particularly the third one, strongly opposed the Tory press and forecast the rancor of the 1790s: "License of the press is no proof of liberty. When a people are corrupted, the press may be made an engine to complete their ruin." The letter also noted notorious abuse of the press and indicted Tories as the least respectful regarding truth and decency. Adams also wrote on America's need to free itself from the British judiciary and congratulated Messieurs Edes and Gill of the *Boston Gazette* for having the courage to publish their convictions.[31]

Adams was a delegate to the First Continental Congress, and he reconciled his parting from Abigail with the promise to her that he would do his duty as conscience dictated. Unfortunately for his personal following, his conscience dictated independence months before popular opinion caught up to him. Although he was considered slightly radical, Adams overreacted and felt slightly ostracized. He had a "faithful Friend" with him en route to Philadelphia in 1776, and that friend, Elbridge Gerry, would remain close to Adams, despite some strain that the friendship suffered over the years because of partisan politics.[32]

While in Congress, Adams's most significant service in terms of future policy was his position on the Board of War, which kept him in constant touch with the statistics of countless tragic deaths. This may explain part of the reasoning behind his gamble for peace in 1799. While on the Board of War, Adams also had occasion to question Washington's military acumen, as well as the entire contemporary American military philosophy, a criticism for which he was abused, but one which was essentially correct.[33]

Another watershed in Adams's career was reached on February 13, 1778, when he and his son, John Quincy, sailed for France aboard the *Boston*. In France, the younger Adams had a ten-year-old playmate, Benny Bache, while the senior Adams had Franklin as a colleague. Franklin admonished Adams to learn French either by taking a mistress or by going to plays, so Adams became a regular at the theater. Adams's real problem in France was that the French thought he was the more radical Sam Adams. Once they came to know John, they fed his pride by telling him, "Monsieur, vous êtes le Washington de la négociation." Adams soon became a publicist for the American cause, using Edmund Jennings in Brussels to plant articles in the British press that were sympathetic to the Americans.[34] Although Adams was irritated by restrictions on the French press, he and the French foreign minister, Vergennes, agreed on the necessity of manipulating the English press. "Mr. Adams," said the count, "the gazettes, the journals govern the world. It is necessary we should attend to them in all parts and in England." Adams also noted prophetically that the day was not far off when French consuls might entangle themselves in American politics.[35]

Adams's role as publicist is matched in significance only by his falling out with Franklin. Although admiring the inventor's genius and wit, Adams doubted his political greatness. He further believed Franklin was willing to hedge on important issues such as the questions of fisheries and western boundaries to retain his popularity with the dignitaries and ladies at court. Adams added, "The Life of Dr. Franklin was a scene of continual dissipation." Adams acted independently of Franklin at times, and his suspicious nature convinced him that Franklin hated him from 1783 onward. As he later wrote to Rush, "Look into Benjamin Franklin Bache's *Aurora* and Duane's *Aurora* for twenty years, and see whether my expectations have been verified."[36]

On February 24, 1785, Congress appointed Adams envoy to Great Britain. The most significant aspect of his three years in London is the newspaper scurrility he faced. The *Public Advertiser* noted, "An Ambassador from America! Good Heavens, what a sound! The Gazette surely never announced anything so extraordinary before." Adams was also criticized as a penny-pincher and a debtor (his salary was indeed low). He was also called "the American commercial agent" and "a proscribed rebel," harsh labels to hurl at a supposedly friendly diplomat. Abigail was mocked for lowering herself to do the family shopping. Adams felt the abuse keenly, and he wrote in his diary: "A Murderer, a Thief, a Robber, a Burglar, is a Tyrant. Perjury, Slander, are tyranny too, when they hurt anyone." Abigail noted the insults also in her correspondence with Jefferson, who expressed regret that the Adamses were the subject of attack, concluding that it would be a victory for John to stand up to "the blackest slanders."[37]

To avoid British calumny, and because duty called, Adams made occasional trips to Holland to seek recognition or loans. He manipulated the press there, publishing a plea for recognition and aid in English, French, and Dutch. He did so over the head of officialdom, as Genet would later do in America. While in Holland, he blurted out to Elkanah Watson that America's defense would someday depend on "twelve sail of the line, supported by a proportion of frigates," a program to which he would later give life.[38]

The final significance of Adams's ten years in Europe relates to the political writings he prepared for export to America during his mission. These writings, which include *Thoughts on Government*, *The Report of a Constitution*, and the *Defence of the American Constitutions*, were read by statesmen at the time, and later by the public. They were verbally twisted, however, and therefore subject to attack in the early years under the Constitution, when Washington was still above attack. Adams looked to balance in government and placed heavy reliance on the representative assembly: "It should be in miniature an exact portrait of the people at large. It should think, feel, reason, and act like them."[39] He also warned that nothing should be kept from the people and would neither attempt to flatter popular prejudices nor fetter the press: "*The liberty of the press, therefore, ought not to be restrained.*"[40] Jefferson wrote to Adams at this time of ongoing literary abuse and mob actions in Paris and regretted that nothing was done to stop it. Adams answered Jefferson: "You are afraid of the one—I, of the few."[41] With these thoughts, Adams returned to America in 1788 with so many books that John Quincy took three days to unpack them. Adams came home to a world that was ten years removed from his memories of America, a world which attacked his writings as inimical rather than helpful to the system of republican forms. "The political world had undergone, in the interval, a great revolution."[42]

The Adams family had also undergone a great revolution. In addition to bringing back cartons of books, John returned with his own published thoughts on government. He also had the distinction of serving in both France and England, which would provide vital experience, as would his functions in Holland, which taught him a poignant lesson about the state of American finances. Adams's eldest son also had gained a modest amount of diplomatic experience, as well as a Harvard education. The son, having learned his trade at his father's elbow, would return to the Old World for many years to come, to be his father's eyes and ears in Europe.

One other person merits serious consideration. Abigail Adams had also been to court in Europe, and she and her daughter-in-law of later years, John Quincy's wife, had an opportunity unique for presidential wives before the twentieth century. While in England, Abigail learned how it felt to be the butt of journalistic venom, and the lesson was not lost on her return to America. More significantly, she would also have a better understanding of the European mind than most of the congressmen who would soon be debating foreign policy. For the 12 years between 1789 and 1801, Abigail would serve John as "minister without portfolio," serve as a leader in the school integration movement, and would also become something of a nativist. If John or John Quincy were years ahead of their time, Abigail was decades ahead of hers.[43]

Within a few months of his return from Europe, Adams was elected vice president under the new Constitution, but the choice had more to do with geography than talent or merit. Washington expected Adams to be vice president and commented: "He will doubtless make a very good one." A month later, however, Washington took, a different view of Adams's election: "I considered it to be the only certain way to prevent the election of an Antifederalist." Thus, our first election was something of a paradox because Washington did not wholeheartedly want Adams because of his attitude toward a standing army during the American Revolution, but needed him to prevent the election of an "anti." Adams's army attitude was probably also the reason why Washington consulted him less and less frequently as his first term progressed.[44] Hamilton would have preferred a vice president who was more pliant than Adams, and he even sent Henry Knox to convince Adams that the second office in the land was beneath him. Fearing, however, that Adams might land some other important position, Hamilton acquiesced in having Adams hidden away in the vice presidency. Hamilton clipped Adams's wings, however, by arranging for votes to be scattered, so that the vain Adams received 34 electoral votes, one less than half of Washington's unanimous 69 electoral votes. Robert Morris hinted at future precedent when he suggested that Adams had been made vice president to keep him quiet.[45]

The weak mandate pierced Adams's thin skin. He noted his feelings of "mortification" that "so great a portion of our Fellow Citizens had been artful and that so many more had been dupes." Adams considered not accepting the office, but he only went so far as to complain. He wrote to Rush in 1790: "I wish very heartily that a change of Vice-President could be made to-morrow. . . . —if I had not been introduced into it in a manner that made it a disgrace. I will never serve it again upon such terms." Adams's grandson and editor pictured Hamilton's move as the first step in a rivalry that would later destroy Federalism, while Adams's concern at the time was fending off his enemies in the name of "the public good."[46]

At the time of his arrival in New York, Adams had, in John Fenno, at least one loyal admirer in the newspaper business. The *Gazette of the United States* for April 18–22 was extremely pro–Adams and devoted many columns to Adams's greatness during and after the Revolution. In a poem, "THE VICE-PRESIDENT," Fenno boasted:

> WHEN Heaven resolv'd COLUMBIA should be free,
> And INDEPENDENCE, spake the great decree,
> Lo, ADAMS rose! a giant in debate,
> And turn'd *that vote* which fix'd our empire's fate.

Fenno would later print Adams's *Discources [sic] on Davila* from April 28, 1790, to April 23, 1791, when they were discontinued due to "the rage and fury of the Jacobinical journals." The *Boston Independent Chronicle* also noted Adams's talents and lamented his weak showing in the recent canvass.[47]

Adams's unpublished papers contain many letters he received from supplicants requesting government appointments. In those he answered, Adams replied that the appointing power was lodged in the president. As for himself, "the Vice-President has no voice excepting in the case of an equal division of the Senators." In that capacity, Adams outworked any vice president since 1797. He broke 20 tie votes in the First Congress alone, including the all-important question of lodging cabinet removal power solely with the president. Abigail sarcastically wrote that the function of "this dangerous *vice*" had probably saved the union. She also noted that her husband was attacked for his vote because it was believed that he was voting power into his own hands.[48]

Adams rashly demonstrated his alleged monarchism in the titles issue. Although the *Federalist* #84 had pointed out that the Constitution prohibited the introduction of titles of nobility, the Senate debated the issue for three weeks. The debate was only interrupted by levity or inflamed rhetoric, as senators called each other "Your Highness of the Senate" and Ralph Izard called Adams "His Rotundity." Adams nevertheless remained convinced of the need for titles to reflect the dignity of high office and asked Dr. Benjamin Rush how he would feel if he were called "Ben" by a servant. Writing again to Rush, Adams concluded that "Titles and Ranks are as essential to government as reason and justice." The opposition jumped on that. Maclay, the personification of early Republicanism, cried out, "O Adams! Adams! what a wretch art thou!" A poem, after lashing Adams directly, snidely asked:

> O WASHINGTON! thy country's hope and
> trust!
> Alas! perhaps her last, as thou wert first;
> Successors we can find—but tell us where
> Of all thy virtues we shall find the heir?[49]

Adams continued to trust public prints, however, and he advised Washington to place paragraphs in newspapers to influence "the public mind." Yet a more sour Adams warned Benjamin Lincoln that "words are employed like paper money, to cheat the widow and the fatherless and every honest man."[50]

By mid–1789, Adams was beginning to recognize trends in the emerging current of American politics. To Roger Sherman he predicted: "We shall very soon have parties formed; a court and country party, and these parties will have names given them." Adams also reflected that he did not share the confidence which the nation had in Washington, and he stated: "A new Vice-President must be chosen before a new President.... I am not am ambitious man. Submission to insult and disgrace is one thing, but aspiring to higher situations is another." Remembering the weaknesses of American finance which had undermined his position in Europe, Adams threw his support behind Hamilton's attempts to reestablish public credit. Writing to John Trumbull, Adams had high praise for Hamilton: "The Secretary of the Treasury is all that you think of him. There is no office in the government better filled." Adams would later regret that Hamilton left the cabinet and that the secretary had been the target of press attacks.[51]

Adams himself became the butt of journals after 1790. Washington's serious illness in that year raised the possibility of succession by Adams. This possibility, combined with Washington's temporary immunity from newspaper attack, Hamilton's political adroitness, and Adams's suspected monarchism, made Adams the logical target for attack. A pamphleteer in

defense of Adams noted the volume of abuse: "Every dabbler in a
newspaper, every manufacturer of a paragraph was sure to have his blow."
Adams's letters to friends at this time reflect nonchalance, but Federalists'
letters to Adams show concern.[52]

Jefferson heated up the simmering newspaper war when his letter to
Philip Mazzei was accidentally printed after repeated translations. The
anti–Federalists of New Haven, Philadelphia, and Boston, spurred on by
Jefferson's criticisms of latent monarchism, increased their attacks against
the "Duke of Braintree." Adams defended himself in a letter to Jefferson,
making reference to the "floods or whirlwinds of tempestuous Abuse,
unexampled in the History of this Country" which he suffered. Jefferson
wrote to Washington regarding Adams, "We differ as friends should do."
The younger Adams, writing as "Publicola," answered the Jefferson-
Mazzei letter. Editors mistook the writing for that of the senior Adams,
who was lavished with praise. Yet by early 1792, Adams was writing that
he should be making a collection of the abuse printed about him.[53]

The year 1792 saw the first real contest for national office. As Washington was still immune from a frontal political assault, the struggle was
limited to a campaign for the vice president's chair. Freneau was the
strongest traducer of Adams at this point, making repeated oblique
references to Adams's monarchical tendencies. He later printed, "RULES,
For Changing a limited Republican Government into an unlimited hereditary one." The campaign was wide open, and even some Federalists may
have opposed Adams. Republicans certainly did. "Valerius," who may
have been John Beckley, attacked Adams as unfit for office. One edition
of Fenno's Federalist journal both praised and attacked Adams. The incumbent vice president fared poorly in the South because of his willingness
to support Hamilton and because of his alleged monarchism. Adams
blamed the lack of Southern support on newspapers: "There is no other
newspaper circulated in the back country of the southern states than
Freneau's *National Gazette*, which is employed with great industry to
poison the minds of the people."[54]

Despite Freneau's influence, real or imagined, evidence indicates that
Jefferson supported Adams in 1792. Hamilton saw Freneau's work as
"something like a very serious design to subvert the government."
Hamilton also urged Adams to return to Philadelphia because his absenteeism was helping his rival, George Clinton.[55]

Adams was reelected by a vote of 77 to 50 over Clinton and was soon
writing to Abigail of his peace of mind in spite of foreign crises and "all
his treacherous friends and open enemies in his own country."[56] Adams's
second term, prior to the election of 1796, was indeed more serene than
the first. Several reasons explain this. First, monarchism had not come to
pass and had lost potency as an issue. Second, increased Federalist strength

in the Senate meant that Adams was no longer the tiebreaker. Finally, although attacks against Adams continued, editors were beginning to fire repeated salvos at Washington, Hamilton, and other Federalists, and their sufferings mitigated Adams's.

During the next three years, 1793 to 1796, Adams was little more than an interested spectator in the maelstrom of crises which swirled around the president and cabinet. In February 1793, Adams noted, "I am weary of reading newspapers," without appending specific reasons for this ennui. Later in the year, Freneau pictured the office of vice president as "superfluous" and found agreement from the incumbent, who wrote his wife, "But my country has, in its wisdom, contrived for me the most insignificant office that ever the invention of man contrived or his imagination conceived; and as I can do neither good nor evil, I must be borne away by others and meet the common fate." Adams also registered his displeasure with events in France, noting that even women might demand the right to vote.[57]

Adams wrote at the outset of 1794 that "anti-federal scribblers" were shifting their abuse to Washington, and he concluded, "I have held the office of Libellee-General long enough." But Adams was still bored listening to hour after hour of debate in which he could not participate. His thoughts also focused on public opinion, which he called "a chaos, a Proteus—any thing, every thing, and nothing. Yet all sides trumpet and dogmatize about the public opinion." He also noted its potential for evil: "*Vox Populi, Vox Dei*, they say, and so it is, sometimes. But it is sometimes the voice of Mahomet, of Caesar, of Cataline, the Pope, and the Devil." In an unpublished letter, Adams vented his spleen against foreign scribblers like Callender, but added that he read their works with "interest and avidity."[58]

A noteworthy incident interrupted the Jay's Treaty hysteria. Adams met Bache as the latter was on his way north to distribute copies of the treaty and denounce its contents. Adams thought the treaty would be accepted once its operation was proved, but Bache evidently dissented, as he pushed ahead to Boston to execrate the treaty. Adams, it should be noted, read the *Aurora*, just as he read Porcupine's pamphlets. Adams was alarmed at the volume of abuse Washington was receiving and was particularly annoyed because his own name, reputation, and talents were often used against the president. Yet Abigail quite correctly warned her husband early in 1796 that if he became president, he would also return to his earlier status of libellee-general.[59]

Before moving on to the election of 1796, it is well to reflect upon a conclusion of Stewart Mitchell, who wrote: "In one respect, our first Vice-President was the most distinguished of all."[60] Adams cast key tie-breaking votes which have since been molded into the American political tradition.

In addition, his courage in the face of attack, particularly before Washington and Hamilton were assailed, prevented the vice presidency from becoming a nonentity. While writers are accustomed to conclude that it was to America's advantage that the first president was a man of strength, the same conclusion applies to America's first vice president.

During his years in Europe, Adams wrote: "Corruption in elections is the great enemy of freedom,"[61] and his phraseology in that instance provides an adequate text to study both presidential elections which involved him. Of immediate concern is the canvass of 1796, which featured enough corruption and political double-dealing to consider it as a dress rehearsal for the Federalist dénouement of 1800.

Adams realized quite early in 1796 that he was the logical successor to Washington, but he knew that a volume of abuse awaited any candidate. He just could not keep himself out of the battle, however. Two letters to his wife demonstrate the enigma. He wrote in January: "I am heir apparent, you know, and a succession is soon to take place. . . . I have no very ardent desire to be the butt of party malevolence. Having tasted of that cup, I find it bitter, nauseous, and unwholesome." But by February he realized he was irresistibly being drawn into the fray: "I am weary of the game, yet I don't know how I could live out of it. I don't love slight, neglect, contempt, disgrace, nor insult, more than others."[62] So Adams put his calculating mind to the task of the election, and his writings reflect both the insecurity of his position and his overall anxiety to be done with politics. Some facet of his personality kept him in motion, however.

In January, Adams realized he could count on little support in the South. When he learned that the South was willing to keep him as vice president under Jefferson, he characteristically answered: "I most humbly thank you for your kind condescension, Messieurs Transchesapeakes." The historian of southern Federalism put it more succinctly: "Adams was mistrusted and disliked universally in the south."[63] Adams's fear of corruption in the election was, however, his guide to action, or inaction, as it was, because he wrote to Jefferson: "Corruptions in Elections has heretofore destroyed all Elective Governments. What Regulations or Precautions may be devised to prevent it in the future, I am content with you to leave to Posterity to consider." Nevertheless, shortly after writing that letter to Jefferson, Adams wrote his wife that he was fed up and wanted out and that he would not accept an election by the House of Representatives. This showed that his letter to Jefferson was a declaration of principles, not a carefully worded political feeler.[64]

The most serious roadblock between Adams and the presidency was not Jeffersonian democracy, but rather Federalist duplicity. Federalists hoped primarily to keep Jefferson out of power, and if that meant running Thomas Pinckney ahead of Adams, Federalist joy would be complete.

They would have a political newcomer, whose political debts to his creators would make him pliable, in the place of the strong-willed Adams. They would also have saved the presidency from the suspected atheist, Jefferson. Federalist newspapers divided on Adams, as Fenno printed columns by "A Federalist" in support of Pinckney. Hamilton, writing years later, claimed he had favored Pinckney over Adams in 1796 and had campaigned actively for the former. George Gibbs claims that Wolcott supported Adams, but the correspondence cited in support leaves the question open. Robert Goodloe Harper, a Federalist leader from South Carolina, saw no need to cloak his preferences as Wolcott did. He wrote to Ralph Izard to urge the election of Pinckney: "He, I think, is our sheet anchor. It is not Pinckney or Adams with us, but Pinckney or Jefferson."[65] A defender of Adams even printed an oblique reference to Federalist duplicity in a pamphlet: "That Mr. ADAMS's election will be disputed is not doubted; but by whom? By those who hate his virtues, dread his talents, and *tremble at his firmness*" (italics added).[66]

Some of the noise of the 1796 campaign was noted in previous chapters, but a few things remain to be added here, as they bear directly on Adams. First, he had to sit through a political humiliation. He wrote in his diary that a Rhode Island representative promised him the support of his state, but "He said they wanted Hamilton for V.P.—I was wholly silent." Second, there was still the *Aurora* to contend with, and the political charges were at best ludicrous. The people were asked to decide "whether we shall have at the head of our executive a steadfast friend to the Rights of the People, or an advocate for hereditary power and distinctions." Borrowing from a letter of Thomas Paine's, the *Aurora* charged that Adams was in favor of hereditary succession in the family of Lund Washington and believed the vice presidency should be kept in the Adams family. Paine, via Bache, concluded: "John Adams is one of those men who never contemplated the origin of government or comprehended any thing of first principles." "Sydney," writing in several October issues of the *Aurora*, exacerbated the situation by taking Adams's political writings out of context. Even Dumas Malone, a Jefferson biographer, admits that Adams's words were distorted far more than Jefferson's. Adams was attacked for having sons, possible successors, while Jefferson had only daughters. Adams was also seen as a party to the "Conway Cabal" during the American Revolution. The *Aurora* reached back to the titles question and reminded readers of the candidacy of "His Rotundity." Hamilton planted articles by "Federalist" in the Democratic-Republican *New World* of Philadelphia, which tried to show that the vice presidency was an empty job and that Adams therefore had no executive experience or knowledge of public affairs. Adams's defenders were upset because they had to repeat the charges in order to refute them.[67] Considering his character traits, the abuse Adams underwent made the canvass of 1796 seem very real to him, although it was not a true election campaign until Washington announced his retirement in mid–September.

Adams's real defenders were the citizens, legislators, and electors who let their voices be heard in his behalf. Perhaps fearing war with England if Jefferson abrogated Jay's Treaty, the people elected Adams in a close contest which took weeks for the final results to become known. French minister Adet's meddling in Pennsylvania politics struck Adams as "an instrument well calculated to reconcile me to private life. It will purify me from all envy of Mr. Jefferson or Mr. Pinckney, or Mr. Burr, or Mr. any body who may be chosen President or Vice-President." While disappointed Republicans were quick to discover voting frauds, Jefferson saw Hamilton as the fraud and wrote to Adams (although the letter was never delivered): "Indeed it is possible that you may be cheated of your succession by a trick worthy of the subtlety of your arch-friend of New York, who has been able to make of your real friends tools to defeat their and your just wishes."[68]

As the results of the election became known, Republican editors who had opposed Adams began to treat the president-elect with a modicum of respect and the lame-duck president with less respect. This surprising turn of events, which came to be the first presidential honeymoon vis-à-vis the press, is the subject of the following chapter. Before that, however, some of the general problems of Adams's presidency must be noted because many of Adams's character traits discussed throughout this chapter would prove fatal to this "honeymoon" and further the deterioration of the executive-press relationship, which was ultimately one basis for the Federalist undoing.

Adams had extremely large shoes to fill as he replaced Washington, and his three-vote victory in the electoral college made the fit even more difficult. The weak mandate, plus precedents established during Washington's terms, all but forced Adams to keep the members of Washington's cabinet in their positions. Hamilton had been the guiding force under Washington while working as a New York attorney, as McHenry admitted and as Wolcott's correspondence clearly proves. Adams was also quick to see the problems any new cabinet member would face: the low salary, the journalistic abuse, and the need to move family and belongings to Philadelphia. Adams later complained to Jefferson that circumstances forced Washington's cabinet upon him, although Wolcott, in a move which became an American political tradition, did tender a resignation, which was refused.[69]

The *Aurora* tried to warn Adams of treachery in his own house, but Adams ignored the warning and wrote to Elbridge Gerry in a secure frame of mind: "Pickering and all his colleagues are as much attached to me as I desire. I have no jealousies from that quarter." It was a great error to keep

Washington's cabinet intact, however, because the cabinet members continued to seek guidance from Hamilton, whose lack of respect for Adams was matched by Adams's lack of respect for him. Hamilton would remain in constant touch with legislative leaders, who looked to him, not Adams, for advice, and the cabinet, hardly a brain trust to begin with, "had this same tropism."[70] Washington, later put in command of the provisional army, pulled the same strings which connected Hamilton to the puppets in the cabinet (Lee and Stoddert excepted), and the cabinet would urge Washington in 1799 to consider running for president once again in 1800.[71] In addition, it should be remembered that the character traits listed at the outset of this chapter would have made Adams a difficult man to work with, even if his cabinet had been composed of saints rather than sinners.

One character trait noted earlier that would plague Adams's presidency was his love for Braintree and his yearly desire to quit the capital and return home at the end of the session of Congress. Adams's absences left governmental business in the hands of a cabinet likened to Ali Baba's "Forty Thieves" and at the mercy of the fledgling postal service. In four years in office (1,460 days), Adams was absent from the seat of government for no less than 559 days (38.2 percent of his term). Virtually none of that time could be construed as having been spent on official business and indeed little of it could be considered a working vacation.[72] Adams could claim precedent, as Washington had absented himself, even in time of crisis, to go to nearby Mount Vernon. But it would be a weak defense. Business was not always completely attended to before Adams's departures, and an illness of Abigail's was not sufficient reason for his abrupt leave-taking in the hectic summer of 1798. There was no emergency whatever behind his 1799 summer absence. While the capital clamored at the prospect of peace in the spring and summer of 1799, Adams alternated his time at home between the manure pile and Voltaire's letters.[73]

One final aspect deserves brief attention. We know that Adams was irascible, bad-tempered, and suspicious as president, as it was his nature from early years. A continuance of these traits in the presidency would only have been strengthened by a problem which modern political scientists have dubbed the "generation gap." Quite simply, from 1774 to his retirement from office in 1801, Adams saw one colleague after another depart from the national scene, either because of a desire to return to private pursuits or through the intervention of the grim reaper. The gap showed up early, as Adams's close friends of the First Continental Congress were generally absent from the Second Congress. By 1783, only four signers of the Declaration of Independence were in the Congress which received the Treaty of Paris for ratification. In 1790, Adams lamented to Rush that the "candidates for fame" were "a sett of young gentlemen who have come out

of Colledge since the revolution." By December 1795, only eight of the
original 26 senators remained in office. In 1797 Adams wrote to Gerry that
his Southern friends were now too old to be reliable information sources.
The same year he wrote, "The friends of my youth are generally gone,"
and a year later, he felt "I am a solitary individual of 1774 men. All the
rest have departed." By 1800, Adams had recognized the situation so clearly
that he began to modify his ideas, and his post–1801 thinking, not largely
at issue here, reflects his acceptance of the generation gap.[74]

We have come full circle with our character study of John Adams. In
addition to the hysteria and rancor of the period, the nature of the journalistic profession, the precedents of the press struggle with George Washington, the traits, foibles, and behavioral mannerisms of our subject complete the background data of our study. The remainder of the book will
attempt to show the interaction of "the age and passion" with the press and
with the unique character of John Adams as it shaped his term, and, in his
own estimation, provided his ultimate undoing.

CHAPTER SIX

Adams and the
American Press I:
Honeymoon

It is universally admitted that Mr. Adams is a man of in-
corruptible integrity, and that the resources of his own
mind are equal to the duties of his station; ... he will not
become the head of a party, and that he will not be the tool
of any man or set of men.
—*Aurora*, March 14, 1797

Republican editors instituted détente with Adams as the results of the election of 1796 became apparent. This détente may have amounted to nothing more than making use of Adams's name as an additional vehicle with which to flay the departing Washington, or it may have reflected a genuine attempt by editors to be conciliatory and adopt a wait-and-see policy while Adams began to channel his many genuine intellectual gifts into workable American policy.

The truth lies in a combination of both reasons. Republican editors proved they would stop at virtually nothing in their abuse of Washington in the closing months of his second term, and the differences between Adams and Washington were too obvious not to exploit. The second factor, the wait-and-see attitude, was stronger, however, because editors realized that Adams might be good for something more than just serving as the object of anti–Washington ink. First, Federalist duplicity in the election indicated that Adams clearly possessed fewer Federalist friends than Washington. Second, Hamilton's ambivalence in the canvass, combined with Adams's strong-willed, independent temperament, meant that the president would probably cease being a reflection of Hamiltonian policy. Finally, it can be inferred from the volume of abuse directed at

Washington in his final year that some Republican editors simply believed that anyone (save Hamilton) would be an improvement over Washington. For those reasons, plus the growing crisis in foreign relations, Adams was to be the object of the first true presidential honeymoon in American history.

If President-elect Adams had chosen to compile a hypothetical political ledger in the weeks before his inauguration, he could have expected Jefferson to lead the opposition politically from the vice president's chair. Former Democratic-Republican leaders Madison and Beckley were soon to retire from their posts in the House of Representatives, the former voluntarily, the latter a victim of Federalist proscription. Adams could also expect the opposition press to be led by Benjamin Franklin Bache in Philadelphia and Philip Freneau in New York.

For adherents, Adams might have concluded that at least minimal support would be forthcoming from the Federalist leader in absentia, Alexander Hamilton, and from the leading Federal sheets, Fenno's *Gazette of the United States* and the forthcoming *Porcupine's Gazette*. As might be expected, the reverse proved true. The *Aurora* and Jefferson ranged in attitudes from elation to tacit acceptance, while Federalist leaders and sheets were noteworthy for either their suspicions or their deafening silence. Bernard Fay has shown that the reversal in attitude goes back to the 1796 election, when some of Adams's friends opposed him. Once he was elected, his quondam friends returned to the fold, and some of his enemies were elated over his election.[1]

All of this did not happen overnight. Although the *Aurora* of December 21, 1796, pictured Adams as "unable to sacrifice his country's interests at the shrine of party," this was more of a brief thaw than a warming trend. Jefferson, writing to Madison, had no regrets at the prospect of serving under Adams and believed that if Adams's monarchism could be kept under control, it might be to Republican as well as to America's advantage "to come to a good understanding with him as to his future elections. He is perhaps the only sure barrier against Hamilton's getting in." A later letter of Jefferson's expressed the hope that Adams would not follow a strict Hamiltonian line.[2]

The *Aurora* reminded readers of Adams's great contribution to independence and wished aloud that Adams would consider pursuing a policy independent of his predecessor. A few sharp volleys preceded the complete, albeit temporary, apostasy of Bache, however. He warned subscribers that Adams's election would mean a war with France, and the following day added that Adams's writings prove that he is "an enemy to the elective principle in government." Nevertheless, Federalist Chauncey Goodrich was essentially correct when he wrote: "The democrats are besetting Mr. Adams with attention. Since his election has become ascertained, the scurrility in Bache's paper has ceased, and it is said the democrats are recommending to him the conciliation of parties." Having correctly gauged Democratic ideology, Goodrich later hinted at future Federalist policy: "We must arm the Executive with powers to curb the lawless efforts of our citizens to embroil us abroad, and repel all insults on the government."[3] This second letter raises two important and largely unanswerable questions. First, if Goodrich admitted that Bache's deportment had improved, who was responsible for "all insults on the government?" Second, whom did Goodrich have in mind when he spoke of arming "the Executive?" This kind of illogical speculation by Federalists will explain part of their undoing.

February 22, 1797, was the day on which Bache began the genuine détente with Adams. Although it was probably a slap at Washington to have his successor lauded on his last birthday in office, the real occasion for Bache's joy was Adams's farewell address as vice president: "The Republicans are well satisfied with the election of Mr. Adams . . . he is a firm and upright patriot. . . . Mr. Adams is also for peace with France." Another column concluded that "America has a right to rejoice" in the coming of "two such distinguished patriots as Mr. Adams and Mr. Jefferson."[4]

On March 4, 1797, John Adams took the oath of office in a crisis-filled atmosphere, although "no one, with the possible exception of Abigail Adams, would have ventured to say that John Adams had replaced General Washington."[5] Yet from March 4 to May 16, a total of 73 days, Adams was on good terms with the opposition press and received far better reviews than his predecessor.

The 73-day grace period was a result of two factors. First, Adams's behavior and words at the time of his inaugural address were conciliatory. Second, he adopted a cautious policy when the French rejected and subsequently curtly dismissed the American envoy, Charles Cotesworth Pinckney, a Southern Federalist. Adams's inaugural message, highlighted by one sentence containing 728 words and an avalanche of semicolons, had an antiparty, antiforeign influence tone reminiscent of Washington's Farewell Address. Adams surpassed Washington, however, when he mentioned "a personal esteem for the French nation" and put monarchism to rest when he claimed that he had never entertained the thought that the executive or the Senate should be made more permanent.[6] Adams also put monarchism to rest visually, as his attire was conspicuous for its absence of jewels or a sword, the usual trappings of royalty. In addition, Adams avoided the ostentation of a large team of matched bays and asked Abigail to have the Quincy coat of arms obliterated from his coach.[7] Charles Francis Adams claimed that the only group dissatisfied with the inaugural was the Hamiltonian faction, whose members "lamented its tone as temporizing."

Adams wrote Abigail that Washington seemed to treat inauguration day as his own triumph. While the letter also noted the approval of Adams's inaugural by Senator Mason, "the treaty publisher," Adams concentrated his thoughts on Washington: "Me thought I heard him say 'Ay! I am fairly out and you are fairly in! See which of us will be happiest.'" Adams later wrote Abigail that his inaugural thoughts were partly "an appeal to posterity. Foreign nations and future times will understand them better than my enemies or friends will own they do."[8] Before gauging the reactions of enemies or friends, one further attempt by Adams at conciliation must be noted.

Adams and Jefferson had not seen each other since January 1794, so when they met in Philadelphia in early 1797 and temporarily shared the same boarding house, it was a good omen. Jefferson's attempts at conciliation have been noted, and Adams matched them. In seeking a Democrat to send to France to join the repudiated Pinckney, Adams thought first of Jefferson. He was the logical choice from the point of view of the French, but the most illogical choice constitutionally. Jefferson did not want to go abroad, and his position as vice president made it imperative that he remain in Philadelphia, a heartbeat, not an ocean, away. Adams then considered Madison, but the cabinet balked at this, so the proposed reconciliation via diplomatic appointment was weakened, although Adams did include the pro–French Elbridge Gerry on the subsequent mission, to the disgust of the Federalists. As Adams sourly commented later regarding his relations with Jefferson: "We parted as good friends as we had always lived; but we consulted very little together afterwards. Party violence soon rendered it impracticable, or at least useless, and this party violence was excited by Hamilton more than any other man."[9] Adams erred here, as Hamilton would have been delighted had a Republican of Madison's stature been a party to the forthcoming and somewhat predictable XYZ fiasco. Dumas Malone, viewing Adams's inaugural as "characteristically ponderous," sees it as an attempt to bring the threatened country together and concludes correctly that his speech did more to relieve Republicans' fears than it did to arouse Federalists' hopes.[10] As an attempt to make bedfellows out of opposition editors, however, the address was a total failure because Federalist silence was still at odds with Republican reporting.

Some of the more moderate Federalist sheets reprinted Adams's inaugural and had praise for both Washington and Adams. One independently Democratic journal, the Hartford *American Mercury*, lamented the departure of Washington, but had high praise for his successor a week later and stated that there was little ideological difference between Adams and Jefferson.[11] The *Readinger Adler*, under the heading *"Americanische Nachrichten,"* noted the arrival of president and vice president. The literary-oriented Philadelphia *Minerva* made an infrequent contribution to political reporting when it commented on the arrival of Jefferson, "that tried patriot." *Claypoole's American Daily Advertiser* used the same three words to describe Jefferson and wrote of a Philadelphia banner welcoming "Jefferson the friend of the People." The same paper printed Adams's inaugural on an extra sheet without comment and then reprinted it two days later in the regular edition and noted the Republican simplicity of the entire ceremony.[12]

The *Boston Independent Chronicle* saw "a new political era" and could hardly conceal its joy at the departure of Washington. Another Boston Democratic-Republican sheet wrote that Adams was working for peace as Federalist newspapers were pushing for war. The *Connecticut Courant*, after printing Adams's inaugural without comment, directed its fire at Congress: "*Melancholy! very Melancholy indeed!* DIED, last evening, of a two years consumption, and under all the horrors of a guilty conscience, the HOUSE OF REPRESENTATIVES of the United States."[13]

The leading Federal organs had little more than left-handed compliments for Adams at the time he took office. On March 6, Fenno lauded Washington and mentioned a pro–Adams toast, but there was no further mention of the new president. The next day Bache was abused, and three days later Adams shared a short column with Washington. Fenno remained silent on Adams's inaugural, choosing rather to refute the *Aurora*'s charges that Washington had committed murder during the American Revolution. William Cobbett's ink flowed along similar lines. His first issue, March 4, noted that Adams was entering office, but devoted much space to a banquet for Washington, adding that this was "no *sans-culotte* civic fete. This is a festival of true patriotism and honor." The same issue flayed the French minister, Adet, and wondered if he would be followed by "some other graduate from the school of insurrection." A few days later, Cobbett execrated Tom Paine, "the Apostle of the Devil, and the Nuisance of the World."[14] John Adams had not yet become good copy to High-Federalists.

Papers less inclined to Federalism paid more attention to issues. The Newark *Centinel of Freedom*, a strongly Democratic journal, exhibited a brief flurry of journalistic ambivalence. Before Adams's inauguration, a poem praised his coming, yet a week later he was attacked as a monarchist. His inaugural, however, brought praise because the characteristic features of the speech were "patriotism and conciliation" and it was seen as "the address of a fellow citizen, who will not deign to become the *President of a Party*." The New York *Argus*, long on Republicanism, chose to be short on rhetoric regarding Adams; it simply concluded: "Let him go on in a career so well begun." The *Aurora* combined its praise for Adams with its dislike for Hamilton, picturing the ex-secretary's ideas as "the menaces or machinations of artful and designing men." Bache also printed a hopefully prophetic conclusion: "Adams has the welfare of his country too much at heart to give in to the measures of that political desperado."[15]

Federalist newspapers which were regional reprints of Fenno were in a quandary. Some chose to write their own copy and were sincere and often lengthy in their praise of Adams. The *New Hampshire Gazette* gave thanks to "the benevolent ruler of the universe" that the second president shared the abilities and talents of his predecessor. The *Salem Gazette* had high praise for Adams, while delivering a carefully worded slap at Jefferson. Some comments on Adams's inaugural amounted to putting words in readers' mouths: "This ceremony and spectacle must have afforded high satisfaction and delight to every genuine Republican."[16] Other Federal writers, left to their own devices, simply reprinted Adams's speech (whether to inform or to fill columns is unclear) and made no comment on it.[17] The lack of comment is highly indicative of Federalist suspicion because it was limited to Federalist newspapers at a time when Republican sheets were following the party line formed by Bache. The absence of comment is the only true indicator of Federalist editorial thinking at this time.

The *Aurora* continued to praise Adams and lash out at "the views of a designing and wicked faction." Later, in an issue which mentioned some mysterious election returns in Philadelphia, Bache had the highest praise for Adams and for his inaugural: "How honorable are these sentiments; how characteristic of a Patriot! ... Adams in his [Washington's] place is endeavoring to soothe the irritated public mind and to harmonize the different parties." The same issue featured the laudatory quotation which introduced this chapter. The *Boston Independent Chronicle*, drawing heavily on Bache, asked, "Who can peruse this address, without giving it his most unreserved approbation?" Although Federalist silence answered the rhetorical question, the *Chronicle* concluded by picturing the address as "A most striking contrast this to the example of his predecessor in office."[18]

In a 1797 letter to Abigail, Adams accurately gauged Federalist sentiment, understated the aim of the Republican press, and gave a forecast of his behavior in 1799 when confronted by a committee of Federalists made irate by the nomination of Murray:

> All the Federalists seem to be afraid to approve any body but Washington. The Jacobin papers damn with faint praise, and undermine with misrepresentation and insinuation. If the Federalists go to playing pranks, I will resign the office, and let Jefferson lead them to peace, wealth and power if he will.

The same letter expressed a desire to keep America free from the influence of either "John Bull" or "Louis Baboon."[19] The letter requires some reflective scrutiny, however, as we know from Adams's character that he needed the presidency badly as an antidote to his manifold anxieties. It may also be that Adams became more willing to adopt Federalist policy in order to prevent the Federalists from "playing pranks." His own character faults may have thus undone his political honeymoon as early as the date of this letter to his wife.

An exchange of letters between Henry Knox and Adams underscored the president's uncertain outlook. Knox wrote to Adams that congratulations upon his elevation were of dubious value because the road ahead undoubtedly had more thorns than roses. Knox added that Adams's inaugural gave general satisfaction, a curious way of offering praise. Adams replied that the election meant little to him, although he would have been upset if someone of less talent, like Jefferson, or "much more such an unknown being as Pinckney" had been elected. He added that he would like to settle the French problem, but pessimistically concluded: "But old as I am, war is, even to me, less dreadful than iniquity or deserved disgrace."[20]

While Adams forecast the possibility of war, the *Aurora* continued its campaign to remind Adams of Federalist duplicity. On March 20, Bache advised his readers that Adams's "insidious friends," who tried to put Pinckney in ahead of him, "cannot forgive the President for the Republican plainness with which he attended at Congress hall to take his inaugural oath." Freneau, now at the helm of the New York *Time Piece*, had little to say on politics primarily because France was now acting as shabbily toward America as were the British, whom Freneau hated. French diplomats in America, acting on the principle that Adams was neither Washington nor Hamilton, generally adopted the same line as Republican newspapers, reversing the earlier trend when Republican newspapers took their editorial cues from French diplomats.[21]

Southern newspapers reflected overall Southern displeasure at the less-than-decorous treatment accorded the South Carolinian Pinckney in Paris. Abraham Hodge's *North Carolina Minerva* led the swing to moderate Federalistm in early 1797, and Pinckney's ouster from France added the influence of other sheets. The *Wilmington Gazette* reprinted Porcupine, while the *State Gazette of North Carolina* and the *North Carolina Gazette* clamored about French ship seizures and about suspected intrigues in the back country.[22]

March 1797 ended with more flattery of Adams by the *Aurora* and occasional anti–Jefferson comment by Federalist sheets, as journalistic honeymoons, like subsequent Sedition Acts, were not tailored to vice presidents. In April, sympathetic editors were still reprinting the *Aurora*, while Bache himself became more subdued regarding Adams. While awaiting the special session of Congress in May, Bache lashed Britain, Jay, Pickering, and C.C. Pinckney, but that was not out of character for

"Lightning Rod, Jr." A Republican, styling himself "THE MEDDLER" wrote in the strongly Federalist Walpole, New Hampshire, *Farmer's Weekly Museum* that he had expected the worst from the combination of Adams and Jefferson. "MEDDLER" expected Adams to import numerous trappings of royalty and Jefferson a like number of guillotines, but the inaugural addresses of both men removed his doubts.[23]

On April 5, 1797, *Kline's Carlisle Weekly Gazette* used large type to announce the special session of Congress called by Adams.[24] At that point, late March and early April, depending on the distance between Philadelphia and an outlying editor's press, the presidential honeymoon of John Adams entered its critical, questioning phase. As it turned out, it was the final phase.

James McHenry, the most inept secretary of war prior to the War of 1812, somehow gauged French military strength accurately when he wrote to Adams on April 8 that the condition of the French fleet ruled out an invasion of America.[25] Other Federalists, however, were more concerned with the condition of American journalism and found much to disgust them in what they saw as pretended praise for Adams. Uriah Tracy saw evidence of "the depravity of our French faction" in certain newspapers. Oliver Wolcott, Sr., wrote to his son of Adams's vanity, lack of prudence, and "far less real abilities than he believes he possesses," which could be played upon by flatterers. The elder Wolcott was correct in this discernment and never more right than when he pictured current events as "no other than what precedes an earthquake." George Cabot added his agreement that a powerful faction was engaged in a grab for power.[26]

An exchange of letters in March and April between Elkanah Watson and Adams shows the former's strong desire to convince the latter that Hamilton, veiled in references as "some New Yorkers," was mortified at Adams's election. Adams replied that Watson was misinformed, because New Yorkers were only upset at the election of Jefferson. A later letter of Watson's went into the details of the Hamiltonian intrigue. Wolcott's editor, George Gibbs, writes that Hamilton stood in the forefront of those who wished Adams a successful administration. Hamilton himself was rather critical of the inaugural, which was the only real presidential act of Adams's term he could have commented on: "It had the air of a lure for the favor of his opponents at the expense of his sincerity."[27]

In mid–April, with McHenry's letter regarding French naval weaknesses notwithstanding, the cabinet urged Adams to announce a preparedness campaign in his special message of May 16. Adams evidently accepted the advice, not aware of its probable Hamiltonian origin, and wrote a letter to Abigail containing a rare mention of the American press. In what amounts to a strong although characteristic distrust of Republican praise, Adams warned his wife: "I warrant you, I shall soon be acquitted of the crime of *Chronicle*, *Argus* and *Aurora* praise. Let it run its rig, however, and say nothing at present." Bache believed that Adams would use the special session to clear up the misunderstandings between France and America and even reminded his readers that Adams had seemingly laid monarchism to rest. Adams's letter to Abigail very accurately forecast the end of the honeymoon, however.[28] The message to the special session, which begins the following chapter, quickly served, as Adams had predicted, to acquit him of the crime of Republican praise.

Federalists must have had some inkling that Adams's coming speech would be as bellicose as his inaugural had been pacific. George Cabot predicted that if Adams spoke of the true national dangers, "he will be supported by the spirit and feelings of the bulk of the people."[29] That ultimately happened.

A few questions remain. Why was Adams, known to be ill-tempered and possessed of so many weaknesses, given a honeymoon by opposition editors? The answer lies in the differences between Washington, Hamilton, and Adams, especially the independence and vanity of the latter. It should be added that Adams was far less popular than Washington, so attacks by rival editors against Adams were not as necessary. As the following chapter will show, attacks grew as his popularity increased.

A larger question revolves around Adams's letter of April 24 to his wife. What circumstances could impel a president of a young and prosperous nation to consider it a crime to be praised by opposition newspapers? Only the hysteria of the age, swirling around in the vortex of Adams's sometimes unfathomable character, can explain such an outburst. In any case, Adams's future policies largely prevented the necessity of a similar outburst. Republican praise ceased being a crime with which Adams had to contend.

CHAPTER SEVEN

Adams and the American Press II: Crisis

If ever an historian should arise fit for the investigation, this transaction must be transmitted to posterity as the most glorious period in American History, and as the most disinterested, prudent, and successful conduct of my whole life.
—Adams to William Cunningham, February 22, 1809, reviewing the years 1798–1801

The seventy-three-day grace period of Adams's political honeymoon came to an abrupt halt on May 16, 1797, when Adams delivered his message to the special session of Congress, a message which in direct language indicated that the United States would not allow itself to be humiliated by the shabby French diplomacy visited upon Charles Cotesworth Pinckney. The relationship between the president and the press then entered its critical phase, lasting from mid–May, 1797, to mid–February, 1799, a total of 21 months. In the first 11 months, the press drew new lines of demarcation. Previously friendly Republican editors, with Bache in the vanguard, hastened to vilify the president. At the same time, Federalist editors found sufficient patriotism in the heretofore suspect Adams to laud the president's martial spirit. Once editorial lines were redrawn, editors on both sides waited for the results of the special mission of John Marshall and Elbridge Gerry, sent to Europe to join Charles Cotesworth Pinckney. Editorial skirmishing was only minimally present, reflecting uncertainty about the three-man mission.

After 11 months of that uncertainty, the results of the "XYZ mission" became known, and Adams's firm stance made him genuinely popular with the citizenry for the first time in his life. From April to October of 1798, while Adams's popularity crested and peaked, Federalists used the newly awakened martial spirit of the nation to justify legislation for internal security and to create an army largely to suit the personal purposes of Alexander Hamilton. With those events before him, Adams began to grow apart from the Federalists in the autumn of 1798, as he began to suspect their dominance in policy. This final phase of the crisis lasted until February 18, 1799, when Adams took steps to convince domineering Federalists that he preferred to create policy, not accept it. Adams's bid for mastery of policy aided his political downfall, but brought peace to the nation. The "threat" of peace, treated in the next chapter, led to yet another press alignment.

On May 16, 1797, Adams calmly shattered Bache's dream that his special message would lay to rest the difficulties existing between France and America. In proposing two additional envoys, Adams held out a tentative olive branch. The basis of the message, in addition to the notion not widely held in Europe that America was here to stay and would not accept or allow inferior treatment, was a collection of general suggestions in the event that the olive branch was spurned. It was a defense proposal, not a war message. Adams believed that "A naval power, next to the militia, is the natural defense of the United States." No army was called for because Adams admitted that distance plus American courage "happily diminish the probability of invasion."[1] While the message did excite Federalists to a great extent, the people at large were less actuated by it, particularly when the quick-to-develop newspaper reporting of the message made it sound like something just short of a declaration of war. Public opinion was not yet prepared to go that far.

On the day that her husband delivered the message, Abigail sent her sister a copy of it and added, "I should like to learn the comments upon it, with a view to discover the Temper and Sentiments of the publick mind."[2] She would not have to wait long for reaction. Although roughly two dozen sheets printed the message without comment in the next two weeks, this silence was bipartisan, supporting the conclusion that the speech was neither the surrender which Bache hoped for nor the war message the Federalists wanted.[3] In short, some editors hesitated, waiting for praise or ridicule to emanate from Philadelphia. Republican editors only had to wait as long as it took the mails to get Bache's first postmessage issue of the *Aurora* to them.

Bache's reporting in the weeks following Adams's message showed that he had lost none of the abusive skills previously aimed at random Federalist targets. On the contrary, his two-and-a-half-month rapport with Adams may have created a backlog of billingsgate, and if so, the floodgates were opened wide after May 17. Adams, Bache told his readers,

had delivered a *"war* speech" and a "war whoop," and Pickering and
Wolcott were accused of feeding Adams's pepperpot "in order to bring his
nerves to a proper anti-gallican tone." Adams, dubbed "President by *three*
votes," was accused of deceiving the people into believing he was "of *no
party*, and that he was under no *extraneous influence*." Bache went on to ac-
cuse Adams of being in his dotage and of being under British influence.
The *Aurora* also told its readers that Adams had appointed his son as
minister plenipotentiary at the court of Berlin. The New York *Time Piece*
echoed Bache and added that Adams was supposedly following precedent,
but Washington never appointed relatives. Bache continued attacks
against "His Serene Highness" and reminded Adams of his three-vote victory. Bache concluded that Adams's speech "Would force a laugh if the
awful crisis of our country would permit levity."[4]

Jefferson also modified his opinion of Adams after the May 16
message, but his position as vice president made total apostasy much more
difficult for him than for Bache. As presiding officer of the Senate, Jefferson was obliged to sign the Senate's reply to Adams's message, which included the passage: "We learn with sincere concern that attempts are in
operation to alienate the affections of our fellow-citizens from their Government."[5]

Bache, with more license than Jefferson, continued the vilification for
several weeks. Adams was unpatriotic, strutting "as if he were the emperor
of all the Russias," part of the British faction, a hypocrite, and "a man
divested of his reason, and wholly under the domination of his passions."
In June, Bache fumed that the House had taken three weeks and spent
$21,000 "for an answer to the speech of a man who is meditating *war* and
ruin to the United States." A week later Bache called for Adams to resign,
"before it be too late to retrieve our deranged affairs."[6]

Other sheets, lacking Bache's instinct for the jugular, featured more
bland reporting and made less interesting reading. The Democratic *Centinel of Freedom* attacked "Porcupine" in its May 17 issue, but had very high
praise for Adams's message a week later. Most Democratic sheets,
however, proved to be servile imitators of Bache, although the *Boston Independent Chronicle* occasionally outdid the *Aurora*. The *Chronicle* was
echoed by the *Boston Gazette*, which made its living reprinting Bache, so
there was solid opposition even in Adams's home state.[7]

On the other side, Adams found able defenders in the previously silent
Federalist press. Porcupine could hardly conceal his joy that "this spaniel"
Bache had to retract his earlier praise of Adams. As to the speech, Cobbett
saw it as a cold blast at the Jacobins, and he trusted that "Congress will
freeze them as stiff as an icicle." The New York *Minerva* lined up with
Adams, writing that he would lose previous *Aurora* and *Argus* support
and would "be abandoned by every body, except . . . *all sound-hearted*

Americans!!" In his native state, Adams could count on the support of the *Columbian Centinel*, the trade-oriented *Boston Price-Current and Marine Intelligencer*, and the *Massachusetts Mercury*.[8]

Outside Massachusetts, many other New England papers lined up behind Adams and radiated High-Federalist doctrine. The *Providence Gazette* was as strong in support of Adams as it was in its denunciation of Jacobinism. The *Farmer's Weekly Museum* of Walpole, New Hampshire, reported events in a very dignified tone which captured the spirit of Adams's message: "The speech is dispassionate but firm. The President, as becomes the chief Magistrate of an independent republic, appears disposed to adjust amicably, if possible, the difficulties, which subsist between the two nations, but resolved, at the same time, to vindicate our rights with energy." The same sheet reported the imbalance of rhetoric over action in congressional proceedings. In Connecticut, the *Norwich Packet* and the *Connecticut Gazette* devoted their ink to "scribblers" or Jacobins who failed to see events in their proper (Federalist) light.[9]

Federalist correspondence echoed Federalist editorials. The leaders of Federalism saw Adams's speech as having the potential to rouse public opinion and to be the antidote to "the French disease" or "the French fever." Washington gave his blessing to the speech and concluded that "Things cannot, ought not to remain any longer in their present disagreeable state." A later letter of Washington's shows that he expected Adams's message to call forth an expression of the public will, but was uncertain when it would happen. The only clue to Adams's reaction to his sudden status change is a letter of William Loughton Smith's, in which he wrote to Ralph Izard that he had dined with the Adamses and told some stories about Cobbett which greatly pleased John and Abigail. Smith concluded: "Porcupine is a great favorite at court."[10]

The same William Smith introduced a Hamilton-inspired legislative package in the House of Representatives on June 5, 1797, which proved that the Federalists were willing to act independently of Adams's leadership, although they remained only too happy to echo the president when it suited their purpose. From the beginning of the congressional debate, however, most of the accusatory or laudatory rhetoric concerning Adams quieted down and a wait-and-see atmosphere again appeared. One individual continued and increased her rhetorical outbursts, however, as it was at this time that Abigail Adams began to lash out at Bache and those in sympathy with him. At the same time she found nothing but truth in Federal journals. After attacking Bache in a series of letters, she concluded: "Fenno has saved me further occasion of detailing the events of the day. He has given them with accuracy."[11]

The most consequential business before Adams's departure for Braintree was the composition of the three-man mission. Adams's decision to appoint the pro–French Elbridge Gerry in place of the reluctant Francis Dana showed that Adams could act as independently of Hamilton and the cabinet as they of him. Adams nevertheless wrote in later years that he "consulted much" on the appointments. Abigail wrote that Bache was abusing Adams, both for his choice of Dana and for his subsequent choice of the Republican Gerry; she wished that "I could tell them what the President says, that their praise for a few weeks mortified him, much more, than all their impudent abuse does."[12]

Once the appointments were settled, Adams was off for home and was out of the capital from July 27 to November 10. The only abuse Bache could muster was editorial complaints, in both August and November, that Adams was being unnecessarily idolized by citizens on his trips to and from the capital. The editor hinted that the populace was required to turn out, since they had never treated Vice President Adams as well. Cobbett, on the other hand, printed a few pro–Adams blurbs during the summer of 1797. But the newspaper war seemed to simmer down while results from the envoys were awaited and the president was absent. Adams's absence would henceforth be a signal for less rhetoric.[13]

While at home, Adams noted press scurrility and asked his correspondent: "Can talents atone for such turpitude? Can wisdom reside with such cullibility?" Yet Adams's tone reflects regrets for his traducers' literary shortcomings rather than anger at their outbursts. At the same time, Adams wrote to Wolcott in a "Federalist-only" frame of mind regarding patronage.[14] As an October issue of Freneau's *Time Piece* attacked Adams for monarchism, Adams wrote that he learned news of his son Thomas in France through the agency of "our Jacobin papers." The next day, however, Adams was writing to Wolcott that the public frenzy on both sides might serve the harmful purpose of weakening congressional resolve.[15]

On their return to Philadelphia, the Adamses went back to their customary pursuits. Abigail wrote her sister of Bache's insinuation that the people were forced to pay homage to her husband and enclosed "a specimen of Bache Gall." Her husband delivered his first annual message to Congress on November 22 and urged the protection of commerce. He also looked to "a manifestation of that energy and unanimity" by the people, plus "the executions of those resources for national defense" which would bolster the bargaining power of the envoys in Paris. In answering the Senate's reply to his message, Adams characteristically forecast: "A mercantile marine and a military marine must grow up together, one can not long exist without the other."[16]

As the wait for news from the envoys lengthened, Adams wrote to the heads of departments listing questions which amounted to asking what should be done if the pending negotiations failed to produce the desired results. The cabinet had to exchange letters with Hamilton, and the time involved in that process made the cabinet's response of little value. In the meantime, Abigail was busy defending John from Bache's abuse, and one letter is worth repeating: "You will see," she wrote her sister, "much said about the Patronage of the President and his determination to appoint none to office, as they say, who do not think exactly with him. This is not true in its full extent." It was not true because no one thought exactly like John Adams. Washington, writing to Pickering at the same time, was dismayed by the "cowardly, illiberal, and assassin-like" methods of the opposition. Letters such as these, plus occasional well-aimed Federalist newspaper blurbs, raised thoughts about a possible restraint of the opposition press.[17]

In late February, the Adamses took umbrage at an invitation to attend a birthday celebration for ex-president Washington. Jefferson believed that the absence of Adams and some of the more moderate Federalists caused a rift in the party, but the incident did little more than weaken the Adamses' uncomfortable and undesired position as social leaders of Philadelphia.[18]

At the very end of February, the political kettle returned to a boil. Both Bache and Washington were writing of the growth of falsehood, misrepresentation, and the growth of party feuds. In Boston, Thomas Adams of the *Chronicle* was content to add: "It is a cardinal error to confound the administration with the government of this country."[19]

On March 4, 1798, after exactly one year as president, Adams received word from the envoys that the olive branch had been spurned and its bearers humiliated. Adams wrote to the cabinet to ask whether the coded dispatches, clear proof of French duplicity, should be given to Congress. He also asked, "Ought the President, then, to recommend, in his message, an immediate declaration of war?" Abigail, in a letter highly laudatory of "the Creature" Porcupine, captured her husband's mood well: "Business thickens upon him. Officering all the frigates, contemplating what can be done at this critical period, *knowing what he thinks ought to be done*, yet not certain whether the people are sufficiently determined to second the Government, is a situation very painfull as well as responsible."[20] John Adams still had a hand on the public wrist to take the public pulse.

The dispatches were withheld, pending translation and the anticipated departure of the envoys. The president also feared that releasing the dispatches was not yet justified. Adams nevertheless reported to the House and Senate on March 19, 1798: "It is incumbent on me to declare that I perceive no ground of expectation that the objects of their mission can be accomplished on terms compatible with the safety, the honor, or the essential interests of the nation."[21]

Republicans, not knowing what the dispatches said, failed to realize that the Federalists now possessed a major tactical advantage. They tried to run a bluff nonetheless. Jefferson called Adams's statement "the insane message." Some newspapers dared the Federalists to go to war, and Bache returned to the fray ready for renewed combat. He viewed Adams's message as "fatal and destructive to the peace of the United States." He also repeated his call for Adams to resign and added, "He should keep in mind that he was not unanimously elected." Freneau, under the pseudonym of "CETERA DESUNT" contributed similar abuse to the *Aurora*. *Carey's United States Recorder* told of a deal made between Adams and British minister Robert Liston.[22] The whole campaign convinced the Federalists, as well as unknowing Republicans, of the need to publish the dispatches. In the long run, it also had deleterious effects on subscriptions to Republican sheets.

Federalists shared Adams's conclusion regarding the national safety, but were fearful of increasing Republican newspaper attacks. George Cabot wrote of "a despondency that is alarming" in describing public opinion. Abigail, more concerned with direct attacks on her husband, asked "What benefit can war be to him?"[23]

The dispatches, however, were the key issue, and both political factions sought the release of the documents. Jonathan Mason, Jr., wrote to Harrison Gray Otis, "We wish much for the papers, if they can with propriety be made public. The Jacobins want them. And in the name of God let them be gratified; it is not the first time they have wished for the means of their destruction." The *Boston Independent Chronicle* also demanded the publication of the papers and accused the monarchical Adams of withholding documents needed by Congress and the public. The *Aurora* went so far as to praise Washington at the expense of Adams because the former president "knew that *those who have neither strength nor weapons to defend themselves, ought at least to be civil.*" Porcupine had the final word, however, because his paper printed the news that Congress received a resolution from John Allen of Connecticut which called for the papers from the special envoys.[24]

In the first 11 months of the critical phase of the relationship between Adams and the press, journalistic lines were redrawn and then a wait-and-see attitude prevailed. During that time, Adams advised Congress of the failure of the envoys, and a bipartisan request for the XYZ papers followed. On April 2, 1798, a coalition of High-Federalists and suspicious Democratic-Republicans carried a vote for the release of the papers. That event, like Adams's message to the special session 11 months earlier, transformed the struggle and pushed Adams and the Federalists into a temporary ascendancy. For the next six to seven months, Federalism symbolized "responsible political conservatism."[25] In addition, John Adams's popularity reached its zenith.

At this point, we must deal with two direct factors and introduce two additional developments. First, we must attempt to gauge the change in public opinion produced by the release of the XYZ papers and note the increasing volume of journalistic praise and concomitant decreasing volume of abuse directed at Adams. It must be added, however, that while the volume of abuse decreased, the tone remained firm. Second, Adams's sudden popularity must be considered. The result of the two factors was a vastly strengthened Federalism, which paved the way for the Alien and Sedition Acts and Federalist attempts to dictate policy over Adams's head. When these final two developments became obvious to Adams, he broke with Federalism and divided an elitist political faction already bent on its own destruction.

There is a historiographical consensus that the XYZ dispatches "produced a revolution in public opinion."[26] Whereas Adams's special session message of May 1797 was in advance of public opinion, the release of the XYZ papers allowed public opinion to catch up to Adams's past rhetoric.

The change was visible in several quarters. Newspapers which were heretofore politically neutral became adherents of Adams. This swing was reinforced by a greater dependence on Federalist-oriented English sources for news in the wake of the Anglo-French war. George Gibbs, Wolcott's editor, sees a new outpouring of "honor, dignity, and independence" after the publication of the XYZ papers. Charles Adams, editor of Adams's *Works*, makes Adams a central figure in the public opinion revolution; the younger Adams believes that his grandfather "roused the country to war, solely as a measure of defense, and to deter France from further persevering in her aggressions."[27] Timothy Pickering, who wrote an attack on Adams in 1823, admitted in the midst of that subsequent abuse that even Hamilton acknowledged Adams's role in rousing the national spirit.[28]

Abigail Adams reflected her husband's sudden popularity when she wrote her sister: "The publick opinion is changing here very fast, and the people begin to see who have been their firm unshaken Friends."[29] Abigail's analysis was correct: Adams became truly popular for the first time in his career. His sudden popularity was a part of the overall public swing to Federalism, but has to be viewed with some circumspection because the public did not balance its respect for Adams and Federalism equally.

Adams learned quickly that the publication of the XYZ papers had increased his popularity. Fenno, editor of the *Gazette of the United States*, reported "uproar and applause from all quarters of the house" when a theater orchestra played "The President's March" three days after the release of the XYZ papers. A month later a New England paper reported that the song was popular "at every Theater in the U.S."[30] Abigail reported that the family were received well wherever they went, but added an exception: "In short we are now wonderfully popular except with Bache & Co who in his paper calls the President Old, querilous, Bald, blind, cripled, Toothless Adams." Federalist newspapers reminded Bache, on a regular basis, of that untimely bit of rhetoric.[31]

The greatest indicator of support for Adams, however, came directly from the people. In petitions or in person, delegations of concerned citizens voiced their approval of Adams's firm stance. The *Providence Gazette* printed an address as early as April 28 in which citizens promised to support the government with their lives. Cobbett wrote of a crowd which marched to Adams's house in Philadelphia: "There could not be less than *ten thousand*. Every female in the city, whose face is worth looking at, gladdened the way with her smiles."[32]

Petitions poured in to the president, and Adams answered them in strong language. Historians Manning Dauer and Dumas Malone agree on the intemperance and bellicosity of Adams's rhetoric in some of those replies. Dauer sees "a violence worthy of such extremists as Pickering and Sedgewick," but correctly concludes that Adams was more belligerent in his rhetoric than in his policy.[33] Federalists recognized both Adams's belligerence and his popularity because Robert Troup wrote Rufus King of the addresses "pouring like a torrent upon the President." Troup concluded: "I supposed the fact to be that since man was created and government was formed no public officer had stood higher in the confidence and affection of his countrymen than our present President does now." William Bingham also wrote to King in the same vein, but was more excited because those events had helped the Federalists at election time.[34]

The belligerence Adams exhibited in his answers to the petitions cannot be doubted, and it reflected two character traits: "Irrational and antisocial under stress." Adams was irrational in pointing a militarily weak nation toward a war with a European power and antisocial in his sudden detestation of all things French. He pictured "no means of averting the storm," but he was ready to meet French overtures although he would make no more.[35] Adams found "a great consolation" in a petition from Philadelphia citizens, and a Virginia petition of support struck him as "peculiarly agreeable." He asked college students, "Is the republic of the United States a fief of the republic of France?" To New Jersey citizens he promised that he would not purchase neutrality and repeated the boast of the citizens of Federalist-controlled Hartford, Connecticut, that government measures "have awed into silence the clamors of faction, and palsied the thousand tongues of calumny."[36] To the citizens of Pott's Town, Pennsylvania, Adams replied, "YOUR confidence, that I will not surrender the rights of the nation, *shall not be betrayed*. If the nation were capable of such a surrender (which it is not) SOME OTHER HAND must affix the signature to the ignominious deed."[37] Adams addressed other citizens' groups in equally strong language. The belligerence was solely the work of Adams, who devoted much of his time to the preparation of answers to the petitions. Adams wrote to Jefferson in later years that he prepared his own replies and was not manipulated by the High-Federalists. Abigail feared her husband would overexert himself and hoped that Congress would soon rise and allow the president some rest or else "they will have Jefferson sooner than they wish."[38]

George Cabot expressed Federalist satisfaction with Adams's conduct in a letter to Treasury Secretary Oliver Wolcott. Bache, not surprisingly, dissented from the adulation and printed a petition from "SEVERAL OF THE MILITIA OF MORRIS COUNTY" highly critical of Adams's policy. Adams fired off a stinging answer, printed in the *Salem Gazette* under the heading "A RAP ON THE FINGERS." Other Federalist sheets stressed the support Adams received from non–Federalist areas, notably Georgia and Virginia.[39]

The patriotism of the petitions and the belligerence of the answers served to make John Adams temporarily sacred to Federalist or quasi–Federalist editors. Day after day, newspapers were filled with pages of addresses and answers, and editors generally added some shrewd bit of Federalist propaganda.

The Boston *Columbian Centinel* lamented that it could not publish all of "the patriotic addresses flowing into the executive" that showed the patriotism and approbation of policy of "nineteen-twentieths of the people." Another sheet printed a petition and reply under the heading "SACRED TRUTHS." Most editors, however, contented themselves by turning out edition after edition of what amounted to rhetoric and counterrhetoric.[40] Crisis, regardless of the stripe, is always good copy.

Adams had thus become virtually the object of a cult of personality at a time when Federalism was also on the rise. The summer of 1798 would see harmony between Adams and the dominant Federalist faction, except in the Alien and Sedition Acts. The autumn would see the beginning of the end of that Adams-Federalist harmony.

In the spring of 1798, as Adams and Federalism together reached their zenith, Republicans realized their error in seeking the XYZ papers and subsequently fought an ineffective rearguard action. Adams found able defenders in Federalist editors who were recent converts to his policies.[41] Freneau's *Time Piece* viewed the unresolved XYZ question as a Federalist bogey and even commended Adams when he delivered the dispatches. Freneau quickly learned his error and lashed out at Adams for his acceptance of the patronage of Fenno and Cobbett and warned that Adams was not "the hereditary monarch of America." Freneau's reaction suggests that Adams was so popular, at least at that moment, that editors were afraid that he might keep his job for life. "Lysander" also contributed several abusive columns to the *Time Piece* which were addressed directly to Adams.[42] *Carey's United States Recorder* added, "All good men pity [Adams's] political insanity and pray for his long life and conversion."[43] Washington was ambivalent in his reactions to opposition measures because he expected no change of policy by the leadership without "a manifest desertion of their followers." The ex-president also added that the *Aurora* had already showed its colors, but he did not expect that the opposition press could remain recalcitrant in the face of events.[44] Abigail Adams added that "the liberty of the press is become licentious beyond any former period."[45]

Fisher Ames wrote to Oliver Wolcott in late April 1798: "Among our wants is that of a good newspaper."[46] This was another example of myopic Federalism because the publication of the XYZ papers gave the Federalists all the newspaper support they needed. Newspaper "extras," one sheet printed on both sides, began to reprint the XYZ documents. At the same time, editorials and poems spoke in the strongest language of patriotism.[47] Jefferson realized that Republicanism was beginning to suffer and wrote to Madison: "The popular movement in the eastern states is checked, as we expected, and war addresses are showering in from New Jersey & the great trading towns." The vice president added that the *Aurora* and *Carey's United States Recorder* "totter for want of subscriptions. . . . If these papers fail, Republicanism will be entirely browbeaten." In a surprisingly prophetic vein, Jefferson later hoped that a land tax and the threat of war would revise popular opinion and concluded: "A little patience, and we shall see the reign of witches pass over."[48]

Jefferson's political acumen and predictions proved correct, but the cure took time. Before the "reign of witches" passed, the Federalists had the journalistic clout they needed. The ambivalent *Centinel of Freedom* of Newark, New Jersey, took a swipe at "presidential infallibility" in early May, but then capitulated and began printing patriotic addresses and replies. Regular Federalist sheets continued to put out the rhetoric that had become their stock-in-trade after Adams's message of May 1797. Cobbett led the way by printing addresses to Adams, the proclamation of the fast day, and a stinging attack on French diplomatic corruption.[49] Still other Federalist sheets continued to declaim about the rise of patriotism, national honor, or French villainy.[50]

Unable to attack patriotism or defend French diplomacy, opposition sheets had only the fast day and Adams's alleged monarchism to fight about. The *Aurora* and contemporary pamphlets saw Adams's proclamation of a fast as unconstitutional. *Carey's United States Recorder* attacked Adams because the fast day would cost Philadelphians $12,000, as 9,000 laborers would lose their daily wage of $1 and taverns would lose their daily income, estimated at $3,000. The *Centinel of Freedom*, after printing addresses and replies, reviled Adams with a song about his monarch-ism.[51]

Public opinion in the South swung toward Federalism and exacer-bated existing Republican demoralization. But Southerners did not become High-Federalists of the Hamiltonian stripe. They adopted the middle course espoused by the president, as they stopped short of war and looked neither to Britain nor France. Instead, they supported a policy of caution and defense of national honor. The reader may find in this attitude the same kind of ideology held by the "war-hawks" a few years later.[52]

With newspaper opposition weak and increased popular support on all fronts, the Federalists looked to decisive action. Hamilton tried to con-vince Washington to make a national tour, but the former president refused. Ames wrote to Pickering to urge a war with France and a sedition law while circumstances were right. But war was blocked by President Adams, who either hesitated to ask for a declaration of war because Elbridge Gerry, his "faithful friend" of 1776, was in France or because he simply could not bring himself to go to war.[53] Adams nevertheless told the Senate and House in mid–June: "I will never send another minister to France without assurances that he will be received, respected, and honored as the repre-sentative of a great, free, powerful, and independent nation."[54]

Adams's earlier rhetoric and his anti–French tone before Congress in-vited attacks. Monroe pictured Adams as "our present Viceroy." Bache saw Congress as "the mere puppets of the Executive." *Carey's United States Recorder* printed a scathing attack which noted the "pleasures, privileges and profits" which would feed Adams's vanity in the event of war. The *Aurora* reminded Adams of the biblical tenet that he belonged to the same race as the Frenchmen he castigated, while editor Bache acknowledged the error of his earlier belief that America could not have a worse president than Washington.[55]

Federalists answered with some equally strong anti–Jefferson report-ing.[56] Other administration supporters outdid each other in reprinting laudatory toasts to President Adams on the Fourth of July.[57]

A week after the patriotic outbursts of July 4, Federalist Stephen Hig-ginson wrote to Treasury Secretary Wolcott concerning Congress's need for "an imposing, firm leader, to direct their measures, and to whip the stragglers from party and duty." The letter concluded: "If the President will go on with his system, he will give the tone to the people, and they to a twaddling, whiffing Congress." At the same time, the *Columbian Centinel* reported Adams's words as "the Gospel of Politicks." The same paper noted a law authorizing distribution of 10,000 copies of the XYZ papers and hoped for distribution in places where Democratic-Republican jour-nals were still influential. On July 13, Washington wrote Adams explaining his own position fully and hinting that matters were reaching a climax:

> Believe me, sir, no one can more cordially approve of the wise and pru-
> dent measures of your administration. They ought to inspire universal
> confidence, and will, no doubt, combined with the state of things, call
> from Congress *such laws and means* as will enable you to meet the full
> force and extent of the crisis [italics added].

At the same time, Federalist newspapers printed the words to the new
patriotic song, "Adams and Liberty," which, as John C. Miller has written,
was "Soon to be given an ironic meaning by the passage of the Alien and
Sedition Acts."[58]

As we have seen, the surge of patriotism, the defense of national
honor, and the sudden popularity and belligerence of Adams combined to
produce an avalanche of rhetoric, but although the emotion and clamor
failed to generate a genuine war, it was subsequently channeled into a program of repressive legislation. If changes in newspaper circulation are
overlooked, the first tangible effects of the strong language and hysteria
were the four legal codes known as the Alien and Sedition Acts. Thus
Adams's sudden popularity and the public swing to Federalism produced
nothing more tangible than four examples of overzealous lawmaking,
which in turn taught Adams a lesson about his position vis-à-vis Federalism and convinced him of the need for independent action.

The Alien and Sedition Acts, "the fruit of an unchecked Federalist extremism," require scrutiny in several directions in order to pinpoint
Adams's precise role in their formation and enforcement.[59] First, because
Adams and the press were in conflict long before the Sedition Act was
passed and long after it became a nullity, the act is but a part of the broad
scope of the relationship between Adams and the press. Second, Adams
was only indirectly involved in the creation of the Sedition Act and only
became an indirect party to two prosecutions. Third, the Sedition Act was
urged, proposed, supported, and enforced by members of the Federalist
party, most of whom either secretly opposed Adams in 1798 or openly opposed him by the time of the election of 1800, when the enforcement of
the act gained its greatest significance. Fourth, the Sedition Act did not
bring down Federalism directly, although it damaged the party by indirection because it combined with other High-Federalist policies to alienate
Adams from the High-Federalists and eventually caused a division in
Federalism which proved fatal to the party.

Historians seem understandably fascinated by the laws. James
Thomas Flexner has written, "no legislation has a more obnoxious reputation" and has concluded that it was "improbable" that Washington would
have signed the laws. Washington might not have done so in the years
1789–1797; had he been president during the XYZ affair, however, this
writer believes he would have signed the law and perhaps done so with
more zeal than Adams.[60] Gilbert Chinard, an early biographer of Adams's,

calls the laws "the most detested legislation ever passed by an American Congress."[61] James Pollard dissents and concludes that any president would have signed the measures under the existing circumstances, as this writer suggested above. John C. Miller used the laws as a yardstick of political wisdom during the McCarthy era.[62]

The initial question must revolve around the degree of significance to be attached to Adams and the Sedition Act. Inasmuch as Adams and the press were intertwined from the last period of the Seven Years' War to the decade of the 1820s, it is hard to picture Adams as the driving force behind the act, and Adams's indirect involvement in the Sedition Act may have been but an episode in an ongoing process. In March and April of 1797, Adams in his correspondence held Republican journalism in contempt. In September 1800, Adams held his clearly identified Federalist traducers in contempt. In retirement, Adams continued to criticize libelers from both sides. Between the outbursts of 1797 and 1800, however, and in the face of increased French intrigue at a time when Federalists suddenly won control of the national spirit, Adams suggested two Sedition Act prosecutions. It should not be overly surprising that he did so. It is perhaps to his credit that those two isolated incidents were the sum of his involvement in an otherwise shabby chapter in American politics.

Leonard Levy has stated: "President Adams willingly signed the Sedition Act and eagerly urged its enforcement." Edward Handler pictures the president as "oppressed by the fear of faction and a licentious press." Irving Brant believes that the "easily overheated Adams" was guilty of "superpatriotic jingoism," but credits subsequent moves against "the political drift toward democracy" to "more purposeful Federalist leaders."[63] Manning Dauer, Gilbert Chinard, and Charles Francis Adams disagree with Levy and Handler, although they note specific cases where Adams suggested the use of the laws.[64]

Despite the historiographical debate, there are no letters in any of the Adams papers collections which provide the slightest hint that Adams wanted a sedition law. Nor did Adams send any messages to Congress proposing such a law. Only in his answers to petitions did he speak of sedition. To the citizens of Easton, Pennsylvania, he wrote: "The spirit of union is much diminished. . . . Unless the spirit of libelling and sedition shall be controlled by an execution of the laws, that spirit will again increase."[65] As noted earlier, it was Adams's often intemperate language in speeches and answers that contributed to the Sedition Act. In addition, he had no constitutional doubts concerning the law, so he signed it. But Adams's later letters provide strong denials of involvement in the passage of the Sedition Act. It should also be noted in defense of Adams that the nonenforcement of the Alien Act was due to his determination to give the law a more strict interpretation than did the extreme Federalists. Adams was unwilling to sign wholesale lots of blank warrants, but did sign three specific warrants. The accused had already left the country, however. In addition, Republicans read extracts from Adams's *Defence* into the record in anti–Sedition Act speeches. Irving Brant credits Adams with upsetting the "whole tipsy edifice" on which the Sedition Act rested when he nominated envoys to negotiate an end to the quasi-war. The final defense of Adams comes from an archenemy of the federal sedition statute, Thomas Jefferson. Writing to Abigail Adams in 1804, Jefferson admitted, "I can say with truth that one act of Mr. Adams' life, and one only, ever gave me a moment's displeasure. I did consider his last appointments to office [the "midnight judges"] as personally unkind."[66] Had Jefferson considered Adams's participation in the Sedition Act culpable, this letter might have assumed an altogether different tone.

It remains to consider the evidence which links Adams to the Sedition Act. Adams wrote in retirement that there was a need for the Alien and Sedition Acts and that he considered the acts "constitutional and salutary, if not necessary." On the other hand, Adams's retirement was also the occasion for a letter to Jefferson in which Adams nonchalantly denied any involvement in the passage of the Sedition Act. Finally, there are the two prosecutions in which Adams involved himself. Adams wrote to Pickering in August 1799 that remarks ascribed to Thomas Cooper in the *Northumberland Gazette* constituted "a libel against the whole government, and as such ought to be prosecuted." In July 1799, Pickering sent Adams an *Aurora*, and Adams agreed that editor William Duane merited prosecution. Duane was charged in connection with the Tench Coxe letter, but the charges were dropped, which indicates that the "truth as a defense" clause in the Sedition Act was operative in one, if only one, case. In most other cases, truth as a defense tended to be overlooked by a partisan Federalist judiciary. This is the sum of Adams's involvement in Sedition Act prosecutions, although it is also a discredit to Adams that he approved of the conduct of Judge Samuel Chase, the leading enforcer of the law in the Judiciary Department. By contrast, although the Jeffersonians tried to impeach Chase, Jefferson himself suggested "selected" prosecution of editors, predicting that such actions would have a "wholesome effect." Jefferson even sent his correspondent a copy of a paper which he felt deserved prosecution under state sedition codes. In defense of Adams, it must be said that he never served as a clipping service for Federalist justice.[67]

In addition, Abigail Adams's writing tends to confirm her husband's lack of interest in repressive legislation. Earlier, it was noted that John confided in her about "the crime of *Chronicle, Argus* and *Aurora* praise." She then passed that information on to her sister six weeks later. Yet from April to July, Abigail wrote a series of stinging letters calling in the strongest language for a sedition bill. Not once did she quote her husband's feelings about such a law, an excellent indicator that he had expressed none.[68] If Adams's 1798 silence and post–1801 denials are genuine, as Abigail's lack of reference to her husband's thoughts seems to confirm, the Sedition Act assumes peculiar significance. First, the data suggests that the Federalist party acted independently of the president, an extremely unwise bit of timing, given the president's sudden popularity. Second, once Adams realized he was not being consulted, the purpose of the Sedition Act was defeated and it was rendered more an engine of subsequent Federalist eclipse than one of Jeffersonian proscription. In acting independently of Adams, the authors of the Sedition Act did not create the one-party system anticipated by High-Federalists. Rather, they alienated Adams, and their action, when combined with other factors, created a brief yet decisive period of a three-party system. This tripartite division proved Adams's popularity with the people, although he lost a close election. But the High-Federalists were crushed under a tidal wave of ballots which they had expected would bear the name of only one party.

The evidence thus tends to show Adams to be a mildly involved accessory after the fact in the matter of the Sedition Act. Adams's involvement was more related to the partisan politics and bombast which generated the Sedition Act. He was linked to very few of the men who agitated for the law, and by 1800 he was alienated politically from the vast majority of Federalists who had sought, supported, or enforced the law. James Morton Smith calls the Sedition Act the "Lloyd-Harper Law," after its authors in both houses. John C. Miller refers to the law as "an intellectual straight jacket fashioned by Harrison Gray Otis and company," a harsh way of agreeing with Samuel Eliot Morison that Otis helped Harper carry the debate against Albert Gallatin and John Nicholas. Irving Brant characterizes Harper as the "most influential of the Federalists" and also stresses the efforts of John Allen of Connecticut. Of the four Federalist prime movers, only one held any loyalty to Adams. Harper had militated against the election of Adams in 1796 and wished Adams personal injury in 1799. Lloyd remained a High-Federalist after the rupture in February 1799. Allen's precise position in the election of 1800 is uncertain, but his attitude throughout the period identifies him far more closely with the program of the High-Federalists than with the subsequent moderation of the Adams-Federalists. Only Otis stood by Adams through the election of 1800, although perhaps more in an attempt to preserve Federalist harmony than out of respect for Adams.[69]

Other Federalists who had directly or in veiled references urged the passage of a sedition bill included Chauncey Goodrich, Oliver Wolcott, Timothy Pickering, George Washington, George Cabot, Robert Troup, Fisher Ames, and Stephen Higginson. With the exception of Washington, who until his death in December 1799 supported Adams, these same individuals, dissatisfied with Adams's peace moves and his disinclination to use the Alien and Sedition Acts for a vigorous purge, reviled him in 1800. Correspondence between Ames, Goodrich, Cabot, Wolcott, and James McHenry looked to the exclusion of Adams in 1800. Benjamin Goodhue thought Adams insane. Wolcott and Hamilton agreed on the need to publish Adams's weaknesses and circulate the publication among High-Federalists. Finally, Timothy Pickering, by historical consensus the "generalissimo of the enforcement effort" of the Sedition Act among members of the Federalist executive, was mistrusted by Adams as early as June 1797, and it has been alleged that Pickering remained in his post as secretary of state to attempt to control Adams's policies and actions. Once ousted from his post by Adams in May 1800, Pickering repeatedly blasted Adams. These facts go a long way to show that there was a solid link between those who wanted the Sedition Act and those who later broke with Adams and worked against him in 1800. Supporting evidence is furnished by the actions of John Marshall, a leading Adams-Federalist, who was a vocal minority spokesperson among Federalists in arguing against any attempt to revive the Sedition Act, although Marshall did consider the act constitutional.[70]

Two final indicators reinforce the conclusion that Adams was not in the coterie which was most closely involved with the Sedition Act. As James Morton Smith wrote, "The most insistent pressure for execution of the law came from Federalist newspapers, which constantly clamored for action against their Republican competitors." It is significant that the newspapers outside of New England, most notably the *Gazette of the United States*, later reviled Adams, a revulsion shared by *Porcupine's Gazette*. The New England newspapers for the most part remained faithful to Adams, although they did not hesitate to praise Charles Cotesworth Pinckney, the High-Federalist presidential aspirant in 1800. Noah Webster in New York remained ambivalent, as he boosted the Sedition Act while supporting Adams's naval policies.[71]

Finally, again quoting James Morton Smith, "Indeed the chief enforcement effort [of the Sedition Act] was tied directly to the presidential campaign of 1800." Irving Brant also tied the Federalist enforcement effort to the election, and here the link between Adams and the judges involved must be raised. While Adams is to be blamed for his acceptance of the conduct of Judge Chase, there is no evidence linking the other judges who enforced the law to the Adams-Federalists. Oliver Ellsworth, chief justice of the Supreme Court during most of the enforcement campaign, was considered by High-Federalists as an alternative to Adams in the election of 1800. There is not much evidence that Adams's appointees to the court engaged in partisan enforcement, and Adams later appointed a chief

justice (Marshall) who was, among Federalists, the least inclined to strenuous use of the enforcement machinery. If enforcement of the Sedition Act
was a part of the electioneering of 1800, it was a part of the High-
Federalists' overall campaign to oust Adams. Adams even considered using the Alien and Sedition Acts against arch–Federalist William Cobbett,
and Thomas Cooper tried to use the Sedition Act against Hamilton after
the latter wrote an anti–Adams pamphlet. It might be well to conclude as
John C. Miller did: "John Adams was sick of the Sedition Act."[72]

Several historians have ascribed the downfall of Federalism in 1800
to the Alien and Sedition Acts, but the relationship is not fully explained.[73]
It is usually left to the reader to conclude that American public opinion
swelled up and produced a backlash which turned out Federalism. There
was a popular backlash, to be sure, but it was not of large proportions,
simply because there were so few individuals directly affected. The initial
backlash generated by the Alien and Sedition Acts stemmed from the fact
that they provided the demoralized Republican press with an issue. Between the publication of the XYZ papers and the Sedition Act, subscriptions to Republican journals fell off. In addition, they had few issues to
question, save the fast day proclamation and the time-worn issue of
Adams's suspected monarchism. In the Sedition Act, Republican leaders
saw a threatened Constitution and editors saw a threatened press, and
both groups united to wage a battle for survival. Leonard Levy has noted
the emergence of a new libertarian theory after 1798, and this theory was
broadcast by a rejuvenated Republican press.[74] According to John C.
Miller, in 1798 there were 20 Democratic-Republican sheets, but by 1800
there were 50, with four new journals in Virginia alone. Miller concluded:
"If the purpose of the Sedition Act had been to multiply Republican
newspapers and to increase vastly their circulation, it could be accounted
an unqualified success."[75] In September, John Hopkins wrote to Wolcott
that the Sedition Act was the only issue the opposition used to attack the
party in power. Two weeks later, Washington expressed much the same
sentiments to William Vans Murray. The issue was kept very much alive
in Virginia from the autumn of 1798 to April 1799, as a factor in the spring
elections.[76]

The Alien and Sedition Acts produced outbursts of rhetoric, to be
sure, but by now, much of it was nothing more than old wine in new bot-
tles. It never reached a fever pitch for several reasons. First, Congress adjourned shortly after the passage of the Sedition Act, so the authors of the
legislation were not available as targets of abuse. Second, although editors
parried insults and questioned the constitutionality of the laws, a wait-
and-see attitude prevailed regarding the enforcement of them. Third, the
fever again stalked Philadelphia and eventually claimed two champion
polemicists, Benjamin Franklin Bache and John Fenno. Finally, Adams

was at home from late July to late November, and, as noted earlier, newspaper abuse slackened in his absence. Editors were also unsure of the degree of Adams's involvement in the Sedition Act.

Adams's absence assumed significance because the earlier mild rift between president and party was given a chance to widen. At the time the Sedition Act was passed, Washington lent his name to the provisional army, and his postpresidential Federalism caused a shift in the allegiance of some Federalists. With Washington on their side, certain Federalists could feel free to act both independently and in defiance of Adams on matters concerning the army. When Adams realized the implications of this political shift, the rift in the party became a rupture.

The 50,000 man provisional army, like the Alien and Sedition Acts, was the work of High-Federalists who acted with Hamilton's eager support. The army, like the repressive legislation, inspired resentment in Adams, who was clearly gearing himself for a change of policy. He wrote a letter to Otis that was critical of Hamilton and apprehensive of the policy he was sponsoring: "This man is stark mad or I am. . . . If Congress should adopt this system, it would produce an instantaneous insurrection of the whole nation from Georgia to New Hampshire." Twentieth-century historians agree that an Adams-Hamilton split was developing, and Hamilton is seen as the moving force in the 1798 legislative program that Adams began to question.[77]

In the summer of 1798, Adams also began to realize that events were reaching the point where the president would have "a master." Later Federalist correspondence echoed this. As George Cabot wrote to Wolcott concerning Adams in the early fall: "If at any time he is absent for the benefit of relaxation, let it be adhered to that he does no business and gives no opinions."[78]

Before leaving for home, Adams nominated Washington as commander in chief of the provisional army. As Abigail wrote in early July, "The knowledge that he lives is a Bulwark." At the same time, Washington wrote to McHenry that there would be no French invasion because Americans were united.[79]

Adams's respect for Washington cannot be doubted. Adams wrote to the former president twice during the summer of 1798 to express the wish that Washington was president again, adding that he would nominate Washington for president if it were in his power.[80] It may also be that Adams believed Washington's presence would temper the extremism of both the Hamiltonians and the Jeffersonians. Newspapers of both factions gave varying support to the appointment of Washington to command.[81]

Once the appointment was made, the army issue generated far more intrigue than patriotism. Washington's staff appointments were one sore-spot with the press. Yet another was the emphasis of the army over the navy, as mercantile sheets were far more concerned with naval arma-ment.[82]

It has been suggested that Washington made appointments with an eye to geography and politics. The appointment of Washington had given renewed energy to Southern Federalism, and he attempted to give an added boost to Federalism in the South with his suggestion that Charles Cotes-worth Pinckney be made second-in-command. The cabinet and other High-Federalists, however, convinced Washington to appoint Hamilton. James Thomas Flexner, reflecting the intrigue of the appointments, en-titles his chapter on that subject "A Sad Affair."[83]

Before Washington's choice was known to Adams, the president be-lieved that he still possessed the last word on appointments. In a letter to War Secretary McHenry, Adams admitted that he would surrender the presidency to Washington if that were possible, but added that, as long as he was president, he would be responsible for the final decisions on ap-pointments. Adams concluded, "There has been too much intrigue in this business with General Washington and me; if I shall ultimately be the dupe of it, I am much mistaken in myself."[84] Adams received countless visits from cabinet members and High-Federalists who were intent on securing the second spot for Hamilton. These visits widened the existing party rift because Adams had hoped to use the appointing power to make new political friends and retreat slightly from Hamiltonian extremism.[85]

Hamilton did get the second post behind Washington, but failed to get a war. The intrigue which put Hamilton directly behind Washington, whom the cabinet considered "but a pageant," further alienated Adams from the High-Federalists. George Gibbs has written of Adams's "hatred of Hamilton" and has concluded that only Washington's threat to resign convinced Adams that Hamilton must be given the command. The net result was the appointment of Hamilton, a split between Adams and the High-Federalists, and a serious weakening of Adams's interest in the army.[86]

Southern Federalists remained attached to Adams. As Adams's mis-trust of some cabinet members and Hamilton grew, it became a reflection of Southern Federalist thinking. Southerners, like Adams, wanted defense but not war. As the split between Adams and the High-Federalists widened, most Southern Federalists tried not to take sides, although John Marshall, campaigning for office in Virginia, realized the necessity of avoiding Ham-iltonian extremes.[87]

Adams's summer at Braintree was indeed troubled. His distrust of the cabinet and military deepened when his son-in-law, Colonel William Smith, was nominated as a general but the appointment was defeated. Adams also began to realize that his own program had a heavy price. He had sought cavalry, artillery, and an increase of the navy. For that, he had

to accept a 50,000 man army under Hamilton, the Alien and Sedition
Acts, higher taxes, and high-interest loans. Federalists worried little over
the cost because they believed the blame would fall on a man "that they
would be glad to see disappear from public life."[88] Adams began to provide
the cabinet with hints of his mistrust in October. On the twentieth, he
wrote to Pickering and asked if he should recommend a declaration of war
in his annual message. That question was but the sugar coating on a bitter
pill because Adams concluded the letter by asking if new negotiations with
France should be tried. Two days later, antimilitarism manifested itself in
a letter to McHenry: "One thing I know, that regiments are costly articles
everywhere. . . . At present there is no more prospect of seeing a French
army here, than there is in heaven."[89] Adams's suspicions were also aroused
when he found Pickering, Hamilton, and Washington together upon his
return to Trenton.[90]

In November, Wolcott parroted the High-Federalist dogma when he
emphasized to Adams that no new envoy should be sent to France. Fisher
Ames was distressed that Congress moved so slowly and was equally annoyed that Noah Webster's newspaper favored a fleet over an army.[91]
Adams shared Webster's anxieties concerning the emphasis given the army
at the expense of the navy. The army, as it existed, had seven officers to
each enlisted man, and was almost entirely the property of Hamilton. Inept War Secretary McHenry gave Hamilton his office "in everything but
name." In addition, it undoubtedly bothered Adams that at the height of
his popularity, he had to defer to Hamilton.[92]

A few minor incidents suggested that a break was coming. Adams
began to consider the appointment of an official government printer,
which hints that he was becoming disenchanted with High-Federalist
sheets. The cabinet later opposed the idea, not realizing that Adams was
taking into account the effect of the Logan mission and the dispatches of
Elbridge Gerry, which aided the revival of the Republican press. Finally,
Adams's brief and moderate message to Congress of December 8, 1798,
indicated his unwillingness to incorporate the ideas of Pickering, Mc-
Henry, Wolcott, or any other Hamiltonian stooges. The message advo-
cated renewed energy in naval matters and suggested that a minister might
be sent to France if proper assurances of his reception were given. Even
the *Aurora* and the *Boston Independent Chronicle* modified their tone ever
so slightly after the message.[93] The message omitted a detailed consideration of the changes in French attitude. That oversight was rectified in a
message of February 18, 1799, which severed the remaining threads between Adams and the High-Federalists.

The French attitude toward America began to turn as soon as Talleyrand realized the folly of his earlier attempts at bribery and intrigue
through his X, Y, and Z intermediaries. John Marshall reported to Adams

on his return from France that the French had tried to bully America, but that public opinion on this side of the ocean might cause a rethinking of French opinion, which is exactly what happened. Washington believed that only a misreading of American opinion had inspired the French folly in the first place. In addition, newspaper accounts, cited above, hammered home the swing in American opinion as a reaction to the shabby cupidity of French diplomacy. Talleyrand's attitude turned rapidly when he received printed copies of the XYZ papers in American journals.[94]

The High-Federalists did what they could to prevent the reconciliation with France. Both Gerry and Logan received Federalist contempt for their efforts, although Boston Federalist Joseph Woodward carried duplicates of Logan's dispatches and arrived back in America before Logan.[95] Adams realized the Federalists were operating at cross purposes to his own. He warned his son John Quincy, who was operating as a listening post in Europe: "Send us all the information you can collect. I wish you to continue your practice of writing freely to me, and cautiously to the office of State." Adams harassed the suspected Pickering when he sent him Gerry's comments on the XYZ affair and asked that they be "inserted in a public print."[96]

Adams's second annual message gave notice to France that America must be treated as a nation. On this policy, John Spencer Bassett has written: "This sentiment exactly expressed the feelings of the country." Adams's message was moderate, but the Senate's reply was not. Replies heretofore had been echoes of Adams, but this reply was far more anti–French than Adams's message.[97] The split was growing.

On January 15, 1799, Adams again harassed Pickering: "The President of the United States requests the Secretary of State to prepare the draught of a project of a treaty and a consular convention, such as in his opinion might at this day be acceded to by the United States, if proposed by France."[98] At the same time, Adams and Washington were both receiving assurances of French willingness to treat from various sources. Washington gave his approval to the reopening of negotiations, which meant Adams had only the High-Federalists to contend with. Stephen Higginson wrote to Wolcott on February 14, 1799, to detail the continued growth of patriotism. At the same time, Higginson warned that Adams's recent annual message would only increase French intrigue and predicted that Adams would have "reason to repent more and more the follies of his *friend* Gerry, and to lament the countenance he has given to him and his silly communications." The following day, Adams sent a message to the House of Representatives which reminded that body that the French still treated American sailors as pirates in certain cases.[99] Three days later Adams sent a tidy incendiary device to the Senate. Federalists, better able to plumb the workings of the bomb, rushed for the exits.

We have thus seen phase two in the Adams-press relationship, which developed in the wake of Adams's message to the special session of May 16, 1797, and ended his brief presidential-press honeymoon. A patriotic upsurge followed, with vastly increased support for both Adams and Federalism. Adams, however, remained more closely attuned to public opinion, as he both mirrored and molded it in his answers to addresses. The Federalists began to outrun public support and promulgated a series of internal security measures which, when combined with the eagerness they demonstrated to dictate legislation and army policy over the president's head, led to a rift between Adams and his party. French assurances to treat convinced Adams to take a risk and propose a new envoy, and the party split.

Adams was somewhat reticent regarding newspaper activity in this period, but he would have plenty to say about it in retirement. The journalistic rhetoric of the period under consideration changed little, except that the lines of demarcation were tightly drawn. Those lines would be sharply redrawn after February 18, 1799, when Adams's gamble for peace ended this second, critical phase of his presidency and hurled both Federalism, on a national scale, and Adams, in his political career, to their dénouement.

CHAPTER EIGHT

Adams and the American Press III: Realignment

The late nominations of the President for the purpose of renewing negotiations with France has given almost universal disgust.... There certainly will be serious difficulties in supporting Mr. Adams at the next election if he should be a candidate.
—Robert Troup to Rufus King, April 19, 1799

The third phase of the relationship between Adams and the press began on February 18, 1799, and ended in the late summer and early fall of 1800, when the presidential election was held. On the first date, Adams sent a message to the Senate which nominated William Vans Murray as minister plenipotentiary to France. On March 3, 1801, shortly after the end of this third phase of the Adams-press relationship, and largely as a result of the nomination of Murray, John Adams packed his belongings and prepared to leave the new Federal City and public office forever. Between the transmittal of Adams's peace message and the election which led to his departure, newspaper editors throughout the country reconsidered their politics, realigned the orientation of their newspapers, and fought a war of words pointing toward the pivotal election of 1800.

We are concerned here with four major events: first, the nomination of Murray; second, the departure of the new peace mission in the fall of 1799; third, the death of Washington in 1799; and finally, the cabinet changes of May 1800. The first event caused the journalistic realignment, and the other three reinforced it. Events of lesser importance, given the temper of the times, further inflamed the reaction to these major events.

On February 18, 1799, John Adams sent a message to the Senate with neither the advice nor the consent of either the cabinet or the High-Federalist party leaders. Jefferson, presiding officer in the Senate, was amazed when he read aloud Adams's message: "Always disposed and ready to embrace every plausible appearance of probability of preserving or restoring tranquility, I nominate William Vans Murray, our minister resident at The Hague, to be minister plenipotentiary of the United States to the French Republic." The message concluded: "Effectual care shall be taken in his instructions that he shall not go to France without direct and unequivocal assurances from the French government, signified by their minister of foreign relations, that he shall be received in character."[1]

Adams's message was a political suicide note, and he knew it. The following day he wrote to Washington that he was seeking peace on honorable terms, but not with an eye to ballots: "In elective governments, peace or war are alike embraced by parties, when they think they can employ either for electioneering purposes." Three days later Adams wrote his wife: "I have no idea that I shall be chosen President a second time; though that is not to be talked of. The business of the office is so oppressive that I shall hardly support it two years longer."[2]

An ad hoc committee of Federalist senators called on Adams in an attempt to alter the president's resolve. To cripple the mission, the Federalists proposed to substitute Rufus King, minister to Great Britain, for Murray. To thwart the Federalists, Adams threatened to resign and substitute Jefferson as president. Oliver Ellsworth, chief justice of the Supreme Court, finally broke the deadlock and convinced the president of the need for compromise. Accordingly, Adams sent a new message to the Senate on February 25, which nominated two additional envoys, Ellsworth and Patrick Henry. The message also addressed itself to the reasons for the change of the embassy: "It appears to me that a new modification of the embassy will give more general satisfaction to the Legislature and to the nation, and perhaps better answer the purposes we have in view."[3]

Reaction to the renewed peace effort was swift and direct, as Adams later noted:

> A great clamor was raised among the members of the House of Representatives, and out of doors, and an abundance of squibs, scoffs, and sarcasms, in what were then called the federal newspapers, particularly Cobbett's *Porcupine* and John Ward Fenno's *United States Gazette*.

Adams also vented his spleen to Abigail: "Rivalries have been irritated to madness, and federalists have merited the Sedition Law, and Cobbett the Alien Bill. But I will not take revenge." Adams also told his ailing wife that the consensus of opinion in Philadelphia believed that her wise counseling would have prevented the new nomination, and he concluded: "This ought to gratify your vanity enough to cure you!"[4]

Washington wrote to Hamilton and concluded that Adams's nomination of Murray was the cure for militarism: "The zeal and enthusiasm which were excited by the Publication of the Dispatches from our Commissioners at Paris are evaporated. It is now no more." Jefferson wrote to Monroe that "the whole was a secret till the nomination was announced. Never did a party shew a stronger mortification, & consequently, that war had been their object."[5]

The letters of Washington and Jefferson demonstrate the two problems central to Federalist thinking at this time. First, Adams did not consult the cabinet. Second, the decision to send a new envoy shattered the surge of nationalism which the Federalists nurtured and desperately needed. John Ward Fenno, Timothy Pickering, and George Gibbs, all writing later, could not conceal their distaste for Adams's decision to stand Federalist ideology on its head without prior notice.[6] Wagers were made in the Senate that the nomination would not be confirmed, but as the late Samuel Eliot Morison has concluded: "Although the Federalists controlled the Senate, they dared not reject the nomination, conscious that public opinion would side with the President."[7] Other writers have agreed that public opinion was on Adams's side and have also seen the nomination as a vehicle to do away with unpopular taxes. Page Smith has suggested that Adams was courting popular support in his peace move (put another way: acting as an elected leader), but has reminded readers that popular support was not electoral support.[8]

Historians generally agree that the nomination of peace envoys made the High-Federalists consider the replacement of Adams, as suggested in the opening quotation which serves as the guidepost for this chapter.[9] Adams recognized that his decision to send a new peace mission was not popular with High-Federalists, but insisted that Logan's junket and Washington's approval of renewed negotiations convinced him to take the step. Adams also defended the failure to consult the cabinet: "If I had asked their reasons, they would be such arguments as Hamilton has recorded; for he, it seems, was their recording secretary. . . . I thought a clamor after the fact would be much less dangerous than a clamor before it."[10]

Adams nevertheless received support from some Federalists. Former Secretary of War Henry Knox wrote to the president to agree with the nomination. He added that although a large majority of Federalists also concurred, Adams should beware of the splinter group. Thomas Adams, the president's son, wrote of similar attitudes in Boston. The president wrote to Attorney-General Charles Lee that the nomination had the good effect of bringing dissidents to the surface and concluded: "If any one entertains the idea, that, because I am a President of three votes only, I am in the power of a party, they shall find that I am no more so than the Constitution forces upon me."[11]

Newspaper editors, like the nation's political leaders, reconsidered their policies and their rhetoric after the nomination of Murray and the subsequent addition of Ellsworth and Henry. Democratic-Republican editors, who now looked to Duane, Bache's successor, were pleased with the appointments. They realized, however, that it was the work of Adams, not the High-Federalists, so they briefly attempted to emphasize the split. But they also moderated their praise of Adams because they had no intention of letting Adams's move for peace interfere with their campaign to defeat him at the next election.[12] The *Aurora* printed the nomination of Murray on February 19 and had praise for Adams, Gerry, and Logan the following day. Adams was well treated in the *Aurora* of February 21, but the High-Federalists were blasted: "to them hell is not so terrible as the thought of peace."[13] Other Republican sheets printed the news of the nominations, and comment generally favored Adams. The Newark *Centinel of Freedom* pictured Hamilton as "loud for war," fell silent on Adams, and hoped for a reduction in taxes. *Kline's Carlisle Weekly Gazette*, under the heading "Important," noted the nominations, but stressed that strong assurances from France were a prerequisite.[14]

Federalist newspapers divided along three lines. One group, which included the papers of Cobbett and Fenno, alternately execrated Adams in the strongest language or lapsed into silence. A second group, comprised mostly of New England sheets, had high praise for Adams's courage and wisdom and execrated Cobbett. A final group exhibited ambivalence, as they noted the nomination but stressed that unequivocal assurances were required.

In February, John Ward Fenno noted the nomination and confirmation of the envoys, but made no comment. On March 4, however, Fenno lashed out at Adams: "It was an accidental government from the outset; good governments are formed on usage and experience."[15] Cobbett was more direct, and his editorial metamorphosis can be read in one column of the February 20, 1799, issue of *Porcupine's Gazette*. He began by mocking the false rumors propagated by Duane and others that Adams had nominated a new envoy. He added: "I have too much respect for the President, too much confidence in his wisdom, to suppose this thing possible." Yet Cobbett concluded the article with a distressingly blunt warning: "but I will just observe, that had he taken such a step, it would have been instantaneously followed by the loss of every friend worth his preserving." Cobbett soon added that Adams would suffer inwardly if praised by the likes of "Mother Bache" (Bache's widow or Duane, choose one). Reporting the nomination of three envoys, Cobbett believed this proved his correct assertion that Adams had not appointed *one*. He added, "Mind, I do not say, that should this last report prove true, that the measure is a proper one."[16] Historians have emphasized that only Cobbett and Fenno opposed the peace mission, but in an era of scissors and paste journalism, that amounted to wire-service opposition.[17]

Adams found able defenders in the columns of the *Columbian Centinel* and *Russell's Gazette* in Boston. The *Centinel* saw the nomination as "the genuine effect of the wisdom, magnanimity, fortitude, and foresight of the American administration and people." *Russell's Gazette* was equally firm: "There is no man in America so well acquainted with the French character as the President.... Under the safeguard of such talents and integrity, then we may well repose our *fullest* confidence. Time will certainly illustrate the propriety of this opinion."[18] The *Massachusetts Mercury*, the *New Hampshire Gazette*, and the *Providence Gazette* all attacked Cobbett for his libels against the president. The *Mercury* was irate: "If he [Cobbett] is not taken up on the Sedition, or sent out of the country on the Alien Act, they are both, what he himself calls them, dead letters." The *Providence Gazette* printed a rumor of Cobbett's arrest under the Sedition Act and concluded: "The complexion of some of his late papers renders this highly probable."[19]

Other sheets simply reprinted the news of the nomination and stressed that assurances were necessary.[20] The *New Hampshire Gazette* continued to push for defense, but believed that the nomination was wise. The Hartford *American Mercury* praised Adams's willingness to treat, but regretted that the president had temporized. The New York *Spectator* and the *Norwich Packet* printed rumors that the appointments were defeated and hoped stronger assurances would be demanded. The *Green Mt. Patriot* added that Adams made the mission a three-man team "at the recommendation of the Senate." Finally, "Union," writing in the *Massachusetts Spy*, concluded: "But to the eye of the discerning patriot, the measure appears expedient and wise."[21]

As editors and politicians were reacting to the news of the new envoys, Adams left Philadelphia on March 11 for what amounted to a vacation at Braintree that included all four of the seasons, as he left in winter and did not return until fall. While there, Adams spent much time reading the works of Frederick of Prussia. In one passage, Frederick wrote: "The mob, which is in the majority everywhere, will always let itself be led by scoundrels." Adams noted in the margin: "There is too much truth in this."[22]

Adams's absence aroused the ire of Hamilton and Pickering, who felt he was abdicating leadership at a critical time. Robert Goodloe Harper was so enraged that he hoped the president's horses would run wild and injure Adams. The New York *Argus* felt that Adams's absence was cause for impeachment if the Fries, or "hot water" rebellion, the second such uprising in Pennsylvania, proved serious. Other Federalists simply lamented the failure to use the Sedition Act and the army and regretted that "the follies of Gerryism" prevented a declaration of war against France.[23]

In late April, Uriah Forrest wrote to Adams to convince him of the danger of his absence: "The people elected you to administer the government. They did not elect your officers, nor do they (however much they respect them) think them equal to govern without your presence and control." At the same time, George Cabot was writing to Wolcott to warn that Henry Knox was trying to convince Adams of the need for cabinet replacements.[24]

Because of the clamor at the time of the nominations, and the subsequent intrigues which developed in opposition to the mission, Philadelphia remained busy throughout the summer of 1799. Adams, on the other hand, spent his time in comparative ease. In May he wrote to Wolcott requesting information about the convicted John Fries.[25] During the summer months, Adams became a party to the two previously cited Sedition Act prosecutions. A series of anti–Adams remarks published in the *Northumberland Gazette* by Thomas Cooper led the president to conclude: "I have no doubt it is a libel against the whole government, and as such ought to be prosecuted."[26] In July the *Aurora* claimed it had proof that British influence had been used in the appointment of a government officer. Pickering sent a copy of the paper to Adams for consideration. Adams replied to Pickering: "Is there any thing evil in the regions of actuality or possibility, that the *Aurora* has not suggested of me? . . . If Mr. Rawle [Philadelphia district attorney] does not think this paper libellous, he is not fit for his office; if he does not prosecute it, he will not do his duty." Washington also wrote to Pickering of his willingness to see the *Aurora* prosecuted. Eventually, charges were brought and then dropped.[27] The accusation of influence and bribery was based on a genuine letter from Adams to Tench Coxe in 1792, so the *Aurora* printed truth in this instance. The Adams-Coxe letter would surface again in the campaign of 1800.

In August, Washington wrote a letter to McHenry that was highly critical of Adams's absence. A week later, however, Washington was writing to John Trumbull to warn against party divisions at all costs. The letter was also an answer to Trumbull's request that Washington stand for election in 1800, and the ex-president's answer was couched in terms of not wanting to be asked, rather than not wanting to run.[28]

In late August, Secretary of the Navy Benjamin Stoddert wrote to Adams to urge the president to return to the capital and meet with the envoys prior to their departure. Stoddert wrote a stronger letter two weeks later, which warned of Federalist intrigue concerning the 1800 election. The second letter struck a nerve. Adams replied that he would leave for the capital shortly, but not for the purpose of electioneering:

> I have only one favor to beg, and that is that a certain election may be wholly laid out of this question and all others. I know the people of

America so well, and the light in which I stand in their eyes, that no alternative will ever be left to me, but to be a President of three votes or no President at all, and the difference, in my estimation, is not worth three farthings.

Adams subsequently notified Pickering to suspend matters pending his return to the capital.[29]

As the summer of 1799 came to a close, William Vans Murray remained at The Hague. Oliver Ellsworth and Governor William R. Davie of North Carolina, who had replaced the unwilling Patrick Henry, were still in America and unsure of their status. To resolve the uncertainty, Adams returned to the temporary capital at Trenton and found the cabinet, Hamilton, and even Ellsworth convinced that the mission should be postponed because they believed a Bourbon restoration in France was an immediate possibility. Adams dismissed the idea as a phantasm. Members of the cabinet repeated their beliefs in a meeting with Adams on October 15 and came away convinced that they had delayed the mission. The following day Adams gave Pickering notice that the envoys should depart within two weeks. George Gibbs accepts the imminent restoration theory and castigates Adams for his decision to send the envoys: "The idea of sending ambassadors for private entertainment and instruction, had certainly the merit of originality." Gibbs also believes that Adams sent the mission because Hamilton was urging delay.[30] Adams later admitted his opposition to Hamilton's and Pickering's reasoning at the time. Abigail reinforced her husband's complaints of meddling and hinted that Pickering's tenure might be tenuous.[31]

The cabinet's intrigue and the president's decision to send the envoys had their effects. The intrigue cost America valuable time because it prevented the envoys from negotiating from the strength of the surge in public opinion. By the time the envoys were nominated, confirmed, collected, and sent, the French Directory had been replaced by Napoleon and America had lost its advantage at the bargaining table. The decision of Adams to send the envoys also put an end to the "unglorious career" of Hamilton-inspired ministerial government. It also made Adams a "doomed man" among High-Federalists. Adams realized this, however, as he wrote to Abigail, "An election is approaching which will set us at liberty from these uncomfortable journeys."[32]

With the departure of the envoys, the High-Federalists were chagrined, but the more moderate Adams-Federalists were satisfied. The two factions were not yet prepared to commence a fratricidal war of words, so Federalist sheets fell temporarily silent on Adams and printed foreign news and rumors of Napoleon's death. Republican sheets hesitated to praise the mission and also temporized about emphasizing the Federalist split. They

concentrated instead on Federalist justice, singling out the cases of Jedediah Peck, the synthetic martyr Jonathan Robbins, and the drunken
Luther Baldwin. In the latter instance, Republican sheets made merry at
the expense of Adams's "posterior."[33] Adams suffered heavily in the case
of Jonathan Robbins, a sailor extradited to British courts and subsequently
executed. An attempt was later made in the House to censure Adams, but
it was defeated 61–35. Jefferson saw great promise in the Robbins case, as
he wrote to Republican Charles Pinckney: "I think no one circumstance
since the establishment of our government has affected the public mind
more. I learn that in Pennsylvania it had a great effect."[34]

Federalist demoralization in the fall of 1799 can be accurately gauged
by reading the letters of High-Federalists in the Wolcott collection edited
by George Gibbs.[35] At the same time, Abigail noted that antigovernment
abuse was still the work of foreigners and added: "John Fenno is become
a coppiest of them. What a disgrace to our Country." Gibbs believes the
reason behind Federalist demoralization and Fenno's defection is clear:
"Mr. Adams' fatal step in instituting the new mission."[36]

Adams's third annual message, delivered on December 3, 1799,
reconciled no one. It spoke of the need for economy and a reorganization
of the judicial system and was answered with belligerent, anti–French
replies from both House and Senate. Republican newspapers, aware of the
fast-approaching elections, saw the message as an appeal to the populace
rather than food for congressional thought.[37] In sum, the message only
added impetus to the Federalist split.

At this time, when the spirit of Federalism seemingly reached its low
ebb, Washington became ill and died. The passing of the former president
drove a deeper wedge between the two wings of Federalism and also put
to rest the "Washington as cloak" practice. Southern Federalism suffered
heavily because Edward Rutledge died within a month of Washington,
and the animosities in the Adams-Hamilton split deepened. The army lost
much of its remaining popularity because Republican newspapers worked
unceasingly to remind their readers of the character of the man in line to
succeed Washington. Washington's passing had one good political effect
for the Federalists, however: news of the event largely obscured the
significance of the "Kentucky Resolutions" of 1799, printed at the same
time, which directly attacked Federalist policies.[38]

Adams was very laudatory of Washington in his eulogy, but Republican politicians, Republican editors, and Abigail Adams believed that
Washington was eulogized beyond his deeds.[39] Wolcott lamented Washington's death because the ex-president seemed to mitigate Adams's
distrust of the cabinet, Wolcott included, as well as his distrust of
Hamilton. The same letter admitted that Adams's peace move, opposed by the cabinet and Hamilton, was widely respected by the people.

Nevertheless, the High-Federalists used Washington's memory against Adams, as they found a striking resemblance between Washington and their presidential hopeful, Charles Cotesworth Pinckney.[40]

A political and journalistic lull followed the passing and mourning of Washington. Once again a wait-and-see attitude prevailed regarding negotiations with France, but the reporting began to look towards the election of 1800 as a topic of great interest. The final remaining issue was the removal of Timothy Pickering and James McHenry from their respective positions in the State and War departments.

In March, government officials in Portsmouth, New Hampshire, were suspected of using their offices for Republican electioneering and were removed by the president. In discussing the removals, Adams asked Benjamin Lincoln, "If the officers of government will not support it, who will?" A month later, William Duane of the *Aurora* gave a prophetic warning: "The cabinet here is in a very discordant condition. They hang together only like wretched mariners on detached planks; if one lets go, the whole go."[41] The "wretched mariners" were cast adrift in early May 1800, at a time when the election campaign was moving into high gear.

Adams called McHenry into conference on May 6, lost control of himself, and browbeat the helpless war secretary into a resignation. Four days later Adams offered Pickering the opportunity to resign. Pickering refused on the grounds that he could not afford to give up the job. The same day Adams fired him. The curt dismissal letter was signed "John Adams, President of the United States."[42] George Gibbs, in the midst of a scathing anti–Adams defense of the cabinet, concluded: "They might have resigned—the interests of their party and the wishes of their friends prevented them. They retained their posts that they might prevent him [Adams] from doing mischief ... they were right in controlling his actions."[43]

After the removal of Pickering and McHenry, editors divided along the same three lines that political factions were following. "The adherents of Hamilton and Adams commenced open hostilities, in which both sides seemed entirely to disregard the fact that their divisions were Jefferson's strength."[44] Republican sheets either contented themselves by simply reporting the removals, or they made merry with the news. The *Aurora*, under the heading "The Hydra Dying" reported: "If ever a man went out of a public station loaded with the universal execrations of an injured country, it is Mr. Timothy Pickering." The *Aurora* and the Salem *Impartial Register* made sport of Pickering's disinclination to retire.[45] New England newspapers generally defended the removals and frequently had high praise for Adams's courageous action at a politically inopportune time.[46] Southern sheets generally followed the High-Federalist party line set down by Fenno. They first reported that the firings were based on political grounds, but later put out a false report promoting nonexistent unity in Federalist ranks.[47] Hamilton tied the cabinet removals to Adams's recent defeat in the New York elections, but added that this was conjecture.[48]

Editors and individuals were quick to see electioneering in the removals. It was reported by newspapers of all three factions that a bargain was made between Adams and Jefferson. The Republican and the Adams-Federalist sheets denied the bargain after reporting it, although the High-Federalist papers stuck to the story. George Gibbs later followed the High-Federalist line. Although a bargain was highly unlikely, the removal of two High-Federalists and their replacement by two Virginians was open to both patriotic and political interpretations. The fired McHenry saw electioneering as well as insanity behind Adams's action.[49]

Republicans got as much mileage out of the removals as possible. The *Aurora* wrote that Adams was now unpopular with the army officers, for "he has dismissed Timothy." Duane later derided the new cabinet man by man and added, "every body knows the *Ides of March are not very distant!*" Abraham Bishop, in an oration, saw "great confusion in the cabinet" and pictured Adams as the blind pilot of a crazy ship. One Republican motto was "When thieves fall out, honest men come by their own."[50]

George Gibbs cites Adams's weaknesses, from jealousy and paranoia to absenteeism, for the reasons behind the dismissals. He also adds that McHenry's talents were esteemed by all concerned, a very misguided and erroneous declaration at best. Wolcott defended Pickering against charges of shortages in the State Department.[51] Adams defended his own policy in the simplest terms because he concluded that either a president had the power to change his secretaries or he was unfit for his office. Noting that the cabinet had been an equal vexation to Washington, Adams admitted that he removed himself from power when he ousted the two secretaries.[52]

Adams's decision of May 21, 1800, to pardon Pennsylvania rabble-rouser John Fries caused a repetition of the agitation which surrounded the cabinet removals. Gibbs and others again view the move from the perspective of electioneering. The *Aurora*, as well as some Adams-Federalist newspapers, viewed the pardon as a signal act of mercy. Public opinion, as well as can be gauged, also approved the move.[53] Fries's pardon, however, was little more than an encore after the cabinet shake-up. Of itself, it caused no realignment and only rehashed existing arguments. The state of thinking among High-Federalists is well shown in a letter from Oliver Wolcott to Chauncey Goodrich written after Adams again left the troubled capital for the serenity of home. Wolcott wrote: "General Marshall was absent about a fortnight, during which time, Mr. Stoddert, Mr. Dexter, and myself, governed the country. We agree in every thing except in the qualifications of our dread lord and master."[54]

Thus there existed a political and journalistic reorientation following John Adams's nomination of peace envoys in February 1799. Those shifts were reinforced by Adams's insistence on the departure of the envoys, by the death of Washington, and by Adams's shake-up of the cabinet. As the election of 1800 approached, a brief period existed in which three factions contended for power.

Lost in all the clamor is the fact that Adams's decisions were largely sustained by the populace. The High-Federalists were beginning to come under popular scrutiny; they fared quite well in the 1799 elections but did very poorly a year later. Republicans for the most part supported Adams's major decisions, but did not allow their admiration for Adams to overcome their overall detestation for Federalism, especially Federalist justice. "Adams-Federalists," or the more moderate element in the party, lined up solidly behind Adams's decisions and continued to support him throughout the year 1800.

CHAPTER NINE

Adams and the American Press IV: Dénouement

To be divided is to be ruined.
—Noah Webster, *letter to Alexander Hamilton,* p. 12

In 1800 the Federalist party suffered the first of five consecutive defeats in presidential elections. Historians have found a variety of reasons for that initial Federalist defeat. Among them were the Alien and Sedition Acts, high taxes, the army, the split in Federalist ranks, and the good organization and campaign strategy of the Democratic-Republicans.

The interaction between Adams and the press also had an effect on the election of 1800 because it resulted in an intricate web of intrigue of High-Federalists and an example of shrewd politics by Democratic-Republicans. An additional key factor in the canvass of 1800 was that Adams was frequently little more than a disinterested witness to Federalist and Republican campaign maneuvers.

In his first two-and-a-half months as president, Adams found himself praised by Republicans and suspected by some Federalists. After May 1797, Republicans refused to place any further trust in Adams, although his subsequent peace moves brought praise. Federalists identified closely with Adams in that second phase, but divided as a party over the question of new envoys to France. Adams's decision to send the envoys and his subsequent cabinet purge aggravated the existing split in Federalism.

As a result, the campaign of 1800 featured three parties: the High-Federalists, led by Hamilton and supported by some Federalist editors; the Adams-Federalists, headed by the president and supported by most moderate Federalist editors; and the Democratic-Republicans, led by Jefferson and Aaron Burr and supported by a rejuvenated press.

Federalist intrigue gave focus to the battle between the two factions of Federalism. Shrewd Republicans concentrated their fire on the High-Federalists, directing their polemics more against Hamilton and Hamiltonian policy than against Adams. The Republican campaign polarized the issues in popular thinking because it seemed that the voters were asked to support either Republicanism or High-Federalism. By omitting much anti–Adams rhetoric from their polemics and by not emphasizing the split in Federalism, the Republicans were able to attack the president through Hamilton. Later on, Republicans opened fire on Adams and the High-Federalists together. Republican organization and manipulation, in combination with Federalist in-fighting, decided the election.

Unpopular issues aided the Republicans and made their campaign believable. But the issues needed a vehicle to reach the voters, and the contemporary Republican and Federalist presses answered that need. When John Adams wrote years later that it was newspapers, not issues, that defeated him, he spoke the truth.

Another factor in the election of 1800 was Republican organization; its early effectiveness in the New York election contributed to the Federalist split. That split, the resulting Federalist duplicity, and Alexander Hamilton's untimely letter against Adams sealed the president's electoral fate. Thus happened the "Revolution of 1800." But was it a revolution?

John C. Miller believes that the Federalists headed into the election year in fairly good shape. Duplicity had not yet completely replaced distrust, so the eventual split was not yet completed. On the positive side, Federalism had peace and prosperity to its credit. Federalism also collected a windfall in the backlash against the Virginia and Kentucky Resolutions. Finally, Federalists delayed the census of 1800, which prevented an increase of electors in middle and southern states.[1]

The campaign of 1800 was an acrimonious one. Abigail Adams believed as early as March that one or two more popular elections would "corrupt and destroy the morals of the people." John C. Miller has commented on the volume of abuse heaped on both Adams and Hamilton (overlooking the much-maligned Jefferson) and has concluded that "there were not enough prisons in the country to hold the newspaper writers, the politicians, and the plain citizens guilty of violating the Sedition Act in the campaign of 1800."[2]

Against this background of vilification, Republicans worked to improve their campaign strategy. In two companion volumes, Noble E. Cunningham, Jr., has shown how this strategy developed and how it was put to use after the Republican victory in 1800.[3] Cunningham's thesis has also been adopted by Stephen Kurtz and Page Smith.[4]

Federalists recognized the impact of Republican organization as early as mid–1800. As Oliver Wolcott wrote to William Bingham, "The victory will be won by the party which conducts its affairs with the greatest skill, consistency, and courage, and these advantages certainly belong to our opponents." A week later Fisher Ames wrote a letter to Wolcott which pinpointed the weakness of Federalism: "The Federalists scarcely deserve the name of party. Their association is a loose one—formed by accident, and shaken by every prospect of labour or hazard."[5]

More recent students of journalism have emphasized the excellent job done by the numerically outnumbered Republican press in rallying public opinion to its cause. Jefferson's work in helping to found newspapers and in circulating subscription lists among his friends was singled out for praise.[6] Uriah Tracy wrote to Wolcott to discuss Republican activity: "They are establishing Democratic presses and newspapers in almost every town and county of the country; and the Federal presses are failing for want of support."[7] Among the resurgent Republican polemicists were Charles Pinckney (not the XYZ Pinckney) and John Beckley. Pinckney wrote to Madison of his efforts in the cause of Republicanism in South Carolina: "I have incessantly laboured to carry this Election here and to sprinkle all the southern states with pamphlets and Essays and every thing I thought would promote the common cause." Beckley, removed from his post as clerk of the House of Representatives in 1797, wrote as "Americanus" to attack Federalism and to reply to charges against Jefferson.[8]

In addition to setting up new presses, the numerical strength of Republican journalism was augmented by converts hitherto undecided or mildly Federalist. Some newspapers had been more or less neutral during the honeymoon phase and had remained neutral during the early months of the crisis phase. The release of the XYZ papers brought the waverers temporarily into line with Federalism. When the High-Federalists rashly outran their popular and editorial support, many of these sheets swung back to neutrality. With Republican journals pointing to a showdown between Jeffersonian Democracy and High-Federalism, many wavering editors now threw their support behind Jefferson. The two most prominent examples were the Newark *Centinel of Freedom* and *Kline's Carlisle Weekly Gazette*. Both sheets supported Jefferson and attacked Adams, reinforcing their swing to Republicanism by a greatly increased dependency on the *Aurora*. In New England, the Hartford *American Mercury* criticized Adams and vilified Hamilton. The paper also echoed the Republican claim that the French threat and the XYZ imbroglio were Federalist ploys, set up to create an army and a despotism. In a September issue, the *Mercury* lashed the seemingly contrived crisis: "But that about the French invasion was the most successful device ever hit upon by any party. 'Tis true, the frolic was rather an unlucky and expensive one to the country."[9]

The final impetus in the growth of Republican journalism was provided by the enforcement of the Alien and Sedition Acts. The Naturalization and Alien laws convinced editors of foreign-language newspapers that Jeffersonian Democracy was preferable to High-Federalism. Newspapers printed in English which were read by aliens also reoriented themselves along Jeffersonian lines. The Sedition Act also changed the scope of journalism. As noted in Chapter 2, the scope of prosecutions under the Sedition Act was limited, and the handful of individuals arrested fell into one of two categories. The first included the leaders of the Jeffersonian press cadre: Bache, Duane, Callender, Holt, Thomas Cooper, and Thomas Adams, who were arrested for publications which aroused High-Federalist pique. If the subsequent convictions had forced the closing of their papers, it would have seriously disrupted the Republican portion of the fledgling scissors-and-paste wire service. Individuals, not newspapers, however, were the focus of the action. The papers continued to publish, and in the cases of Callender, Cooper, and Holt, the writers increased their calumnies subsequent to their adjudication.

The second group of individuals detained under the Sedition Act was an eclectic group of bothersome thorns in the side of High-Federalism: Luther Baldwin, Matthew Lyon, Anthony Haswell, William Durrell, Jedediah Peck, David Brown, Benjamin Fairbanks, and David Frothingham. Although the truth of an allegation could be used as a defense and criminal intent had to be proved, Leonard Levy sees these guarantees as "an empty protection of the accused."

Despite the small scope of the Federalist enforcement efforts, the prosecutions under the Sedition Act were viewed by non–Federalist editors as a part of the 1800 election and were treated accordingly. Adams's urging of the prosecution of Duane and Cooper was unknown to Republican editors and therefore did not become a press issue, nor did it contribute to or materially alter the nature of the interaction between Adams and the press. Noah Webster, a moderate Federalist, epitomized overall Federalist displeasure with the Republican press in a letter to Wolcott. After commenting on the need for government to mirror public opinion, Webster concluded: "I go further and aver that no government can be durable and quiet under the licentiousness of the press that now disgraces our country. Jacobinism will prevail, unless more pains are taken to keep public opinion correct."[10] New Republican presses were begun in response to the Sedition Act, and the quantity of these new presses greatly outnumbered, and therefore filled the void of, the few already existing Republican presses whose editors were affected or endangered by the Sedition Act. Nevertheless, the new presses joined the chorus of those already in existence in reviling the Sedition Act. The *Constitutional Telegraph* reported that Federalists recognized the *Aurora*'s impact on public opinion

and were preparing to eliminate the paper or its editor. The *Aurora* stoked
the anti–Sedition Act fire when it printed a notice that Thomas Cooper,
convicted under the Sedition Act, had refused a pardon. Cooper, writing
from his cell, refused to be "the voluntary cats-paw of electioneering
clemency." James Callender also published from his cell. His second
volume of *The Prospect Before Us*, written during his imprisonment, saw
Adams as "that scourge, that scorn, that outcast of America.... He is, in
private life, one of the most egregious fools upon the continent."[11]

The yeoman efforts of the Republican press were seconded by the
work of some very able Republican political leaders. Aaron Burr of New
York and Charles Pinckney of South Carolina were very influential in
helping Jefferson carry those two key states. In New York, Burr worked
diligently to put together a slate of electors which contained the most able
Republican leaders in the state. Hamilton's electoral state, by comparison,
was a group of nonentities. Burr's efforts were indirectly aided by Adams's
1799 decision for peace. Renewed negotiations with France seriously
weakened Anglo-American relations and British captures and impress-
ments became an issue. On the eve of the spring elections, a British warship escorted several captured American ships into New York harbor.[12]

Burr's legwork, Hamilton's apathy, untimely incidents, and strong
Republican press efforts combined to give Jefferson New York's 12 electoral votes. The early defeat in New York disheartened Federalists of every
hue. High-Federalists dropped what little respect they still had for Adams
and made a bold attempt to elevate Charles Cotesworth Pinckney. Hesi-
tant moderates deserted Federalism for the party of Jefferson. Although
South Carolina proved to be the pivotal state as the election closed, the
victory in New York kept Republicanism alive. Writing to Adams years
later, Benjamin Stoddert believed that if Burr's efforts in New York had
failed, Jefferson would have thrown his support to Adams and waited four
more years. (Jefferson's letter of January 1, 1797, to Madison showed that
Jefferson preferred Adams to Hamilton at a time when his own defeat was
imminent.)[13]

The results of the New York election also convinced moderate Federalists of the need for action independent of Hamilton's control. The candidates for the New York Legislature put forward by Hamilton, in effect
the electoral slate, had included "a ship chandler, a baker, a potter, a book
seller, two grocers, a bankrupt, a shoe-maker, and a mason." It was a clear
indicator of Hamilton's lack of concern regarding Adams's reelection.
Henceforth, the Adams-Federalists tried to present their nominee as an independent or third-party candidate.[14]

As early as February 1800, the *Aurora* printed a breakdown of
Federalist factionalism, more an attempt to conquer than to divide.
Duane viewed the Adams-Federalists as "The New England Party, the

Connecticut Illuminati, [and] the Office Hunting Party." Hamilton's minions were treated to a lengthier political analysis, as they were seen to include "The Old Tory and Refugee Party, the army, navy, place and profit hunting party, the funding, banking, and loan party, the British Agency and Speculating party, [and] the monarchical and anti–Gallican party." The *Aurora* reprinted a description of the split in May, but blasted both factions.[15]

Fisher Ames, writing to Wolcott in the summer of 1800, pictured "three parties in the United States" and believed one of the Federalist wings was led by a man of great weakness and little talent. As if the party split neither existed nor mattered, Ames asked: "Why not then, without delay, begin a series of papers to prove the dreadful evils to be apprehended from a Jacobin President?" That same summer Adams was visited at Quincy by moderate leaders concerned with the 1800 election. The High-Federalists' conspicuous absence distressed Adams.[16]

In his study of Southern Federalism, Lisle Rose discovered a paradox. While Northern Federalism was being weakened by the Adams-Hamilton split, Southern Federalism was becoming stronger. The Southern press was also becoming more articulate in its support of Adams. Although Adams was distrusted in Virginia for suspected monarchism and it was Jefferson's home state, Virginia Federalists worked hard for their candidate. The *Virginia Federalist* made Old Testament heroes out of Washington and Adams. The president was also lauded in a series of essays throughout 1800 in the *Federal Carolina Gazette*.[17]

Adams also retained much of his popularity with the people throughout 1800. He was warmly greeted by citizens in Alexandria, Virginia, on his return from visiting Martha Washington at Mount Vernon. He was also met by friendly crowds on his trip home to Massachusetts and on his return trip to the new Federal City in the fall.[18]

As the campaign intensified, the leaders of the High-Federalist party deserted Adams. At a time when Republicanism was making rapid strides, High-Federalists conducted a campaign of intrigue surpassing in intensity their maneuvers against Adams in all past elections. The influence of Federalist duplicity upon the election of 1800 equaled that of Republican journalism and legwork. In the long run, however, such duplicity was more distressing to Adams and Federalism because Republican efforts at least had the merit of being predictable.

Adams began to cut himself loose from the High-Federalists at the height of his popularity in late 1798. The peace mission to France, the passing of Washington, and the cabinet shake-up completed the split. The High-Federalists sought a replacement for Adams and considered Oliver Ellsworth briefly. Ellsworth, however, was too closely identified with the Sedition Act because of his position on the high court, and his potential candidacy also suffered from his absence in France as negotiator to an as yet unknown treaty.[19] Finally, High-Federalists agreed to support Charles Cotesworth Pinckney over Adams, and the in-fighting commenced.

George Gibbs, in discussing the problems faced by Federalism in the summer of 1800, singles out two: "The attacks of the opposition" and "the still more fatal dissensions in [Federalist] ranks."[20] Gibbs then prints a series of letters by many of the leading High-Federalists that were couched in the strongest anti–Adams language.

Fisher Ames wrote to Chauncey Goodrich of the need "to keep an *anti* out . . . at the risk, which everyone I converse with suggests, of excluding Mr. A." George Cabot wrote of Adams's weakness and theorized that Pinckney would be elected to keep Jefferson out. Wolcott answered Cabot, "We shall never find ourselves in the straight road of federalism while Mr. Adams is President." Benjamin Goodhue wrote to Wolcott of "Mr. Adams' insufferable madness and vanity." Wolcott happily wrote to his former colleague James McHenry, "At any rate, the prospect is almost certain that the country will be freed from the greatest possible curse, a Presidential Administration which no party can trust." Cabot pictured an even darker Federalist gloom: "There are even men among the Federalists who would prefer Jefferson to a *federal* rival of Mr. A. and there are certainly some who would prefer Mr. J. to Adams." Thomas Fitzsimmons was ambivalent: "Jefferson's interest must surely prevail. I really know not whether we shall be much worse off with him than with the present man." Wolcott, in a letter to Fisher Ames, saw Jefferson capable of the same mischief as Adams. Later, Wolcott made a paradoxical promise to McHenry: "I shall do all in my power, consistently with truth and integrity, to promote the election of General Pinckney." Later letters in the Gibbs collection concentrate on the "unfitness of one of the federal candidates to fill the office of President."[21]

Cobbett wrote to Edward Thornton predicting Jefferson's election and noting Federalist attempts to put in Pinckney. Fisher Ames pinpointed Adams's sin in a letter to Pickering: "He is implacable against a certain great little man whom we mutually respect [Hamilton]."[22]

The High-Federalist press reflected the tone of the leadership of the party. Adams was no more popular in their newspapers and pamphlets than he was in the pages of Wolcott's letterbook. John Ward Fenno, in a strongly anti–Adams pamphlet, had high praise for Pinckney. Fenno had become so fearful of one-man rule that he proposed a new system of government.[23] Cobbett wrote to a friend about the *Anti-Jacobin Review*, a High-Federalist polemic which reviled Adams for his peace moves.[24]

High-Federalist newspapers worked against Adams by indirection, channeling their duplicity into laudatory adulation about Charles Cotesworth Pinckney. The *Gazette of the United States* regularly boosted Pinckney

beyond his merit and eventually printed "A Sketch of the Life and
Character of Charles Cotesworth Pinckney." That column was reprinted
in the *Boston Columbian Centinel*, the *Middlesex Gazette*, the *Salem Gazette*,
and the *Norwich Packet*. The printing of that column was the best indicator
that a newspaper was either strongly or latently High-Federalist. The
Salem *Impartial Register*, an Adams-Federalist sheet, urged voters to vote
for Thomas Kittridge, an elector pledged to Adams, and against "the
Pinckney Party (alias the anti–Adams junto)." A Democratic sheet, the
New York *American Citizen*, used the strategy noted earlier when it reported: "The real controversy for President is between Mr. Jefferson and
Mr. Hamilton: as for Mr. Adams, he has been cast off by the most influen-
tial men of his party to give way to Mr. Pinckney."[25]

Federalist duplicity found its champion in Alexander Hamilton. His
efforts in 1789 to reduce Adams's vice presidential vote were ominous of
future discord. In 1800, Hamilton went on an inspection tour of New
England troops and used the opportunity to laud Pinckney at the expense
of Adams. But his biggest contribution to the cause of Pinckney and, as
it turned out, to the cause of Republicanism was his "Letter concerning
the Public Conduct and Character of *John Adams, Esq.* President of the
United States." Historians of the twentieth century have agreed with
Adams-Federalists on the complete irresponsibility of that pamphlet.
Adrienne Koch sees the Hamilton-Adams split as stronger than the
Republican-Federalist split. John C. Miller believes that Hamiltonians
wrote more seditious material against Adams than Republicans were
capable of or convicted for. Marshall Smelser calls Hamilton's pamphlet
"the most eccentric bit of self-gratification in American political history,"
concluding, "but it was hate's labor lost."[26]

Hamilton wrote to Wolcott in July of 1800 requesting information on
Adams. If Wolcott provided the information, Hamilton concluded, "I can
set malice at defiance." A month later Hamilton repeated his intention to
write a letter about Adams for private circulation. Wolcott answered
Hamilton that it was a good idea to expose Adams's weaknesses, but warned
Hamilton not to publish under his own signature. That the whole episode
was self-gratification is shown by Wolcott's conclusion: "Mr. Jefferson will
certainly be elected President. The antis have command of the press—the
current of public opinion is in their favour." In late September, Hamilton
replied that the letter was ready, adding, "I hope from it two advantages—
the promotion of Mr. Pinckney's election and the vindication of ourselves."[27]

Burr procured a copy of Hamilton's philippic before it reached its intended audience and had parts of it printed in the *Aurora* and the New
London *Bee*. As extracts were more damaging than the whole, Hamilton
released the entire pamphlet. The polemic itself made little sense and only

served to satiate the collective High-Federalist ego. Hamilton wrote of Adams's weaknesses, "Which unfit him for the office of Chief Magistrate." After repetition of further presidential foibles, Hamilton concluded: "Yet with this opinion of Mr. Adams, I have finally resolved not to advise the withholding from him a single vote."[28] After 50 pages of insults, Hamilton thus performed a volte-face and gave a weak endorsement of Adams in one sentence.

Moderate Federalists rushed into print to defend Adams, but the damage was done. Noah Webster viewed Adams's naval policies as being far wiser than Hamilton's army. Webster pinpointed High-Federalists' displeasure with Adams in his conclusion: "That the President is *unmanageable*, is in a degree, true, that is, you and your supporters cannot manage him." Adams was also defended in pamphlets written by Uzal Ogden and William Pinckney.[29]

The split in Federalism was demonstrated by newspaper reaction to Hamilton's pamphlet. The Salem *Impartial Register* remarked, "The Pinckney Party, thank Heaven, have prematurely developed their views— Our illustrious President has been dragged before the public tribunal by a confessed *Adulterer!*" The same sheet repeated Noah Webster's idea that Hamilton would prefer a puppet to the unmanageable Adams. To bolster High-Federalism, the Charleston *City Gazette* serialized Hamilton's pamphlet. The *Gazette of the United States* told its readers of the pamphlet and even how to obtain it. The Washington *National Intelligencer* quoted the pamphlet at great length to prove that the election was a contest between Republicanism and High-Federalism, "for Mr. Adams is out of the question." The New York *American Citizen* repeated the charge that Hamilton was supporting a candidate he could control, but added that Hamilton would have been jailed if he had said such things as a Republican. The *Courier of New Hampshire* defended Hamilton against the attempts of Thomas Cooper to have him arrested under the Sedition Act. The Democratic *Boston Independent Chronicle* printed "Hamiltonian delusions" as a Federalist epitaph. The *Farmer's Museum, or Literary Gazette* believed the regrettable pamphlet would have no effect on the voters.[30]

A few individuals added interesting comments on the results of Hamilton's pamphlet. William Duane, editor of the *Aurora*, wrote: "This pamphlet has done more mischief to the parties concerned than all the labors of the *Aurora*." Abigail Adams expressed much the same sentiments, viewing Hamilton's scurrility as at least the equal of Duane's "grose lies." John Adams believed "Never was there a grosser mistake of public opinion than that of Mr. Hamilton." But Adams was not greatly upset at Hamilton, as he viewed the attack as but a continuation of the Hamiltonian distrust which began when Adams supported Gates over Schuyler in May 1776.

Adams saw the removal of the war threat and the dismantling of the regiments as the immediate cause for the rhetoric. To Uzal Ogden, Adams wrote: "The last pamphlet I regret more on account of its author than on my own, because I am confident it will do him more harm than me." Finally, in a letter to Rush in 1806, Adams mentioned that Hamilton's work in 1800 did not bother him nearly as much as the pamphlet Hamilton threatened to write against Washington if he was not given an important post at Yorktown. Adams lashed out: "I lose all patience when I think of a bastard brat of a Scotch pedlar daring to threaten to undeceive the world in their judgment of Washington by writing an history of his battles and campaigns. This creature was in a delirium of ambition."[31]

The overall effect of the pamphlet is difficult to gauge. It weakened the Republican strategy of linking Adams to the High-Federalists, but probably changed few Republican votes. Also, Republicans were beginning to attack both Adams and Hamilton by late fall. The pamphlet may have made a few converts for Adams because some High-Federalists undoubtedly recognized the lack of rationale behind Hamilton's work. Beyond that, the pamphlet finalized the split in Federalism.

Before the pamphlet, Adams enjoyed the support of the majority of Federal newspapers, and the pamphlet only served to confirm that support. Some sheets signified their support for Adams by attacking the High-Federalists. Others lashed Jefferson, under the headings "Burleigh" or "The Jeffersoniad." Still others praised Adams directly: "First in the list of Merit, John Adams, the Achme of the Pyramid." Additional Adams-Federalist newspapers implored wandering Federalists to return to the fold. Russell's Gazette endorsed Adams and warned that the French were waiting for a "first consul" [Jefferson] to be installed in America in March 1801.[32]

In comparison to what High-Federalists said about Adams in their letters and newspapers, the Republican campaign against him was considerably milder. Adams, Hamilton, the High-Federalists, and unpopular issues were attacked, but the intensity of earlier rhetoric was moderated, in part because some of the leading character assassins were in jail, dead, or absent for other reasons.

Scurrility was also moderated by an absence of unpopular issues which could be tied to Adams directly. The June 17, 1800, Aurora listed "Some of the blessings of Mr. Adams's administration," citing the miscues of High-Federalism: the army, the sedition law, taxes, loans, and an increased debt. Although inspired by High-Federalists, the legislation received Adams's signature, so he shared the editorial indictment with the authors of the measures. The Virginia Argus, published in the safest Republican state, featured directness over name calling:

> We insinuate nothing against the opposite ticket. Let the contest be considered as it really is, between Thomas Jefferson and John Adams. The former you know to be a sincere and enlightened Republican; whose greatness has been promulgated through the unavailing calumnies of his enemies, though he stands unshielded by a sedition law.

The *Aurora* found an issue in early August, when it attacked Adams for accepting a $25,000 yearly salary while "at Braintree *superintending the faithful execution of the laws.*"[33]

In late August, the *Aurora* printed a letter sent by Adams to Tench Coxe in May 1792. This episode gave rise to the most serious charges that Republicans were able to level at Adams, although the incident was little more than a rhetorical charade. The letter, given by Coxe to the *Aurora*, proved that Adams suspected "much British influence" in the appointment of Thomas Pinckney to succeed him in London. The *Aurora* printed the letter on August 28 and again on the following day. It was scrutinized sentence by sentence for maximum effect. Writing to Wolcott two days later, McHenry accepted the veracity of the letter and rehashed Adams's weaknesses. Wolcott simultaneously wrote an uncharacteristic defense of Adams. The *Aurora* continued to hammer away at "British influence" and was seconded by the New York *American Citizen*. Both sheets printed all the horrors of Federalism that stemmed from the British faction in America.[34]

The *Gazette of the United States* was the High-Federalist barometer in the Adams-Coxe episode. Defending Pinckney, it printed a report that the letter was a forgery or a misrepresentation. The *Aurora* correctly asserted that the letter was genuine. The *Gazette* then printed the letter, concluding that its readers might be loath to purchase the *Aurora*. The *Gazette* added: "Whatever improprieties Mr. A may be guilty of, Tench Coxe is not the man to reproach him."[35] Adams-Federalist sheets defended the president against the charges that he knew of British influence. Defense, however, meant further reprints of the charges.[36]

Rumors frequently mingled with calumny. The *Virginia Argus* reported that Adams preferred Jefferson to Pinckney. Newspapers even invented maladies for Adams. As Abigail wrote: "We are all at present well, tho the newspapers very kindly gave the President the Ague and fever. I am rejoiced that it was only in the paper that he had it."[37]

As the campaign neared its close, rhetoric tended to polarize. Adams and war or Jefferson and peace was the standard Republican motto. Federalists answered with "God and a religious president or *Jefferson and no God.*" That attack on deism led to the founding of a deistical newspaper in New York, the *Temple of Reason*. The New York *American Citizen* printed "SERIOUS CONSIDERATIONS, WHY JOHN ADAMS SHOULD NOT BE REELECTED PRESIDENT." The paper then matched the crimes alleged to

George III in the Declaration of Independence with 28 alleged similar crimes of the Federalist administrations. James Callender's purpose in writing *The Prospect Before Us* was to publicize "the multiplied corruptions of the Federal Government, and more especially the misconduct of the President, Mr. Adams." Calling Adams a "hoary-heady incendiary," Callender coupled logic with invective. For the purpose of Southern listeners, he wrote that the Alien Act gave the president the power to banish aliens. Since slaves were aliens, could they be banished by presidential fiat? Callender's second volume of *The Prospect* had additional impact because it was written "in the stench and suffocation of a jail."[38]

As state after state reported election returns, it became clear that South Carolina would decide the outcome. Several factors operated to give the state to Jefferson and Burr. First, although the Adams-Hamilton split had not affected Southern politics during most of the canvass, it became a serious issue in the late fall in South Carolina. The Washington *National Intelligencer* addressed an editorial "To the Legislature, and Electors of President, for South Carolina." The article reviewed Hamilton's pamphlet and stressed that the pamphlet would cause Adams-Federalists to abandon South Carolina's favorite son, Charles Cotesworth Pinckney. The pamphlet was thus used against Adams, rather than in favor of Pinckney, as its author intended. Adams's chances also suffered from the indefatigable machinations of Republican Charles Pinckney. Turning out numerous polemics, Pinckney accused Adams of being a "stock-holder" and the "spokesman of the moneyed group." Pinckney also prevented a Federalist strategy session by getting to the meeting hall prior to the appointed hour and posting a sign "No Meeting here this night."[39]

Despite Pinckney's efforts and the split in their own ranks, Federalists believed they had carried South Carolina and the election. Adams-Federalist newspapers reported that their candidate was successful in South Carolina. The *Middlesex Gazette* denied the *Aurora*'s report that Jefferson had carried the key state. The High-Federalist *Gazette of the United States* wrote of the Jacobins' lament because they had lost the election.[40]

Republican newspapers, more content to wait for official returns, had the last word. The Newark *Centinel of Freedom* used large type to announce "Jefferson elected." In its elation, the *Centinel* printed an attack on Federalism which downplayed Adams: "A complete victory is obtained by virtue over vice, republicanism over aristocracy, and the consequent downfall of the Hamiltonians, Pickeronians, British Agents, and Old Tories."[41]

As the issue was decided, Adams was more or less neglected in the remaining months of his term. Fisher Ames wrote to Christopher Gore in late December to blame Adams for the defeat, but it was more a defense of High-Federalist duplicity: "The truth is we were assaulted, rashly and unaccountably, by the head of the party, and we stood in our own defence with as much temper, forecast, and spirit, as men could." Adams, writing to Gerry in early February, believed that the loss was Hamilton's fault. The same letter exonerated Pinckney from charges of duplicity. Finally, the *Aurora* took a parting shot at Adams in March: "To-morrow will be a very festive day in this place. Mr. Adams will leave the city early in the morning under a discharge of cannon fired for joy at his departure."[42]

Lastly, the idea of a "revolution of 1800" requires attention. The notion that the election of 1800 was a revolution gained credence in early historical reports which tended to overdramatize the events. In that interpretation, an unpopular group of haughty aristocrats had not deigned to trust the populace and the populace turned them out. In terms of congressional voting, there was a revolution in 1800. Federalists held a margin of 20 seats, 63–43, in the Sixth Congress, but lost 22 of its seats in 1800, giving the Jeffersonians a 24 seat margin, 65–41.[43]

The presidential election, however, was less revolutionary. Jefferson and Burr outpolled Adams by eight electoral votes, but the real margin of victory was a slender 214 popular vote difference in New York City which determined the outcome in that state. Although it cannot be denied that there was an ideological chasm between Jefferson and Adams, the differences in thought are mitigated as revolutionary barometers by the lack of significant difference in the administration of government before and after March 1801. Leonard White, who has studied both the Federalist and Jeffersonian administration of government, has found few significant differences. Leonard Levy notes the closing of the ideological chasm by concluding, "Many of the Jeffersonians, most notably Jefferson himself, behaved when in power in ways that belied their fine libertarian sentiments of 1798." In addition, Levy points out that, excepting New York, Adams ran better in the electoral college in 1800 than he did in 1796 and "he was stronger with 'the people' in 1800 than he had been in 1796." Marshall Smelser, in his consideration of the election, sees Adams as "the hero of the piece." Candidates identified with Adams also did fairly well. Republican Elbridge Gerry, running as a friend of Adams, the people, and peace, lost the governorship of Federalist Massachusetts by only 200 votes. Charles Francis Adams and Samuel Eliot Morison have both written that considering the unpopularity and duplicity of Federalism, it is surprising not that Jefferson won, but rather that Adams came so close.[44] Having looked at both sides of the "revolution of 1800" question, it is well to conclude that the revolutionary character of the election of 1800 remains open to several historical interpretations.

Thus we have seen the effects of the relationship between Adams and the press on the events and the outcome of the election of 1800. Adams faced duplicity and a hostile press from the High-Federalists, who preferred

Pinckney to the incumbent. Hamilton's pamphlet symbolized the dotage of old-guard High-Federalism and reinforced the Federalist duplicity that was a cause of Adams's defeat. Republicans concentrated their fire on the issues created by the High-Federalists and had only the Tench Coxe "British influence" letter as an issue against Adams, although a rejuvenated press and methodical organization greatly aided Republican chances for success. Between the High-Federalists and the Jeffersonians stood the Adamsites, who were devoted to the principles of Adams and moderate Federalism and were fearful of the extremes of the two contending parties. This group, with solid newspaper backing, attacked the pretensions of Jefferson and Pinckney and brought their candidate to within 214 popular votes of victory.

Finally, the conclusion to be reached from these last four chapters is that newspapers played a vital role in the politics of John Adams's term as president. Fisher Ames, who blamed Adams for the Federalist defeat in a moment of anger, later reappraised the election. He concluded: "The newspapers are an overmatch for any Government. They will first overawe and then usurp it. This has been done; and the Jacobins owe their triumph to the unceasing use of this engine; not so much to skill in the use of it, as by repetition."[45]

John Adams also believed that the press was the key factor in the election of 1800, but he did not agree with Ames about which press was to blame. A rare outburst by Adams against the press during his presidency forecast the election results and the reasons behind them. Writing to John Trumbull in September 1800, Adams argued:

> Porcupine's Gazette, and Fenno's Gazette, from the moment of the mission to France, aided, countenanced, and encouraged by soi-disant Federalists in Boston, New York, and Philadelphia have done more to shuffle the cards into the hands of the jacobin leaders, than all the acts of administration, and all the policy of opposition from the commencement of the government. . . . If the election of a Federal President is lost by it, those who performed the exploit will be the greatest losers.[46]

This statement, plus Adams's remarks about "Chronicle, Argus and Aurora praise" and a few statements of similar tone, are as far as Adams went in discussing the press while in office. In retirement, he would make good the deficit.

CHAPTER TEN

John Adams:
Afterthoughts on the Press

The causes of my retirement are to be found in the writings of Freneau, Markoe, Ned Church, Andrew Brown, Paine, Callender, Hamilton, Cobbett, and John Ward Fenno.... Without a complete collection of all these libels, no faithful history of the last twenty years can ever be written, nor any adequate account given of the causes of my retirement from public life.
—Adams to Skelton Jones, March 11, 1809

In the early, predawn hours of March 4, 1801, John Adams left the capital for the final trip home. His haste in leaving before Jefferson was inaugurated is unexplained, but there are several possible reasons. The primary reason, I believe, is that Adams had suffered at the hands of the Hamiltonians and did not care to be the embodiment of Federalist defeat on March 4. Second, the recent death of his son Charles no doubt meant that there was much more on his mind that morning than just politics. Finally, there was a lack of precedent for a change of administrations because this was the first popular, nonviolent change of government in history. These are the reasons we could cite in defense of Adams's behavior. On the other hand, Adams's untimely departure from the capital may be further evidence of his more serious character weaknesses.[1]

When Adams left the capital, he took with him the privilege of franking his mail for the rest of his life. He also took a multitude of scars from 12 years of journalistic abuse and a deep, abiding mistrust of politics and politicians. The combination of the franking privilege, the scars, and the mistrust would create a volume of letters in which Adams would articulate his beliefs on the press and public opinion.[2]

Page Smith believed that "John Adams came back to Quincy to die,"

136

a statement indicative of the historical contempt usually accorded Adams's retirement. In fact, Adams went to Quincy (Braintree renamed) to make the most of his remaining days and devoted a great deal of his time in retirement to the reevaluation of his thoughts on American politics. He had ample time for that reevaluation because his 25 years and four months of retirement are second only to the 31 years and seven months of Herbert Hoover's retirement. In his remaining years, Adams established and maintained a lively correspondence with numerous individuals, mostly Republicans. He exchanged ideas regularly with Benjamin Rush, William Cunningham, Benjamin Waterhouse, Thomas Jefferson, John Taylor, and James Lloyd. In those letters, Adams left a legacy of comment which atoned for much of his presidential silence.

George Gibbs is convinced of the motivation behind Adams's post-presidential actions: "He had retired to private life, soured and discontented, to vent his spleen on all men, and principally on the federalists." L.H. Butterfield believes Adams's retirement was a time in which he "relived his public life in long, self-justifying letters and memoirs." Finally, in a review of the Butterfield edition of *The Adams Papers*, John F. Kennedy concludes: "That Adams had considerable self-esteem and a strong propensity to self-justification is unmistakable."[3]

Many of Adams's letters of this period were indeed characterized by harsh rhetoric and self-justification. But both of those traits were present throughout his life, and no understanding of the period is possible without either. As if to balance the rhetoric, Adams occasionally wrote in quiescent prose, even in the third person. By contrasting Adams's extreme rhetoric with his more philosophical outpourings, a clear picture emerges.

Several things become evident from the study of Adams's post–1801 writing. First and foremost, it is clear that Adams believed that he had been ousted from the presidency by the press. Adams blamed both High-Federalist and Republican sheets and never hesitated to pinpoint individuals. He wrote at length of cabinet duplicity, but Hamilton was usually singled out for extensive posthumous rhetorical attack. Finally, Adams's writings in retirement gave additional substance to what friends and enemies had said about him since 1776, in terms of character weaknesses. When Adams himself, after 1801, occasionally alluded to these weaknesses, that made them more believable.

Finally, Adams's post–1801 penchant for nostalgia and rehashing will give us another opportunity to examine the major themes of this work and will demonstrate that the Adams-press relationship was a function of many factors: the passions of the age, the nature of the press, the precedent of abuse set under Washington, Adams's character, and the various phases of his presidency.

Newspapers reacted in different ways to Adams's final act as president, his early morning escape from Washington. Federalist newspapers lamented either the passing of Federalism or Adams's hasty departure. Republican sheets were generally glad to be rid of Adams and any additional departing governmental machinery that smacked of Federalism. The *Constitutional Telegraph* used medical metaphors to note the passing of Federalism from "a lingering consumption ... after he voided some very nauseous Pickeronian worms." The paper later added that Adams's term and Callender's jail sentence expired together. The Republican *American Citizen* of New York lamented that "Citizen Adams" was barely noticed as he passed through New York City, at a time when "Oliver Wolcott, the Secretary, is toasted and idolized."[4] Finally, moderate Federalist sheets were willing to give Jefferson a journalistic honeymoon. They generally repeated the kind of rhetoric used by Bache to welcome Adams in 1797. Federalists regretted, however, the appointment of Gallatin as secretary of the treasury: "That any *foreigner* should be placed in office is as *dangerous* as it is *degrading*."[5] This may well have been an indirect Federalist slap at Hamilton for his published treachery.

As early as September 1800, Adams believed that High-Federalist newspapers were to blame for the renewed vigor and strength of Republicanism. His retirement confirmed that this was his conviction. Before beginning his correspondence, he spent a great deal of time with his books. Commenting on Viscount Bolingbroke, Adams asked whether "the war of gazettes," as conducted by Cobbett and Fenno as well as Republicans, was in the spirit of liberty or of faction. In 1807, Adams wrote to defend himself from Mercy Warren and included her with his other libelers: Porcupine, Fenno, and Hamilton. In replying to William Cunningham about the removal of Pickering, Adams hinted that a volume would be necessary. He added that other persons, including Hamilton, numerous High-Federalists, plus John Ward Fenno "and a Porcupine Cobbett," were guilty of equal sins. In 1809, Adams wrote to Joseph Lyman concerning the 1799 peace mission to France: "If for this service I had no thanks from the republicans, I had nothing but insolence and scurrility from the federalists. Look back and read the federal newspapers in Boston, New York, and Philadelphia of that period, you will then see how I was treated." Adams later commented that the mission brought on the abuse of "Cobbett ... and every Briton in Europe and America, who wished us at war with France and in alliance with England."[6]

In 1811, Adams hinted to Benjamin Waterhouse that he was rather enjoying the current abuse of Federalists who were displeased with the defection of the Adamses to Republicanism. A year later Adams mentioned Cobbett and Hamilton in a letter to Jefferson. In 1815, writing to James Lloyd, Adams gave his version of the election of 1800: "The party committed suicide; they killed themselves and the national President (not their President) at one shot, and then, as foolishly as maliciously, indicted me for the murder." Years later, Rufus King, lacking his earlier High-Federalist zeal, wrote to President-elect John Quincy Adams: I consider your election as the best amends for the injustice of which he [Adams Sr.] was made the victim."[7]

Adams made fewer remarks about the cabinet, but his tone was the same. Historians have accepted Adams's statements, and the cabinet as a whole has received poor marks. Manning Dauer has praised Adams's moderate stand in opposition to the extremists in his own party, but has added that Adams lacked the ability to make them follow his program. Irving Brant has inferred that Adams's political fate was sealed before his term began, citing Adams's refusal to accept cabinet resignations over the issue of sending Madison to France. Lisle Rose believes the Federalist collapse was due to "the overwhelming of the party's many progressive impulses by a reactionary national leadership." Charles Francis Adams states that Federalism could have survived the contemporary issues, "But it could not be expected to endure the cross of *bad faith*." Stephen Kurtz believes that if Washington's general approval of the 1799 peace mission had been known, Adams would have been spared much of the subsequent ordeal. George Gibbs disagrees with this view and answers Adams's post–1801 justification with two volumes of High-Federalist justification. Gibbs concludes that "the conduct of Mr. Adams" was responsible for the Federalist defeat in 1800.[8]

Adams wrote a lengthy letter to William Cunningham in reply to questions about Pickering. Adams's answer included charges that Pickering obstructed nominations and negotiations and was adroitly two-faced. Adams added: "I could get nothing done as I would have it. My new minister, Marshall, did all to my entire satisfaction." A later letter to Cunningham included Pickering with other "Anglomaniac Federalists."[9]

In 1809, Adams wrote in the *Boston Patriot* that Washington had been vexed by the cabinet "and resigned his office to get rid of them." On the day of Madison's inauguration, Adams compared his own presidential beginnings to Madison's: "Mine was the worst, however, because he has a great majority of the officers and men attached to him, and I had all the officers and half the crew always ready to throw me overboard." Adams later wrote of a British faction which was bent on making Hamilton head of the army and the president: "Peace with France was therefore treason against their fundamental maxims and reasons of state." In 1812, Adams reflected that while he was working for peace in 1799, "the arm of the nation was palsied by one party." A year later Adams described the High-Federalists to Jefferson as "puppets upon the Wires of two Jugglers behind the Scene: and these Jugglers were Hamilton and Washington."[10]

Wolcott expected Adams to attack the conduct of the cabinet, so he obtained copies of Pickering's correspondence from John Marshall.[11] The securing of a defense before charges were brought suggests some erratic behavior in the cabinet. The cabinet's collective answer, however, did not come until 1823. In that year, William Cunningham died. His son gave his father's and Adams's letters to Timothy Pickering. The former secretary of state scrutinized the correspondence in detail and found fault in many places. Pickering published a *Review* of the correspondence, but warned his readers "every page is characterized by [Adams's] vanity and self-love." Adams's vanity and disappointed ambition were Pickering's repeated themes. As to the renewed correspondence between Adams and Jefferson, Pickering believed it to be an attempt to improve the political fortunes of John Quincy Adams. Pickering also harped on the theme of Adams's absences, believing that Adams treated his office "nearly as a sinecure." Pickering also asked why it took a man of Adams's self-admitted talents over three years to recognize the want of talent in a secretary. Finally, Pickering concluded that the peace mission, the cabinet shake-up, and Fries's pardon were all part of an agreement between Adams and the Republicans.[12]

Pickering published his attack in 1823. Adams, then in his eighty-eighth year, was too old and too apathetic to lower himself to reply. Another reason for Adams's silence was that Adams had earlier singled out Alexander Hamilton for attack. Having denounced the Federalist chieftain, Adams saw no reason in 1823 to answer Pickering, a mere warrior.

Bernard Fay believes that Federalism "died of the yellow fever, and of Hamilton's hatred of Adams, and of its contempt for the immigrants." Page Smith believes that "behind all the Federalists' missteps stood the sinister figure of Alexander Hamilton." Stewart Mitchell states that three men deprived Adams of a second term: Jefferson, Burr, and "Alexander the great Hamilton, ... 'the brain' of their party." Joseph Charles uncharacteristically gives Adams good marks for not using the war fever to entrench himself politically and for thwarting Hamilton's schemes in 1799.[13]

Adams planned to reply to Hamilton's pamphlet in 1801, but for some reason did not. By the time he did, the ex-secretary had already been felled in Weehawken, New Jersey, by a bullet fired by the current vice president. Adams nevertheless often included Hamilton in the list of Federalist writers who contributed to the Federalist loss in 1800. In addition, Adams never hesitated to single Hamilton out for criticism. To William Cunningham, Adams wrote: "Hamilton's ambition, intrigues, and caucuses have ruined the cause of federalism, by encumbering and entangling it with men and measures that ought never to have been brought forward." A later letter to Cunninham linked Pickering to Hamilton: "He was so devoted an Idolater of Hamilton, that he could not judge impartially of the sentiments and opinions of the President of the U. States. Look into Hamilton's pamphlet."[14] Writing to the *Boston Patriot* of the British faction, Adams commented: "They all panted for a war between the United States and France as sincerely, though not so ardently, as Alexander Hamilton." Adams considered Hamilton the "recording secretary" of the pre–1800 cabinet and viewed Hamilton's pamphlet as a folly presented to the opposition press for the most serious exploitation. One letter to the *Boston Patriot* showed that Adams was glad that he was retired by his party because he believed that he could not long have withstood the repeated character attacks. Adams added that his retirement was due largely to "Alexander Hamilton and his satellites." A later letter discussed Hamilton's proposals at the outset of Adams's presidency. Adams stated that he read the proposals, but "thought the man was in a delerium. . . . Mr. Hamilton's imagination was always haunted by that hideous monster or phantom, so often called a *crisis*, and which so often produces imprudent measures." Adams concluded: "They passed a bill to raise an army, not a large one, but enough to overturn the then Federal government."[15]

Adams also believed that Hamilton had excited the "party violence" which prevented Adams from naming a Republican to the first three-man mission, although Adams later sent Elbridge Gerry as a replacement over cabinet objections. Writing to James Lloyd in 1815, Adams confessed: "My hobby-horse was a navy; Alexander Hamilton's an army." Adams further believed that Hamilton was aiming for the presidency. Finally, in 1824, John Taylor wrote to Adams about Hamilton's pamphlet. Believing that the pamphlet prevented Adams's reelection, Taylor considered the work "the most malicious, foolish, and inexcusable composition, which was ever produced by a tolerable mind."[16]

Having thoroughly denounced his pretended friends, Adams did not hesitate to castigate his open enemies. Yet Adams's thoughts on Republican editors were far less personal than his feelings about unfaithful Federalists. They reflected philosophical detachment rather than petty vindictiveness.

John Bach McMaster and Margaret Woodbury have both written that William Duane did more to make Jefferson president than any other person. This is an overstatement based on a misreading of a letter Jefferson wrote to President Monroe in 1823.[17] Members of the opposition press did greatly affect the outcome of the election of 1800, but they could not have done it without Federalist aid.

Almost as soon as he arrived back in Quincy, Adams wrote to Benjamin Stoddert of the overthrow of Federalism by "Freneau, Duane, Callender, Cooper, and Lyon, [and] their great patron and protector." Adams added: "A group of foreign liars, encouraged by a few ambitious native gentlemen have discomfited the education, the talents, the virtues, and the property of the country." A month later Adams asked Christopher Gadsden: "Is there no pride in American bosoms? Can their hearts endure that Callender, Duane, Cooper, and Lyon should be the most influential men in the country, all foreigners and degraded characters?" In a letter to Cunningham, Adams linked his enemies to Jefferson: "He always professed great friendship for me, even when, as it now appears, he was countenancing Freneau, Bache, Duane, and Callender." Abigail Adams wrote to Jefferson to lament "the blackest calumny, and foulest falsehoods," which aided Jefferson's election. In his *Autobiography*, Adams mentioned the smallpox inoculation which caused serious damage to his teeth: "I should not have mentioned this, if I had not been reproached with this personal Defect, with so much politeness in the *Aurora*."[18]

Subsequent letters to Rush and Cunningham listed the leaders of the opposition and attacked the editors with appropriate innuendo. Adams later linked the *Aurora*'s scurrility to his quarrels with Franklin in the 1780s. Rush sent Adams an *Aurora*, to which Adams replied: "Thanks for 'the light and truth' as I used to call the *Aurora*, which you send me." In a letter to Jefferson, Adams strongly doubted that the writings of Callender and others were "Public Discussions," and he asserted, "The Ravings and Rantings of Bedlam, merit the Character as well." Additional letters to John Taylor and James Lloyd repeated much of this rhetoric. Strangely enough, Adams received a letter from Charles Holt, convicted under the Sedition Act, which apologized for earlier misbehavior. Adams replied that others had changed their opinion and recognized the personal sacrifice made by the president in 1799. Holt responded on March 4, 1825, when John Quincy Adams was sworn in as president: "The long wished time has at length arrived, when good sense has triumphed over political hostility."[19] At a time when Adams was being attacked in print by his former secretary of state, he was receiving cordial greetings from a convicted sedition peddler.

Having vented his anger against individuals, Adams tried to justify his role in the Sedition Act. Much of this procedure involved Jefferson. The Sedition Act expired on March 3, 1801, as Adams was preparing to leave office. A few months later Jefferson boasted to Philip Mazzei, "We have found a way of carrying on affairs without any need for an Act of Sedition." Yet Jefferson did suggest state sedition codes be used against editors who let their rhetoric outrun their judgment.[20] In a letter to Abigail Adams, Jefferson spoke of the attacks of Porcupine, Fenno, and Russell. Believing that Adams was not involved in those attacks, Jefferson noted that he was equally blameless for the attacks of Duane, Callender, or Freneau. Abigail replied with a defense of the Sedition Act. Adams himself denied authorship of the laws, but "knew there was enough for both [Alien and Sedition

Acts], and therefore I consented to them." Writing to Rush, Adams noted that Jefferson did not approve the laws, "which I believe to have been constitutional and salutary, if not necessary." Adams later hedged on that stand, however, when he wrote to Jefferson to remind him that they both signed the law. Adams concluded: "I know not why you are not as responsible for it as I am. Neither of us were concerned in the formation of it." In 1823, Pickering claimed the law had been enacted, among other reasons, to protect Adams "from the torrents of calumny pouring upon him from all the streams of democracy." In sum, the post–1801 justifications of the Sedition Act amounted to the pot and the kettle calling each other white. Eventually, in 1832, after the disputants had largely left the arena, the House Judiciary Committee denounced the Sedition Act. This action made it possible to have the fines repaid.[21]

What were Adams's afterthoughts on his own character, the presidency, and the press? Hints of what was to come have already appeared above. A much younger Adams wrote in his *Novanglus Essays* that "License of the press is no proof of liberty. When a people are corrupted, the press may be made an engine to complete their ruin." It has also been noted that parts of Adams's 1797 inaugural address were directed to posterity.[22] Adams's retirement would provide posterity further food for thought.

Adams began his *Autobiography* on October 5, 1802. As early as the third sentence he noted:

> My Excuse is, that having been the Object of much Misrepresentation, some of my Posterity may probably wish to see in my own hand Writing a proof of the falsehood of that Mass of odious Abuse of My Character, with which News Papers, private letters and public Pamphlets and Histories have been disgraced for thirty Years.[23]

From his *Autobiography*, Adams turned to the books in his library. Reading the Abbé de Mably's comments on the Roman office of censor, Adams asked, "What would our newspapers make of such an officer?" On Mary Wollstonecraft's discussions of libels, Adams commented: "Is there any nation that will distinguish between the license and the freedom of the press? Not the English. Nor the Americans most certainly." Condorcet claimed that the press freed the education of the populace from all political and religious fetters. "Oh! That it had!" Adams wished.[24]

The correspondence which was to broadcast Adams's regrets and justifications began in 1803. Writing to Mercy Warren, Adams concluded: "It can not be long before We must exchange this Theatre for some other. I hope it will be one, in which there are no Politicks." Three years later Rush triggered rhetoric from Adams by writing: "A newspaper, once the vehicle of pleasing and useful intelligence is now the sad record only of misery and crimes." In letters to Rush, Adams admitted his lack of reserve, but balanced that negative assertion with the positive claim that he had never been a politician. Regarding Jefferson, Adams wrote: "I have no resentment against him, though he has honored and salaried every villain he could find that had been an enemy to me." In 1809, Adams wrote Rush of his weariness of newspaper abuse and also accurately reflected a conclusion presented in Chapter 5 of this book: "Mausoleums, statues, monuments will never be erected to me. I wish them not." Rush also received a sample of Adams's anxiety: "If a button maker becomes a button at last, the Lord knows what I am to be: a newspaper, I fear. I had rather be anything else." Finally, after Madison's inauguration, Adams gave himself the credit for Jefferson's reputation: "I am bold enough to say I was his preceptor in politics and taught him everything that has been good and solid in his whole political conduct."[25]

Adams maintained a similar tone in his correspondence with William Cunningham. Regarding the press, Adams wrote: "Regret nothing that you see in the papers concerning me. It is impossible that newspapers can say the truth. They would be out of their element." Adams also believed both parties had concealed his worthy services between 1789 and 1809, and he was writing to the *Boston Patriot* to rectify the omissions. He advised Cunningham that he expected heaps of abuse: "Let them come. They cannot sink me lower than the bottom, and I have been safely landed there these eight years." Adams's suspicious nature convinced him that he had been the object of "secret hatred for ten years, for twenty years, for all my life indeed."[26]

Writing to his son Thomas of his agricultural pursuits, Adams predicted a host of names that a hostile press would invent for him: "Monarch of Stony Field, Count of Gull Island, Earl of Mount Arrarat [sic], Marquis of Candlewood Hill, Baron of Rocky Run." Later, Adams wrote to Benjamin Waterhouse to warn that "Republicans would be as much offended as the Federalists by my History" if he attempted such a project. In a more generous mood, Adams wrote Josiah Quincy in 1811: "However lightly we may think of the voice of the people sometimes, they not unfrequently see farther than you and I, in many fundamental questions." When Rush proposed that Adams write an address to Americans, Adams answered with 15 reasons why he would not. The second reason was: "If I am to judge by the newspapers and pamphlets that have been printed in America for twenty years past, I should think that both parties believed me the meanest villain in the world."[27]

As Adams warmed to his subject, he alternated between pessimism and optimism, politics and philosophy, concern and apathy. In March 1812, he was specific about the shortcomings of the administrations of Washington and Jefferson, as well as his own. A second letter to Waterhouse was more philosophical: "All Parties have been violent Friends of Order, Law, Government, and Religion, when in Power; and all Parties libellous, Seditious, and Rebellious, when out of power. Such is our destiny." He reminisced in the third person to Rush: "Then he was 8 years Vice-President, ... a constant object of the billingsgate, scurrility, misapprehensions, misconstructions, misrepresentations, lies and libels of all parties.... He was then President for 4 years. A tale told by an idiot, full of sound and fury, signifying nothing."[28]

Adams told Jefferson that he cared "not a farthing" about his own reputation. Yet three letters to Jefferson in the next 18 days proved that Adams did indeed care about his reputation.[29] Adams was more philosophical to John Taylor. He wrote Taylor that "Mankind do not love to read any thing upon any theory of government. Very few read any thing but libels." Adams also admitted his weakness and vanity to Taylor. Subsequent letters to Taylor repeated the idea that the press misinformed public opinion.[30]

To James Lloyd, Adams wrote that the Federalists would have been trounced in 1800 without his peace move. He added, "I desired no other inscription over my gravestone than: 'Here lies John Adams, who took upon himself the responsibility of peace with France in the year 1800.'" Adams also catalogued the achievements of his term and indicated that they were all done with less support and more opposition "than has ever fallen to the lot of any administration before or since."[31]

Adams confided in Jedediah Morse that "I have little faith in history" and wrote in a male-chauvinist vein to Elbridge Gerry that "History is not the Province of the Ladies."[32] Yet the volume of rhetoric cited above proves that Adams was concerned with posterity. In 1820, John Adams cast a ballot for James Monroe in the electoral college that indicated his total apostasy from a now moribund, irrelevant Federalism. In 1823, Adams learned that Jefferson had made a collection of the slanders against himself, and Adams wished he had made a similar collection: "If we had I am confident I could have produced a more splendid Mass than yours." Adams also wrote to Jefferson and to Charles Francis Adams to express parental joy concerning the accomplishments of John Quincy Adams, but noted that scurrility was still present in politics. On April 17, 1826, in the last letter between Adams and Jefferson, Adams concluded a 50-year friendship with Jefferson with a final comment on the state of public opinion: "Public affairs go on pretty much as usual: perpetual chicanery and rather more personal abuse than there used to be."[33]

On July 4, 1826, the fiftieth anniversary of the event which both men had worked so hard to create and maintain, Thomas Jefferson and John Adams died. Marcus Cunliffe noted the event, "a symbolic symmetry rare in history and not lost upon their contemporaries."[34]

The passing of Jefferson and Adams on America's birthday was far more than historical and actuarial coincidence, however; it ended the age of justification that followed the era of rhetoric. It also meant that the two primary targets of journalistic scurrility in the years 1789–1809 would no longer be available for abuse. Jefferson had fared better than Adams in retirement, although irate northern Federalists never forgave Jefferson for the embargo. Adams had been attacked in print as late as 1823. After July 4, 1826, the people mourned the loss of two Founding Fathers. Editors, however, had already transferred their abuse to a former Jeffersonian from Tennessee and to an offspring of John Adams's. The new generation was treated to abuse reminiscent of the scurrility accorded to the Founding Fathers.

This conclusory chapter has tried to demonstrate that Adams held strong convictions about the low state of the American press. It has also shown that Adams's tacit acceptance of newspaper abuse during his presidency was an uncharacteristic display of decorum on the part of the president. Once his obligations to the electorate were completed, Adams answered past newspaper vilification with harsh rhetoric and self-justification, and the vain, ill-tempered patriot of Quincy certainly gave as good as he got. We have also seen that Adams was capable of matching Washington's outbursts against the press, although Adams made his comments primarily as a private citizen.

Finally, this chapter reinforces the theory posited in the previous chapter that Adams's reelection was prevented by the press. There, the press and historians provided the evidence. Here, Adams and his largely sympathetic correspondents provide the evidence. Despite his penchants for hyperbole and justification, Adams's role as the defeated candidate in 1800 gives his beliefs concerning the reasons for his defeat a credibility which continues to have a fundamental validity.

In this book, I have probed the interplay between John Adams and the press, with the critical stress on the years 1797 to 1801. I agree with Donald Stewart's conclusion that newspapers were the primary reason for the defeat of John Adams in 1800. But while Stewart emphasizes that it was Republican newspapers which toppled Adams, that was only half the story.[35] A few Federalist editors and pamphleteers also worked unceasingly to defeat Adams, and considering Jefferson's slender margin of victory, the work of the Federalists cannot be overlooked. In essence, Adams lost New York City, New York State, and the presidency by 214 popular votes.[36] If Adams had received 108 of those votes, he would have been reelected, to the disgust of High-Federalists and Republicans alike.

The Federalist period was a passionate age in which the survival of the republic was tied to every important issue and some trivial incidents as well. The American press grew towards maturity in the years 1789–1801, although scurrility, lack of objectivity, and a preference for partisanship at the expense of truth hindered the emergence of the newspaper as we know it. The press slowly began to question presidential policies during Washington's final term and by the end of that term was abusing the president in the most coarse vernacular. With this precedent established, John Adams's presidency was the first full-scale confrontation between the chief executive and the press.

In its first phase, the relationship between Adams and the press was a wait-and-see period in which Republicans hoped by the tone and volume of their praise to lure Adams away from suspicious Federalist extremists. When Adams announced a Federalist program, he was execrated by his former Republican admirers, but was well treated by earlier silent Federalists. When the results of the XYZ affair became known, Adams and Federalism reached heights of popularity hitherto unknown. Federalism, however, was not able to gauge public sentiment as well as Adams was; Federalists rashly flew in the face of public opinion while Adams acted with respect for it. As Federalists pushed internal security and looked for war, Adams divorced himself from the extremists in his party. On February 18, 1799, the president made a move for peace which sealed his political fate. For the next two years, Adams was popular with a moderate element of Federalism which carried him to within 214 votes of victory. At the same time, Republicans found satisfaction in many of Adams's policies, but they continued to work for their own candidate. Having been denied a war, High-Federalists also had a candidate to oppose Adams.

The election of 1800 presented the electorate with essentially three parties from which to choose. The campaign involved several critical issues: the army, taxation, the Alien and Sedition Acts, and the contrasting philosophies of government centralization and states' rights. Strong-willed personalities and catalytic issues both found their definitive focus in the newspapers of the three contending factions. It was ultimately the presses, grown strong by ten years of strenuous effort, abusive rhetoric, and political polarization that decided the outcome of the election of 1800. The issues were given a vehicle to reach Americans by the press of the Federalist period. Adams realized the impact of the press on his presidency because he took note of it in his "Jacobin papers damn with faint praise" letter to Abigail and in his "crime of *Chronicle, Argus* and *Aurora* praise" letter, also to Abigail. He noted press scurrility in his private correspondence and in harsh answers to petitions, and by September 10, 1800, while still president, Adams included leading Federalist newspaper editors among his traducers. These outbursts, coupled with the volume of his postpresidential writings, articulated his conviction that High-Federalist and Republican editors had been his undoing and that the press was a poor vehicle with

148   CHAPTER TEN

which to inform the public. These actions also demonstrate the breadth of the confrontation between Adams and the press.

The election of 1800 was the beginning of the end for old-guard High-Federalists. Although Federalism retained some of its regional strength and garnered a handful of electoral votes in the next few presidential elections, its contempt for the people became too conspicuous and its ideology became too irrelevant to make it a nationally viable political force. Historians have several possible epitaphs for Federalism, but Fisher Ames prophetically wrote a letter to Wolcott containing an epitaph with which Federalists could have identified: "Among our wants is that of a good newspaper." Ames later wrote a sentence that would suffice as an epitaph for any president of a party that had suffered at the hands of editors: "The newspapers are an overmatch for any government."[37]

The passing of Federalism in the years between 1801 and the deaths of Jefferson and Adams in 1826 by no means marked the end of acrimonious presidential-press relations. In the years since the final decade of the eighteenth century, presidents as well as the press have rethought and refined their treatment of each other. Some presidents after Adams have been at least as ill-treated, although they have usually reacted more strongly than Adams did. Editors, for their part, have become more articulate and more objective, although in crisis times they have seemingly had a touch of Benjamin Franklin Bache. The executive-press confrontation is an ongoing process, but its beginnings can be traced to the four stormy years which concluded the eighteenth century. In those crisis-filled years, both the press and the president discovered their respective strengths. The resulting clash willed posterity a legacy of interaction between president and press that still exists today.

Abbreviations List

JA	John Adams, vice president under George Washington; second president of the United States.
AA	Abigail Adams, wife of John Adams.
JQA	John Quincy Adams, son of John and Abigail Adams; sixth president of the United States.
GW	George Washington, first president of the United States.
TJ	Thomas Jefferson, secretary of state under Washington, vice president under Adams, and third president of the United States.
AH	Alexander Hamilton, first secretary of the treasury.
OW	Oliver Wolcott, secretary of the treasury under Washington and Adams; references to OW Sr. are to his father, a Federalist patriarch.
AQ	*American Quarterly*
RP	*Review of Politics*
AHR	*American Historical Review*
WMQ	*The William and Mary Quarterly*
MHS	*Massachusetts Historical Society*
VaMHB	*Virginia Magazine of History and Biography*
PaMHB	*Pennsylvania Magazine of History and Biography*
NEQ	*New England Quarterly*

References

Chapter One

1. GW to John Trumbull, July 25, 1798, in John C. Fitzpatrick, ed., *The Writings of George Washington* (Washington, D.C.: U.S. Government Printing Office, 1939), 36:367; JA to Benjamin Waterhouse, October 29, 1805, in Worthington Chauncey Ford, ed., *Statesman and Friend* (Boston: Little, Brown, 1927), p. 31.

2. Marshall Smelser, "The Federalist Period as an Age of Passion," *American Quarterly* 10 (1958), *passim*; Frank Luther Mott, *Jefferson and the Press* (Baton Rouge: Louisiana State University Press, 1943), p. 38; Marshall Smelser, *Congress Founds the Navy, 1787–1798* (Notre Dame, Ind.: University of Notre Dame Press, 1959), p. 156.

3. Doris A. Graber, *Public Opinion, the President, and Foreign Policy: Four Case Studies from the Formative Years* (New York: Holt, Rinehart, and Winston, 1968), p. 18; Leonard D. White, *The Federalists: A Study in Administrative History, 1789–1801* (New York: Free Press, 1948); Alexander DeConde, *Entangling Alliance: Politics and Diplomacy Under George Washington* (Durham, N.C.: Duke University Press, 1958), p. 505.

4. John C. Miller, *Crisis in Freedom: The Alien and Sedition Acts* (Boston: Little, Brown, 1951), p. 210.

5. Gaillard Hunt, "Office Seeking During the Administration of John Adams," *AHR* 2 (1896–1897): 242; Richard Hofstadter, *The American Political Tradition and the Men Who Made It* (New York: Vintage Books, 1948), p. 18.

6. Thomas Cooper, *Political Essays*, 2d ed. (Philadelphia: Robert Campbell, 1800), p. 17.

7. Page Smith, *John Adams*, 2 vols. (Garden City, N.Y.: Doubleday, 1962), 2:758; Claude G. Bowers, *Jefferson and Hamilton: The Struggle for Democracy in America* (Boston: Houghton Mifflin, 1966), p. 295; Smelser, *Congress*, p. 145.

8. James Thomson Callender, *The Prospect Before Us*, 2 vols. (Richmond: James Thomson Callender, 1800), 1: title sheet; George Clinton, *An Oration, Delivered on the Fourth of July, 1798* (New York: Davis and Davis, 1798), p. 3.

9. *Boston Gazette*, December 26, 1791; Donald H. Stewart, *The Opposition Press of the Federalist Period* (Albany: State University of New York Press, 1969),

151

p. 60; Callender, *Prospect* 1:35; Marcus Cunliffe, *The Nation Takes Shape, 1789–1837*, Chicago History of American Civilization Series (Chicago: University of Chicago Press, 1959), p. 26.

10. Worthington C. Ford, ed., "Letters of William Duane," *MHS Proceedings* 20 (1906–1907):258; John Bach McMaster, *A History of the People of the United States, From the Revolution to the Civil War*, 5 vols. (New York: D. Appleton, 1885), 2:433.

11. John C. Miller, *The Federalist Era, 1789–1801*, New American Nation Series (New York: Harper and Row, 1960), p. 109.

12. Charles Warren, *Jacobin and Junto; or Early American Politics as Viewed in the Diary of Dr. Nathaniel Ames, 1758–1822* (Cambridge: Harvard University Press, 1931), p. 93; Irving Brant, *James Madison, Father of the Constitution*, vol. 3 of *James Madison* (Indianapolis: Bobbs-Merrill, 1950), p. 387.

13. George C. Rogers, Jr., *Evolution of a Federalist: William Loughton Smith of Charleston (1758–1812)* (Columbia: University of South Carolina Press, 1962), p. 302.

14. Miller, *Crisis*, p. 25.

15. *Federal Gazette* (Boston), January 30, 1798; John Ward Fenno, *Desultory Reflections on the New Political Aspects of Public Affairs in the United States of America Since the Commencement of the Year 1799* (New York: John Ward Fenno, 1800), 2:7.

16. Stewart, *Opposition Press*, pp. 540–41; McMaster, *History*, 2:330; *Philadelphia General Advertiser*, July 23, 1793; hereafter cited as *Aurora*.

17. Brant, *Madison*, 3:443; Bowers, *Jefferson and Hamilton*, p. 23.

18. JA to Benjamin Rush, January 25, 1806, and July 7, 1805, in *The Spur of Fame; Dialogues of . . . John Adams and Benjamin Rush, 1805–1813*, ed. John A. Schutz and Douglass Adair (San Marino, Calif.: Huntington Library, 1966), pp. 30–31, 48; JA to B. Waterhouse, May 21, 1821, in Ford, *Statesman*, pp. 157–58.

19. McMaster, *History*, 2:330; Samuel Eliot Morison, *The Life and Letters of Harrison Gray Otis, Federalist, 1765–1848*, 2 vols. (Boston: Houghton Mifflin, 1913), 1:183; Callender, *Prospect*, 1:4; Brant, *Madison*, 3:451; Samuel Bemis nevertheless sees Pickering as a "facile penman." Samuel Flagg Bemis, "Washington's Farewell Address: A Foreign Policy of Independence," *AHR* 39 (1934):265.

20. DeConde, *Entangling Alliance*, p. 316; *Aurora*, June 17, 1797; Morison, *Life-Otis*, 1:56; Stewart Mitchell, ed., *New Letters of Abigail Adams, 1788–1801* (Boston: Houghton Mifflin, 1947), p. xxviii; Dumas Malone, *Jefferson and the Rights of Man*, vol. 2 of *Jefferson and His Time* (Boston: Little, Brown, 1951), p. 263; Harry Ammon, *The Genet Mission* (New York: Norton, 1973), p. 50; *American Citizen* (New York), October 10, 1800.

21. George Gibbs, *Memoirs of the Administration of Washington and John Adams: Edited from the Papers of Oliver Wolcott, Secretary of the Treasury*, 2 vols. (New York: William Van Norden, 1846), 2:157–58; William Loughton Smith, *The Pretensions of Thomas Jefferson to the Presidency Examined: And the Charges Against John Adams Refuted* (Philadelphia, n.p., 1796), pp. 6–7.

22. Gibbs, *Memoirs*, 2:231; *Courier of New Hampshire* (Concord), February 2, 1799; Marshall Smelser, "George Washington and the Alien and Sedition Acts," *AHR* 59 (1953–1954):332; Frederick B. Tolles, "Unofficial Ambassador: George Logan's Mission to France, 1798," *WMQ*, 3d ser., 7 (1950):4.

23. Smith, *JA*, 2:1023; Richard Hildreth, *The History of the United States of America*, 6 vols. (New York: Harper and Brothers, 1880), 5:343; Miller, *Federalist*

Era, p. 77; Beckley's biographers have seen him as better than a scandalmonger, see infra; William Cobbett, *Porcupine's Works*, 12 vols. (London: Cobbett and Morgan, 1801), 10:107. McMaster, *History*, 2:364.

24. Ammon, *Genet*, p. 22; John Lowell, *An Oration, Pronounced July 4, 1799* (Boston: Manning and Loring, 1799), p. 8.

25. DeConde, *Entangling Alliance*, p. 39; Miller, *Federalist Era*, p. ix; Bowers, *Jefferson and Hamilton*, respectively, pp. 35, 69, 25; Samuel F. Bemis, *Jay's Treaty; A Study in Commerce and Diplomacy* (New Haven: Yale University Press, 1923), p. 275; Joseph Charles, *The Origins of the American Party System: Three Essays* (New York: Harper and Row, 1956), p. 37; Manning J. Dauer, *The Adams Federalists* (Baltimore: Johns Hopkins University Press, 1953), p. 6; Henry W. Elson, *History of the United States of America*, 5 vols. (New York: Macmillan, 1905), 2:185.

26. Leland D. Baldwin, *Whiskey Rebels; The Story of a Frontier Uprising* (Pittsburgh: University of Pittsburgh Press, 1939), p. 178.

27. William Nisbet Chambers, "Party Development and Party Action: The American Origins," *History and Theory* 3 (1963):101; DeConde, *Entangling Alliance*, pp. 508–09.

28. William Maclay's journal entry of December 14, 1790, in William Maclay, *The Journal of William Maclay* (New York: Frederick Unger, 1965), p. 341; Maclay's *Journal* provides the best source of Republican opinion during the writer's brief incumbency in the Senate of the United States.

29. James Thomas Flexner, *George Washington: Anguish and Farewell (1793–1799)*, volume 4 of *George Washington* (Boston: Little, Brown, 1972), pp. 4, 194; Charles R. King, *The Life and Correspondence of Rufus King*, 6 vols. (New York: G.P. Putnam's Sons, 1894), 1:518; Bemis, *Jay's Treaty*, p. 269; Miller, *Federalist Era*, p. 153; DeConde, *Entangling Alliance*, p. 102.

30. William Vans Murray to OW, October 2, 1795, in Gibbs, *Memoirs*, 1:249; Miller, *Federalist Era*, p. 168; Bemis, *Jay's Treaty*, p. xii; Dumas Malone, *Jefferson and the Ordeal of Liberty*, vol. 3 of *Jefferson and His Time* (Boston: Little, Brown, 1962), p. 268; Charles Francis Adams, ed., *The Works of John Adams, Second President of the United States*, 10 vols. (Boston: Charles C. Little and James Brown, 1851), 1:477; Callender, *Prospect*, 1:16.

31. B. Rush to TJ, January 4, 1797, in L.H. Butterfield, ed., *Letters of Benjamin Rush*, 2 vols. (Princeton, N.J.: Princeton University Press, 1951), 2:784; *Boston Independent Chronicle*, September 25, 1797; Gibbs, *Memoirs*, 1:487, 2:166; JA to B. Rush, September 30, 1805, in Schutz and Adair, *JA-Rush*, p. 42.

32. Bemis, *Jay's Treaty*, p. 23.

33. AA to Mary Cranch, May 30, 1790, in Mitchell, *Letters-AA*, pp. 48–49.

34. Smelser, "Passion," pp. 392–93; Miller, *Federalist Era*, pp. 47, 152.

35. GW to P. Henry, October 9, 1795, in Fitzpatrick, *GW*, 34:335; *Aurora*, August 17, 1795; OW to AH, April 29, 1796, in Gibbs, *Memoirs*, 1:334.

36. Smith, *Pretensions*, p. 61; OW Jr. to OW Sr., March 29, 1797, in Gibbs, *Memoirs*, 1:482; Smelser, *Congress*, pp. 116–17; *Connecticut Courant* (Hartford), March 19, 1798.

37. *Aurora*, March 21, 1798; AA to Mary Cranch, May 10, 1798, in Mitchell, *Letters-AA*, pp. 171–72; Clinton, *Oration*, p. 10.

38. *Green Mt. Patriot* (Peacham, Vermont), February 28, 1799; *Porcupine's Gazette* (Philadelphia), March 12, 1799.

39. Edward Channing, "Washington and Parties, 1789–1797," *MHS Proceedings* 47 (1913–1914):36; Charles A. Beard, *Economic Origins of Jeffersonian Democracy* (New York: Free Press, 1965), p. 99.

40. Channing, "Washington," pp. 35, 43.

41. For nicknames, see above; for doggerel, see *Massachusetts Centinel* (Boston), August 22, 1789; Malone, *TJ*, 2:261.

42. *Journal* (New York), July 6, 1790; Noble E. Cunningham, Jr., *The Jeffersonian Republicans; The Formation of Party Organization, 1789–1801* (Chapel Hill: University of North Carolina Press, 1957), p. 5; Miller, *Federalist Era*, p. 56.

43. *National Gazette* (Philadelphia), April 2 and May 3, 1792.

44. TJ to the president of the United States, May 23, 1792, in Paul Leicester Ford, ed., *The Writings of Thomas Jefferson* (New York: G.P. Putnam and Sons, 1894), 6:5.

45. James Truslow Adams, *The Adams Family* (Boston: Little, Brown, 1930), p. 96; *Gazette of the United States* (Philadelphia), October 24, 1792; Flexner, *GW*, 4:76, sees TJ's resignation as press-induced; *Columbian Centinel* (Boston), July 18, 1792.

46. *National Gazette*, May 7, 1792; Gibbs, *Memoirs*, 1:172; Beard, *Economic Origins*, p. 113; *National Gazette*, June 11, 1792; TJ to the president of the United States, September 7, 1792, in Andrew A. Lipscomb and Albert Ellery Bergh, eds., *The Writings of Thomas Jefferson*, 10 vols. (Washington: Thomas Jefferson Memorial Association, 1905), 8:406.

47. James Thomas Flexner, *George Washington and the New Nation (1783–1793)*, vol. 3 of *George Washington* (Boston: Little, Brown, 1969), p. 381; Gibbs, *Memoirs*, 1:78; Adams, *Works of JA*, 1:456; Miller, *Federalist Era*, p. 89.

48. GW to John Francis Mercer, September 26, 1792, in Fitzpatrick, *GW*, 32:165; JA to AA, January 2, 1794, in Adams, *Works of JA*, 1:461.

49. *Carlisle Gazette and the Western Repository of Knowledge*, December 19, 1792.

50. Stewart, *Opposition Press*, p. 118; Ammon, *Genet*, p. 114.

51. Samuel Eliot Morison, *Harrison Gray Otis; 1765–1848; The Urbane Federalist* (Boston: Houghton Mifflin, 1969), p. 91; Smith, *JA*, 2:831; Miller, *Federalist Era*, pp. 126–27; Flexner, *GW*, 4:5; Gibbs, *Memoirs*, 1:103.

52. *National Gazette*, April 20, 1793; Charles D. Hazen, *Contemporary American Opinion of the French Revolution* (Baltimore: Johns Hopkins University Press, 1897), p. 258; Bowers, *Jefferson and Hamilton*, p. 211.

53. Ammon, *Genet*, p. vii; Flexner, *GW*, 4:41; Gardiner W. Allen, *Our Naval War with France* (Boston: Houghton Mifflin, 1909), p. 4; Eugene Perry Link, *Democratic-Republican Societies, 1790–1800* (New York: Columbia University Press, 1942), p. 46; Edwin Emery, *The Press and America; An Interpretive History of Journalism*, 2d ed. (Englewood Cliffs, N.J.: Prentice-Hall, 1962), p. 153; Ammon, *Genet*, p. 55; Lewis Leary, *That Rascal Freneau; A Study in Literary Failure* (New Brunswick, N.J.: Rutgers University Press, 1941), pp. 232ff; Malone, *TJ*, 3:94.

54. Smelser, "GW and Sedition," p. 323ff; Gibbs, *Memoirs*, 1:97; Hazen, *Opinion*, p. 294; Thomas Woodrow Wilson, *A History of the American People*, 5 vols. (New York: William H. Wise, 1931), 3:123.

55. DeConde, *Entangling Alliance*, p. 270; Ammon, *Genet*, p. 112; Hazen, *Opinion*, p. 169; McMaster, *History*, 2:104.

56. JA to TJ, June 30, 1813, in Lester J. Cappon, ed., *The Adams-Jefferson Letters; The Complete Correspondence Between Thomas Jefferson and Abigail and John Adams* (Chapel Hill: University of North Carolina Press, 1959), 2:347; JA to William Cunningham, October 15, 1808, in *Correspondence Between the Hon. John Adams, Late President of the United States, and the Late William Cunningham, Esq., Beginning in 1803 and Ending in 1812* (Boston: E.M. Cunningham, 1823), p. 36.

57. Bemis, *Jay's Treaty*, p. 253; Brant, *Madison*, 3:377, 384; Bowers, *Jefferson and Hamilton*, p. 228; Miller, *Federalist Era*, pp. 132, 137; Link, *Societies*, pp. 126ff, 191–92.

58. Malone, *TJ*, 3:140; Brant, *Madison*, 3:405–06; Bowers, *Jefferson and Hamilton*, pp. 234ff; McMaster, *History*, 2:129–30.

59. McMaster, *History*, 2:121; *Mirrour* (Concord), December 16, 1793; JA to AA, April 1, 1794, in Adams, *Works of JA*, 1:470; Smelser, *Congress*, pp. 74–75; Stewart, *Opposition Press*, p. 502.

60. Brant, *Madison*, 3:391–93; Bemis, *Jay's Treaty*, p. 261; Smith, *JA*, 2:858.

61. Edward Channing, *A History of the United States*, 6 vols. (New York: Macmillan, 1917), 4:16; McMaster, *History*, 2:29 and 190ff; Flexner, *GW*, 4:163, 168; Baldwin, *Whiskey*, pp. 23, 81; Gibbs, *Memoirs*, 1:157.

62. Baldwin, *Whiskey*, pp. 232–33, 248–49; Brant, *Madison*, 3:415–16.

63. GW to Henry Lee, August 26, 1794, in Fitzpatrick, *GW*, 33:475; see also GW to Burges Ball, September 25, 1794, 33:506.

64. Link, *Societies*, pp. 6, 13ff, 57; Flexner, *GW*, 4:162; Brant, *Madison*, 3:417; Link, *Societies*, pp. 186ff; Marshall Smelser, "The Jacobin Phrenzy: Federalism and the Menace of Liberty, Equality, and Fraternity," *Review of Politics* 13 (1951): 470.

65. OW to OW Sr., April 14, 1794, in Gibbs, *Memoirs*, 1:134; GW to Maj. Gen. Daniel Morgan, October 8, 1794, and GW to Charles Mynn Thruston, August 10, 1794, in Fitzpatrick, *GW*, respectively 33:524, 464–65.

66. Link, *Societies*, respectively, pp. 86–87, 66ff; Bemis, *Jay's Treaty*, p. 147; Miller, *Federalist Era*, p. 146; Link, *Societies*, pp. 19, 200ff; Margaret Woodbury, "Public Opinion in Philadelphia, 1789–1801," *Smith College Studies in History* 5 (1919–1920):113.

67. Stewart, *Opposition Press*, p. 177.

68. Stewart, *Opposition Press*, p. 190; JA to AA, April 19, 1794, in Charles Francis Adams, ed., *Letters of John Adams, Addressed to His Wife*, 2 vols. (Boston: Charles C. Little and James Brown, 1841), 2:156.

69. Bowers, *Jefferson and Hamilton*, p. 269; TJ to E. Rutledge, November 30, 1795, in Ford, *TJ Writings*, 7:40; Bemis, *Jay's Treaty*, p. 373; DeConde, *Entangling Alliance*, p. 110; TJ to Mann Page, August 30, 1795, in Lipscomb, Bergh, *Writings of TJ*, 9:307; Bowers, *Jefferson and Hamilton*, p. 271; Bernard Fay, *The Two Franklins: Fathers of American Democracy* (Boston: Little, Brown, 1933), p. 234.

70. JA to AA, June 9, 1795, in Adams, *JA-AA*, 2:180.

71. John Spencer Bassett, *The Federalist System, 1789–1801*, vol. 11 of the American Nation Series (New York: Harper and Brothers, 1906), p. 130; McMaster, *History*, 2:221; Morison, *Life-Otis*, 1:59.

72. Bowers, *Jefferson and Hamilton*, p. 283; Warren, *Jacobin*, p. 58; McMaster, *History*, 2:222; Flexner, *GW*, 4:217; McMaster, *History*, 2:214, 219; Smith, *JA*, 2:875.

73. William Jay, *The Life of John Jay*, 2 vols. (New York: J. & J. Harper,

1833), 1:355–56; Gibbs, *Memoirs*, 1:218; McMaster, *History*, 2:217–18; Warren, *Jacobin*, p. 59; Jay, *John Jay*, 1:357.

74. Wilson, *History*, 3:140; *Boston Independent Chronicle*, November 23, 1795.

75. Lisle A. Rose, *Prologue to Democracy: The Federalists in the South, 1789–1800* (Lexington: University of Kentucky Press, 1968), pp. 220–21; *Richmond and Manchester Advertiser*, July 30, 1795.

76. Jay, *John Jay*, 1:362.

77. GW to the vice president of the United States, August 20, 1795, in Fitzpatrick, *GW*, 34:280; Brant, *Madison*, 3:438; *Debates and Proceedings in the Congress of the United States* (Washington, D.C.: Gales and Seaton, 1849), 4th Cong., 1st sess., 1259; JA to AA, April 30, 1796, in Adams, *JA-AA*, 2:227.

78. *Pittsburgh Gazette*, July 9, 1796, cited in Stephen G. Kurtz, *The Presidency of John Adams: The Collapse of Federalism, 1795–1800* (New York: A.S. Barnes, 1961), p. 71; Stewart, *Opposition Press*, p. 203; DeConde, *Entangling Alliance*, p. 256.

79. Smelser, "Passion," p. 405; Irving Brant, "Edmund Randolph, Not Guilty!" *WMQ*, 3d ser., 7 (1950); Kurtz, *Presidency*, p. 264.

80. DeConde, *Entangling Alliance*, p. 129; Flexner, *GW*, 4:250.

81. Kurtz, *Presidency*, pp. 34–35.

82. Beard, *Economic Origins*, p. 284; Fisher Ames to Thomas Dwight, August 24 and December 30, 1795, in Seth Ames, ed., *Works of Fisher Ames, with a Selection from His Speeches and Correspondence*, 2 vols. (Boston: Little, Brown, 1854), pp. 172, 180; *Maryland Gazette* (Annapolis), December 31, 1795.

83. JA to AA, April 1, 1796, in Adams, *Works of JA*, 1:489; OW Sr. to OW Jr., April 25, 1796, in Gibbs, *Memoirs*, 1:332; Bassett, *Federalist*, p. 196, gives the import-export data; Jay, *John Jay*, 1:377; Kurtz, *Presidency*, p. 145.

84. Gilbert Chinard, *Honest John Adams* (Boston: Little, Brown, 1964), p. 255.

85. Kurtz, *Presidency*, respectively, pp. 36, 203, 57, 61.

86. Rose, *Prologue*, pp. 90ff; JA to AA, January 7, 1796, in Adams, *JA-AA*, 2:188; Smith, *JA*, 2:885.

87. JA to AA, February 15, 1796, and March 25, 1796, in Adams, *JA-AA*, 2:200, 214; OW to GW, July 4, 1796, in Gibbs, *Memoirs*, 1:365.

88. Kurtz, *Presidency*, pp. 80ff; Flexner, *GW*, 4:295; Smelser, "Phrenzy," p. 476.

89. Smelser, "Passion," p. 406; Woodbury, "Public Opinion," p. 125; Kurtz, *Presidency*, pp. 78, 92; Cunningham, *Jeffersonians*, pp. 97, 107; Malone, *TJ*, 3:273; Bassett, *Federalist System*, p. 252; Warren, *Jacobin*, p. 50; Hofstadter, *Tradition*, p. 26; Stewart, *Opposition Press*, pp. 78, 344.

90. E. Wilson Lyon, "The Directory and the United States," *AHR* 43 (1938): 516; Bemis, "Washington," p. 257; Miller, *Federalist Era*, p. 205; Elson, *History*, 2:198; Kurtz, *Presidency*, pp. 124ff.

91. Warren, *Jacobin*, p. 71; Kurtz, *Presidency*, pp. 105ff; OW to OW Sr., October 17, November 27, and December 12, 1796, in Gibbs, *Memoirs*, 1:387, 402, 408–09.

92. TJ to JA, December 28, 1796 (forwarded to Madison and never sent to JA), in Lipscomb, Bergh, *Writings of TJ*, 9:355; TJ to Tench Coxe, September 10, 1795, in Ford, *Writings of TJ*, 7:30; TJ to JA, December 28, 1796, in Lipscomb, Bergh, *Writings of TJ*, 9:356; Kurtz, *Presidency*, p. 200; TJ to E. Rutledge, December 27, 1796, in Ford, *Writings of TJ*, 7:93–94.

Chapter Two

1. OW to JA, April 25, 1797, in George Gibbs, *Memoirs of the Administration of Washington and John Adams; Edited from the Papers of Oliver Wolcott, Secretary of the Treasury*, 2 vols. (New York: William Van Norden, 1846), p. 509; Adams is quoted on AH's "delerium" in Gibbs, *Memoirs*, 1:483; *Aurora*, May 19 and May 24, 1797; George Cabot to OW, May 24, 1797, in Gibbs, *Memoirs*, 1:536; *Aurora*, June 13, 1797; *Boston Independent Chronicle*, June 15, 1797.

2. TJ to E. Rutledge, June 24, 1797, in Andrew A. Lipscomb and Albert Ellery Bergh, eds., *The Writings of Thomas Jefferson*, 10 vols. (Washington, D.C.: Thomas Jefferson Memorial Association, 1905), 9:411; Samuel Eliot Morison, *The Life and Letters of Harrison Gray Otis, Federalist; 1765–1848*, 2 vols. (Boston: Houghton Mifflin, 1913), 1:62; Gibbs, *Memoirs*, 1:555–56.

3. JA to AA, in Charles Francis Adams, ed., *Letters of John Adams, Addressed to His Wife*, 2 vols. (Boston: Charles C. Little and James Brown, 1841), 2:240; *Centinel of Freedom* (Newark, N.J.), June 21, 1797; Irving Brant, *James Madison, Father of the Constitution*, vol. 3 of *James Madison* (Indianapolis: Bobbs-Merrill, 1950), p. 443; "Party Violence, 1790–1800," *VaMHB*, 29 (1921):173; John C. Miller, *The Federalist Era; 1789–1801*, New American Nation Series (New York: Harper and Row, 1960), p. 165; Alexander DeConde, *The Quasi-War; The Politics and Diplomacy of the Undeclared War with France, 1797–1801* (New York: C. Scribner's Sons, 1966), pp. 32–33; GW to the secretary of war, August 14, 1797, in John C. Fitzpatrick, ed., *The Writings of George Washington*, 39 vols. (Washington, D.C.: U.S. Government Printing Office, 1939), 36:8.

4. Page Smith, *John Adams*, 2 vols. (Garden City, N.Y.: Doubleday, 1962), 2:947; *Norwich Packet*, April 20, 1797; GW to the secretary of state, August 29, GW to Charles Cotesworth Pinckney, December 4, and GW to John Marshall, December 4, 1797, in Fitzpatrick, *GW*, 36:19, 90, 94; OW to JA, September 1797, in Gibbs, *Memoirs*, 1:561.

5. *Time Piece* (New York), February 1, 1798; Claude G. Bowers, *Jefferson and Hamilton; The Struggle for Democracy in America* (Boston: Houghton Mifflin, 1966), p. 360; Morison, *Life-Otis*, 1:78; AA to Mary Cranch, February 15 and 21, 1798, in Stewart Mitchell, ed., *New Letters of Abigail Adams; 1788–1801* (Boston: Houghton Mifflin, 1947), pp. 132–33, 135; *Farmer's Weekly Museum* (Walpole, N.H.), July 17, 1798; *Salem Gazette*, March 5, 1799.

6. James Morton Smith, *Freedom's Fetters: The Alien and Sedition Laws and American Civil Liberties* (Ithaca, N.Y.: Cornell University Press, 1966), p. 238; Bowers, *Jefferson and Hamilton*, pp. 386–88; Edwin Emery, *The Press and America; An Interpretive History of Journalism*, 2d. ed. (Englewood Cliffs, N.J.: Prentice-Hall, 1962), p. 160; J. Smith, *Fetters*, p. 244; Leonard W. Levy, *Freedom of Speech and Press in Early American History; Legacy of Suppression* (New York: Harper and Row, 1963), pp. 146–47; *New Hampshire Gazette* (Portsmouth), March 6, 1799; William Cobbett, *Porcupine's Works*, 12 vols. (London: Cobbett and Morgan, 1801), 10:69–70.

7. E. Wilson Lyon, "The Directory and the United States," *AHR* 43 (1938):521; Morison, *Life-Otis*, 1:83.

8. Timothy Pickering, *A Review of the Correspondence Between the Hon. John Adams, Late President of the United States, and the Late Wm. Cunningham, Beginning in 1803 and Ending in 1812* (Salem, Mass.: Cushing and Appleton, 1824), p. 126; Smith, *JA*, 2:931; *Farmer's Weekly Museum*, May 15, 1798.

9. Bowers, *Jefferson and Hamilton*, p. 364; Morison, *Life-Otis*, 1:81; Dumas Malone, *Thomas Jefferson and the Ordeal of Liberty*, vol. 3 of *Jefferson and His Time* (Boston: Little, Brown, 1962), p. 371; Charles Francis Adams, ed., *The Works of John Adams, Second President of the United States*, 10 vols. (Boston: Charles C. Little and James Brown, 1851), 1:519.

10. Smith, *JA*, 2:953–55; Gibbs, *Memoirs*, 2:39; Lisle A. Rose, *A Prologue to Democracy; The Federalists in the South, 1789–1800* (Lexington: University of Kentucky Press, 1968), pp. 143, 179–80; DeConde, *Quasi-War*, p. 20.

11. *Time Piece* (New York), June 18, 1798; GW to the secretary of state, April 16, 1798, in Fitzpatrick, *GW*, 36:249.

12. *Middlesex Gazette* (Middletown, Conn.), June 28, 1798; Smith, *Fetters*, p. 3; DeConde, *Quasi-War*, p. 93; Donald H. Stewart, *The Opposition Press of the Federalist Period* (Albany: State University of New York Press, 1969), p. 315; John Wood, *The Suppressed History of the Administration of John Adams (From 1797 to 1801) as Printed and Suppressed in 1802* (Philadelphia: John H. Sherburne, 1846), p. 91.

13. Bowers, *Jefferson and Hamilton*, p. 426; Samuel Eliot Morison, *By Land and by Sea: Essays and Addresses* (New York: Knopf, 1953), p. 195; Miller, *Federalist Era*, p. 214; Marshall Smelser, "The Federalist Period as an Age of Passion," *AQ* 10 (1958):411; T. Pickering to JA, November 5, 1798, in Adams, *Works of JA*, 8:616; GW to the secretary of state, February 10, 1799, in Fitzpatrick, *GW*, 37:127; Gibbs, *Memoirs*, 2:148.

14. Doris A. Graber, *Public Opinion, the President, and Foreign Policy: Four Case Studies from the Formative Years* (New York: Holt, Rinehart, and Winston, 1968), p. 70; Smith, *Fetters*, p. 21; Smelser, "Passion," p. 409.

15. Wood, *Suppressed History*, pp. 124–25; Smelser, "Passion," p. 412; Morton Borden, *Parties and Politics in the Early Republic, 1789–1815* (New York: Thomas Y. Crowell, 1967), p. 30; James M. Banner, *To the Hartford Convention: The Federalists and the Origins of Party Politics in Massachusetts* (New York: Knopf, 1970), pp. 99ff; Smith, *Fetters*, p. 131; Smelser, "Passion," p. 395.

16. Smith, *Fetters*, p. 14; Miller, *Federalist Era*, p. 113; Joseph Charles, *The Origins of the American Party System; Three Essays* (New York: Harper and Row, 1956), p. 6; John C. Miller, *Crisis in Freedom: The Alien and Sedition Acts* (Boston: Little, Brown, 1951), p. 14; Borden, *Parties*, p. 34; Morison, *Life-Otis*, 1:108; GW to Sir John Sinclair, December 11, 1796, in Fitzpatrick, *GW*, 35:326; "An American" [Joseph Hopkinson], *What Is Our Situation? And What Our Prospects? A Few Pages for Americans, by an American* (Philadelphia: n.p., 1798), p. 19.

17. Marshall Smelser, "The Jacobin Phrenzy: Federalism and the Menace of Liberty, Equality, and Fraternity," *RP* 13 (1951):458; Banner, *Hartford Convention*, pp. 31–32; Miller, *Crisis*, p. 58.

18. GW to the secretary of war, March 27, and GW to Alexander White, March 1, 1798, in Fitzpatrick, *GW*, respectively, 36:175–76, 91; JA to TJ, June 14, 1813, in Lester J. Cappon, ed., *The Adams-Jefferson Letters; The Complete Correspondence Between Thomas Jefferson and Abigail and John Adams*, 2 vols. (Chapel Hill: University of North Carolina Press, 1959), 2:329; Smith, *Fetters*, p. 61; Morison, *Life-Otis*, 1:115.

19. Smith, *Fetters*, pp. 48, 50ff; Malone, *TJ*, 3:384.

20. DeConde, *Quasi-War*, pp. 84, 86; Rose, *Prologue*, pp. 63–64; *Gazette of the United States*, March 31, 1798, and March 24, 1798.

21. John Bach McMaster, *A History of the People of the United States, From the*

Revolution to the Civil War, 5 vols. (New York: D. Appleton, 1885), 2:380; Bowers, *Jefferson and Hamilton*, p. 368; *New Hampshire Gazette* (Portsmouth), June 12, 1798; *Middlesex Gazette* (Middletown, Conn.), June 8, 1798; DeConde, *Quasi-War*, p. 88; Banner, *Hartford Convention*, pp. 18–19; DeConde, *Quasi-War*, p. 75; Bowers, *Jefferson and Hamilton*, p. 474.

22. Borden, *Parties*, pp. 36–37; Brant, *Madison*, 3:457, sees JA's answers to the addresses as "the most grotesque scene in the whole tragicomedy." *U.S. Chronicle* (Providence), May 24, 1798; *Providence Gazette*, May 12, 1798; *Debates and Proceedings in the Congress of the United States* (Washington, D.C.: Gales and Seaton, 1849), 5th Congress, 2d session, 1679; *Aurora*, May 9 and May 2, 1798.

23. For AA's part in the Sedition Act, see Smith, *Fetters*, pp. 96, 191; Miller, *Crisis*, p. 72; Malone, *TJ*, 3:390, in addition to letters of AA cited below; *Courier of New Hampshire* (Concord), July 10, 1798; *Russell's Gazette* (Boston), June 11, 1798.

24. JA to the young men of Boston, Massachusetts, May 22, 1798, in Adams, *Works of JA*, 9:194; *Porcupine's Gazette*, June 18, 1798; *Courier of New Hampshire*, July 17, 1798; Hopkinson, *Situation*, p. 8; Miller, *Federalist Era*, p. 219; David Osgood, *Some Facts Evincive of the Atheistical, Anarchical, and in Other Respects Immoral Principles of the French Republicans, Stated in a Sermon, Delivered on the 9th of May, 1798* (Boston: Samuel Hall, 1798), p. 13; Charles A. Beard, *Economic Origins of Jeffersonian Democracy* (New York: Free Press, 1965), p. 366.

25. *Connecticut Courant* (Hartford), July 2, 1798; *Porcupine's Gazette*, June 12, 1798; *Middlesex Gazette*, June 29, 1798; AA to Mercy Warren, April 25, 1798, in Worthington Chauncey Ford, ed., *Warren-Adams Letters; Being Chiefly a Correspondence Among John Adams, Samuel Adams, and James Warren*, 2 vols. (Boston: MHS, 1925), 2:337; *Porcupine's Gazette*, June 7, 1798; Hopkinson, *Situation*, p. 34; *American Mercury* (Hartford), September 6, 1798.

26. Bowers, *Jefferson and Hamilton*, pp. 372–73; Miller, *Crisis*, p. 187; DeConde, *Quasi-War*, p. 79; Stewart, *Opposition Press*, pp. 326–27; *Commercial Advertiser* (New York), June 1798, cited in Smith, *Fetters*, p. 14; *Wilmington Gazette*, May 31, 1798; *Farmer's Weekly Museum*, July 10, 1798.

27. *Providence Gazette*, July 7, 1798.

28. Smith, *JA*, 2:970; McMaster, *History*, 2:413; JA to OW, September 13, 1798, in Adams, *Works of JA*, 8:595.

29. *Salem Gazette*, July 17, 1798; *Kline's Carlisle Weekly Gazette*, June 6, 1798; *Claypoole's American Daily Advertiser* (Philadelphia), July 12, 1798; Charles Warren, *Jacobin and Junto; or Early American Politics as Viewed in the Diary of Dr. Nathaniel Ames, 1758–1822* (Cambridge: Harvard University Press, 1931), p. 75; *Norwich Packet*, July 24, 1798; Warren, *Jacobin*, p. 84; *Political Repository* (Brookfield, Massachusetts), August 14, 1798.

30. DeConde, *Quasi-War*, p. 82; *Carey's United States Recorder* (Philadelphia), June 26, 1798; Warren, *Jacobin*, p. 100; *Boston Independent Chronicle*, July 5, 1798; *Aurora*, July 14, 1798; Stewart, *Opposition Press*, p. 450.

31. *Farmer's Weekly Museum*, July 3, 1798; *Time Piece* (New York), June 20, 1798; Smith, *Fetters*, p. 188; *Aurora*, July 16, 1798; Morison, *Life-Otis*, 1:156; *Aurora*, July 20, 1798; *Political Repository* (Brookfield, Mass.), August 14, 1798.

32. *Porcupine's Gazette*, July 27, 1798; on GW and appointments, see GW to AH, August 9, GW to the secretary of war, July 14, July 25, September 30, October 15 and 22, 1798; GW to Edward Carrington, October 22, and GW to William R.

Davie, October 24, 1798, in Fitzpatrick, *GW*, respectively, 36:394–95, 335, 366, 474, 491, 505, 513, and 516.

33. For JA's suspicions, see JA to J. McHenry, secretary of war, August 18, 1798, in Adams, *Works of JA*, 8:582; for his willingness to appoint Republicans, see Chapter 1, note 31.

34. Rose, *Prologue*, pp. 20ff and 206.

35. Miller, *Federalist Era*, p. 249; James Thomson Callender, *The Prospect Before Us*, 2 vols. (Richmond, Va.: James Thomson Callender, 1800), 2:120ff; *Debates and Proceedings*, 4th Congress, 2d session, 2090; Warren, *Jacobin*, pp. 114–15; George Clinton, *An Oration, Delivered on the Fourth of July, 1798* (New York: M.L. Davis and W.A. Davis, 1798), p. 13.

36. Brant, *Madison*, 3:466; Marshall Smelser, "George Washington Declines the Part of El Libertador," *WMQ*, 3d ser., 11 (1954): 42, 47–51; Stephen G. Kurtz, *The Presidency of John Adams: The Collapse of Federalism, 1795–1800* (New York: A.S. Barnes, 1961), p. 356; JA to James Lloyd, March 27, 1815, in Adams, *Works of JA*, 10:146.

37. GW to Charles Carroll, August 2, and GW to William Heth, July 18, 1798, in Fitzpatrick, *GW*, respectively, 36: 384, 352; Manning J. Dauer, *The Adams Federalists* (Baltimore: Johns Hopkins University Press, 1968), p. 159; Gibbs, *Memoirs*, 2:75; Marshall Smelser, "George Washington and the Alien and Sedition Acts," *AHR* 59 (1953–1954):322.

38. Leonard W. Levy, "Liberty and the First Amendment: 1790–1800," *AHR* 68 (1962): 35; Smelser, "Phrenzy," p. 480; Stewart, *Opposition Press*, pp. 469–70; Frank M. Anderson, "The Enforcement of the Alien and Sedition Acts," *AHA Annual Report for the Year 1912* (1914): 125–26; Smith, *Fetters*, p. 348.

39. Miller, *Federalist Era*, p. 234; Miller, *Crisis*, p. 131; Smith, *Fetters*, pp. 359ff and 385ff; Anderson, "Enforcement," p. 62; Smith, *Fetters*, pp. 257ff; Callender, *Prospect*, 2:88.

40. Levy, *Legacy*, pp. ix, 215, 248; Walter Berns, "Freedom of the Press and the Alien and Sedition Laws: A Reappraisal," *Supreme Court Review* (1970): 111, 121–22.

41. On Republican willingness to use state laws dealing with sedition and aliens, see Levy, *Legacy*, p. xiii; Berns, "Freedom," pp. 121, 131, 142; see also Irving Brant, *Madison*, vol. 3, and *The Bill of Rights; Its Origins and Meanings* (Indianapolis: Bobbs-Merrill, 1965), pp. 232, 260; "Address of the General Assembly to the People of the Commonwealth of Virginia," January 23, 1799, in Gaillard Hunt, ed., *The Writings of James Madison*, 9 vols. (New York: G.P. Putnam's Sons, 1900–1910), 6:333–34; Leonard W. Levy, *Jefferson and Civil Liberties: The Darker Side* (Cambridge, 1963), p. 46.

42. Brant, *Madison*, 3:459ff; Frank M. Anderson, "Contemporary Opinion of the Virginia and Kentucky Resolutions," *AHR* 5 (1899): 48; TJ to S.T. Mason, October 11, 1798, in Lipscomb, Bergh, *TJ Writings*, 10:61–62; On Madison toning down Jefferson, see Berns, "Freedom," p. 127; see also Adrienne Koch, *Jefferson and Madison* (New York: Oxford University Press, 1964).

43. Frederick B. Tolles, "Unofficial Ambassador: George Logan's Mission to France, 1798," *WMQ*, 3d ser., 7 (1950):9; GW to William Vans Murray, August 10, 1798, in Fitzpatrick, *GW*, 36:407; JA to Pickering, November 2, 1798, in Adams, *Works of JA*, 8:615; *Debates and Proceedings*, December 28, 1798, cited in Dauer, *Federalists*, p. 228.

44. Edward Channing, *A History of the United States*, 6 vols. (New York: Macmillan, 1917), 4:202; "Memorandum of an Interview," November 13, 1798, in Fitzpatrick, *GW*, 37:18–20; Cobbett, *Porcupine's Works*, 10:17; Warren, *Jacobin*, p. 121; Tolles, "Logan," respectively, pp. 25, 23; DeConde, *Quasi-War*, p. 172.

45. GW to Alexander Spotswood, November 22, GW to Marquis de Lafayette, December 25, and GW to John Marshall, December 30, 1798, in Fitzpatrick, *GW*, 37:23–24, 66, 69, and 76.

46. *Providence Gazette*, February 23, 1799; *New Hampshire Gazette* (Portsmouth), February 22, 1799.

47. Letter 5 to the *Boston Patriot*, in Adams, *Works of JA*, 9:249–50; Smith, *JA*, 2:1003; Miller, *Federalist Era*, p. 246.

48. Letter 12 to the *Boston Patriot*, in Adams, *Works of JA*, 9:279; Smith, *JA*, 2:1005; Miller, *Federalist Era*, p. 247; Smith, *JA*, 2:1034.

49. *Russell's Gazette* (Boston), March 21, 1799; *Norwich Packet*, March 20, 1799; McMaster, *History*, 2:441; "Robert Slender" [Philip M. Freneau], *Letters on Various Interesting and Important Subjects* (Philadelphia: D. Hogan, 1799), p. 13; DeConde, *Quasi-War*, pp. 189–90.

50. DeConde, *Quasi-War*, p. 197; *U.S. Chronicle* (Providence), May 16, 1799.

51. JA to Pickering, May 25, 1799, in Adams, *Works of JA*, 8:652; for the threat, see pp. 652–53n.

52. Jabez D. Hammond, *The History of Political Parties in the State of New York: From the Ratification of the Federal Constitution to December, 1840*, 2 vols. (Cooperstown, N.Y.: H. and E. Phinney, 1846), 1:132; *Aurora*, October 12, 1799; Smith, *Fetters*, p. 271.

53. *Constitutional Telegraph* (Boston), October 5, 16, 1799; Callender, *Prospect*, 1:84.

54. Miller, *Crisis*, p. 178; Morison, *Life-Otis*, 1:180.

55. JA to Thomas Johnson, April 11, 1800, in Adams, *JA Works*, 9:49; OW to JA, August 13, 1798, in Gibbs, *Memoirs*, 2:106; GW to Maj. Gen. AH, August 9, 1798, in Fitzpatrick, *GW*, 36:394–95; *Aurora*, May 15, 1800.

56. Warren, *Jacobin*, pp. 124, 126; *Aurora*, June 7 and 24, 1800; *Boston Independent Chronicle*, September 8, 1800.

57. "Burleigh," in the *Connecticut Courant* (Hartford), in the fall of 1800, but especially September 15 and 29, 1800; Malone, *TJ*, 3:479; *Gazette of the United States*, October 7, 1800; Callender, *Prospect*, 1:167.

58. *American Citizen* (New York), October 23, 1800; *Courier of New Hampshire* (Concord), November 8, 1800; Stewart, *Opposition Press*, p. 589; Miller, *Federalist Era*, p. 258; Callender, *Prospect*, 1:157ff.

59. Gibbs, *Memoirs*, 2:478; *National Intelligencer* (Washington), November 10, 1800; Warren, *Jacobin*, p. 159.

60. Smith, *JA*, 2:1055.

61. Smelser, "Passion," p. 418.

Chapter Three

1. Morton Borden, *Parties and Politics in the Early Republic, 1789–1815* (New York: Thomas Y. Crowell, 1967), p. 28; Harry Ammon, *The Genet Mission* (New

York: Norton, 1973), pp. 140–41; Frank Luther Mott, *Jefferson and the Press* (Baton Rouge: Louisiana State University Press, 1943), p. 57.

2. GW to Edmund Pendleton, September 23, 1793, in John C. Fitzpatrick, *The Writings of George Washington*, 39 vols. (Washington, D.C.: U.S. Government Printing Office, 1939), 33:15.

3. Jay to Pickering, August 17, 1795, in William Jay, *The Life of John Jay*, 2 vols. (New York: J. & J. Harper, 1833), 1:372; *Gazette of the United States*, March 4, 1799.

4. *Gazette of the United States*, March 4, 1799.

5. Allan Nevins, *American Press Opinion, Washington to Coolidge* (Boston: D.C. Heath, 1928), p. 11; John T. Morse, Jr., ed., *John Adams*, American Statesman Series (Boston: Houghton Mifflin, 1884), p. 269; Saul K. Padover, "Wave of the Past," *New Republic*, 116 (1949):16; Page Smith, *John Adams*, 2 vols. (Garden City, N.Y.: Doubleday, 1962), 2:944.

6. Nevins, *Press Opinion*, p. 5; Stephen G. Kurtz, *The Presidency of John Adams: The Collapse of Federalism, 1795–1800* (New York: A.S. Barnes, 1961), p. 37; James M. Banner, Jr., *To the Hartford Convention: The Federalists and the Origins of Party Politics in Massachusetts* (New York: Knopf, 1930), p. 23; Charles Warren, *Jacobin and Junto; or Early American Politics as Viewed in the Diary of Dr. Nathaniel Ames, 1758–1822* (Cambridge: Harvard University Press, 1931), p. 93; for partisanship, see Marshall Smelser, "The Federalist Period as an Age of Passion," *AQ* 10 (1958):396; Bernard A. Weisberger, *The American Newspaperman*, Chicago History of American Civilization Series (Chicago: University of Chicago Press, 1961), p. 34; Frank L. Mott, *American Journalism; A History: 1690–1960* (New York: Macmillan, 1962), p. 113; Donald H. Stewart, *The Opposition Press of the Federalist Period* (Albany: State University of New York Press, 1969), p. 12.

7. Richard Hildreth, *The History of the United States of America*, 6 vols. (New York: Harper and Brothers, 1880), 5:228–30; Stewart, *Opposition Press*, pp. 487, 519, 543; "Party Violence, 1790–1800," *VaMHB* 29 (1921):172; Doris A. Graber, *Public Opinion, the President, and Foreign Policy: Four Case Studies from the Formative Years* (New York: Holt, Rinehart, and Winston, 1968), p. 23; Marshall Smelser, "The Jacobin Phrenzy: Federalism and the Menace of Liberty, Equality, and Fraternity," *RP* 13 (1951):460; Dumas Malone, *Jefferson and the Ordeal of Liberty*, vol. 3 of *Jefferson and His Time* (Boston: Little, Brown, 1962), p. 391.

8. Graber, *Public Opinion*, p. 24; Clarence S. Brigham, *Journals and Journeymen: A Contribution to the History of Early American Newspapers* (Philadelphia: American Antiquarian Society, 1950), p. 63.

9. Nevins, *Press Opinion*, p. 4, agrees that "the true newspaper, independent of politics, had not yet been born." McMaster, *History*, 2:58ff; *Farmer's Weekly Museum* featured "entertaining scraps" on, for example, March 7, 1797; Mott, *Journalism*, pp. 114–15, stresses commercial news.

10. Leland D. Baldwin, *Whiskey Rebels: The Story of a Frontier Uprising* (Pittsburgh: University of Pittsburgh Press, 1939), p. 221, and Smelser, "Passion," p. 399, stress repetition; *Russell's Gazette* (Boston), June 18, 1798, and *Aurora*, October 23, 1790, admitted the lack of gossip; *Green Mt. Patriot* (Peacham, Vt.), May 14, 1800, printed the apology.

11. Charles D. Hazen, *Contemporary American Opinion of the French Revolution*, vol. 16 of Johns Hopkins University Studies in History and Political Science, edited by Herbert Baxter Adams (Baltimore: Johns Hopkins University Press,

1897), pp. 219–20; Brigham, *Journals*, p. 88; Lewis Leary, *That Rascal Freneau: A Study in Literary Failure* (New Brunswick, N.J.: Rutgers University Press, 1941), p. 276.

12. Stewart, *Opposition Press*, p. 19; McMaster, *History*, 2:63, cites the absence of religious papers and erroneously claims an absence of trade or literary papers. The New York *Temple of Reason* defended deism in its brief existence.

13. Brigham, *Journals*, p. 12; Weisberger, *Newspaperman*, p. 8.

14. Weisberger, *Newspaperman*, pp. 3, 24; Mott, *Journalism*, pp. 113, 138; Stewart, *Opposition Press*, pp. 14–15, and Weisberger, *Newspaperman*, p. 51, give the statistics for the years 1790 through 1820; Leary, *Rascal Freneau*, p. 196; Mott, *Journalism*, p. 143.

15. Mott, *Journalism*, pp. 159, 162.

16. Brigham, *Journals*, pp. 20–21, 27; Edward Channing, *A History of the United States*, 6 vols. (New York: Macmillan, 1917), 4:23 stresses medical ads.

17. Brigham, *Journals*, p. 23ff; *American* (Baltimore), *October 20, 1800*, cited in Stewart, *Opposition Press*, p. 18; Weisberger, *Newspaperman*, p. 25; Carl Bridenbaugh, "The Press and the Book in Eighteenth Century Philadelphia," *PaMHB*, 65 (1941):7; on the value of the press to citizens, see Nevins, *Press Opinion*, pp. 5–6; Kurtz, *Presidency*, p. 137; and Graber, *Public Opinion*, p. 25.

18. Brigham, *Journals*, pp. 46–47; Philip M. Marsh, *Philip Freneau: Poet and Journalist* (Minneapolis: Dillon, 1967), p. 195.

19. Bridenbaugh, "Press," p. 13; Mott, *Journalism*, p. 114; Stewart, *Opposition Press*, p. 27; Brigham, *Journals*, pp. 71, 73, 108; Worthington Chauncey Ford, ed., "Letters of William Duane," *Massachusetts Historical Society Proceedings* 20 (1906–1907):257.

20. Mott, *Journalism*, p. 121; Stewart, *Opposition Press*, p. 386.

21. Mott, *Journalism*, p. 155; Stewart, *Opposition Press*, pp. 22–23; *Massachusetts Mercury* (Boston), March 7, 1797; Napoleon's death was noted in *Norwich Packet*, March 6, 1799; *Massachusetts Spy* (Worcester), March 6, 1799; *Middlesex Gazette*, March 8, 1799; *Courier of New Hampshire*, March 9, 1799; *Farmer's Weekly Museum*, March 11, 1799; and *New Hampshire Gazette* (Portsmouth), March 12, 1799.

22. Miller, *Crisis*, pp. 30–31; Leary, *Rascal Freneau*, p. 240; Brigham, *Journals*, pp. 56–57; *Claypoole's American Daily Advertiser* (Philadelphia), March 4 and May 17, 1797; *Courier of New Hampshire*, March 28, 1797; *Boston Gazette*, May 29, 1797.

23. Stewart, *Opposition Press*, p. 19; DeConde, *Quasi-War*, p. 35; F. Ames to Thomas Dwight, September 25, 1798, in Seth Ames, *Works of Fisher Ames, with a Selection from His Speeches and Correspondence*, 2 vols. (Boston: Little, Brown, 1854), 1:240.

24. *Green Mt. Patriot*, June 1, 1798; *New Hampshire Gazette*, March 25, 1797; *Porcupine's Gazette*, March 8, 1797; *Aurora*, May 6, 1796, for example.

25. Warren, *Jacobin*, p. 90.

26. Dr. Lemuel Hopkins to OW, August 21, 1793, and OW Sr. to OW Jr., November 23, 1795, in George Gibbs, *Memoirs of the Administration of Washington and John Adams; Edited from the Papers of Oliver Wolcott, Secretary of the Treasury*, 2 vols. (New York: William Van Norden, 1846), 1:104, 261; Gibbs adds his own comments on aliens on p. 358; John C. Miller, *Crisis in Freedom: The Alien and Sedition Acts* (Boston: Little, Brown, 1951), p. 58; Weisberger, *Newspaperman*, p. 37.

27. Edwin Emery, *The Press and America: An Interpretive History of Journalism*, 2d ed. (Englewood Cliffs, N.J.: Prentice-Hall, 1962), p. 136; *Gazette of the United States*, April 27, 1791; Margaret Woodbury, "Public Opinion in Philadelphia, 1789–1801," *Smith College Studies in History* 5 (1919–1920):11; Claude G. Bowers, *Jefferson and Hamilton: The Struggle for Democracy in America* (Boston: Houghton Mifflin, 1966), pp. 153–54; Marsh, *Freneau*, respectively, pp. 144, 141; Robert W. Jones, *Journalism in the United States* (New York: Dutton, 1947), p. 174; JA to Rush, January 8, 1812, in John A. Schutz and Douglass Adair, eds., *The Spur of Fame: Dialogues of . . . John Adams and Benjamin Rush, 1805–1813* (San Marino, Calif.: Huntington Library, 1966), pp. 204–05; F. Ames to J.W. Fenno, February 1800, in Ames, *Fisher Ames*, 1:274.

28. Miller, *Crisis*, p. 26; Woodbury, "Public Opinion," p. 24; Bowers, *Jefferson and Hamilton*, p. 155; Mott, *Jefferson*, p. 28; Mott, *Journalism*, p. 128; Brigham, *Journals*, p. 67.

29. Alexander DeConde, *Entangling Alliance: Politics and Diplomacy Under George Washington* (Durham, N.C.: Duke University Press, 1958), p. 58; Bowers, *Jefferson and Hamilton*, p. 156ff; Ammon, *Genet*, p. 35. William Loughton Smith, *The Pretensions of Thomas Jefferson to the Presidency Examined; And the Charges Against John Adams Refuted* (Philadelphia: n.p., 1796), p. 48; Noble E. Cunningham, Jr., *The Jeffersonian-Republicans: The Formation of Party Organization, 1789–1809* (Chapel Hill: University of North Carolina Press, 1957), p. 13; and Malone, *TJ*, 2:351, cite the Jefferson-Freneau link; Mott, *Jefferson*, pp. 18, 22; Stewart, *Opposition Press*, pp. 487–88; Malone, *TJ*, 2:427–28; John C. Miller, *The Federalist Era, 1789–1801*, New American Nation Series (New York: Harper and Row, 1960), pp. 90–91, discusses Freneau's concerted efforts against AH; Marsh, *Freneau*, pp. 206, 217–28; James Morton Smith, *Freedom's Fetters: The Alien and Sedition Laws and American Civil Liberties* (Ithaca, N.Y.: Cornell University Press, 1966), pp. 204–05.

30. Hildreth, *History*, 5:121; G.D.H. Cole, ed., *Letters from William Cobbett to Edward Thornton Written in the Years 1797 to 1800* (London: Oxford University Press, 1937), p. xi and following; *Centinel of Freedom* (Newark), March 8, 1797; William Reitzen, "William Cobbett and Philadelphia Journalism," *PaMHB* 59 (1935):243; Cole, *Cobbett-Thornton*, p. xxix; Reitzen, "Cobbett," p. 229; Woodbury, "Public Opinion," p. 15.

31. McMaster, *History*, 2:338; Gibbs, *Memoirs*, 2:293; Stewart, *Opposition Press*, respectively, pp. 620, 10.

32. Jones, *Journalism*, pp. 153ff and 162.

33. Emery, *Press*, p. 142; Warren, *Jacobin*, p. 55; Ammon, *Genet*, p. 139; Philip M. Marsh, "John Beckley; Mystery Man of the Early Jeffersonians," *PaMHB* 72 (1948):60–61.

34. *Constitutional Telegraph* (Boston), October 5, 1799; James Thomson Callender, *The Prospect Before Us*, 2 vols. (Richmond: James Thomson Callender, 1800), 1:33; David Osgood, *Some Facts Evincive of the Atheistical, Anarchical, and in Other Respects, Immoral Principles of the French Republicans, Stated in a Sermon, Delivered on the 9th of May, 1798* (Boston: Samuel Hall, 1798), p. 22.

35. *The Spectator* (New York), August 1, 1798; *Porcupine's Gazette*, June 7, 1798; *Middlesex Gazette*, June 29, 1798; *Farmer's Weekly Museum*, July 3, 1798; *Gazette of the United States*, March 7, 1797.

36. *Courier of New Hampshire*, April 18, 1797; OW to the editor of the *Aurora*,

October 24, 1795, in Gibbs, *Memoirs*, 1:260; *Debates and Proceedings in the Congress of the United States*, 5th Cong., 2d sess., 1972–1973 (Washington, D.C.: Gales and Seaton, 1849); *Porcupine's Gazette*, May 18, 1797; *Farmer's Weekly Museum*, July 3, 1798.

37. Smith, *Fetters*, p. 129, cites Porcupine; Mott, *Journalism*, p. 128; De-Conde, *Quasi-War*, p. 79; *Russell's Gazette* (Boston), September 21, 1798.

38. William Cobbett, *Porcupine's Works*, 12 vols. (London: Cobbett and Morgan, 1801), 10:97; John Wood, *The Suppressed History of the Administration of John Adams (from 1797–1801), As Printed and Suppressed in 1802* (Philadelphia: John H. Sherburne, 1846), p. 195.

39. John Swanwick, *A Rub from Snub* (Philadelphia: n.p., 1795), pp. 7, 16; Hazen, *Opinion*, p. 242; *Constitutional Diary* (Philadelphia), December 24, 1799.

40. *American Mercury* (Hartford), February 4, 1793; *Gazette of the United States*, September 26, 1792; *Minerva* (New York), September 21, 1797.

41. Miller, *Crisis*, pp. 214–15; *Massachusetts Spy* (Worcester), August 22, 1798.

42. *Connecticut Courant*, June 18, 1798; *Salem Gazette*, July 17, 1798; Callender, *Prospect*, 1:160; Miller, *Crisis*, p. 195.

Chapter Four

1. James Thomas Flexner, *George Washington: Anguish and Farewell*, vol. 4 of *George Washington* (Boston: Little, Brown, 1972), pp. 388, 422.

2. The Boston *Columbian Centinel*, December 31, 1796, for example, attacked Bache's assertion that Washington could have been made vice president under Adams in the election of 1796.

3. GW to the secretary for foreign affairs, July 18, and GW to AH, August 28, 1788, in John C. Fitzpatrick, ed., *The Writings of George Washington*, 39 vols. (Washington, D.C.: U.S. Government Printing Office, 1939), 30:15–18, 65–67; James Thomas Flexner, *George Washington and the New Nation (1783–1793)*, vol. 3 of *George Washington* (Boston: Little, Brown, 1969), p. 167; James E. Pollard, *The President and the Press* (New York: Macmillan, 1947), pp. 6–7; Bernard Fay, *The Two Franklins: Fathers of American Democracy* (Boston: Little, Brown, 1933), p. 238.

4. Donald H. Stewart, *The Opposition Press of the Federalist Period* (Albany: State University of New York Press, 1969), p. 503; William Maclay, *The Journal of William Maclay* (New York: Frederick Unger, 1965), p. 341; Marshall Smelser, "The Jacobin Phrenzy: Federalism and the Menace of Liberty, Equality, and Fraternity," *RP* 13 (1951):461; Dumas Malone, *Jefferson and the Rights of Man*, vol. 2 of *Jefferson and His Time* (Boston: Little, Brown, 1951), p. 421; AA to Mary Cranch, April 20, 1792, in Stewart Mitchell, ed., *New Letters of Abigail Adams*, 1788–1801 (Boston: Houghton Mifflin, 1947), p. 83; Flexner, *GW*, 4:9.

5. Stewart, *Opposition Press*, pp. 520, 531; GW to Gouverneur Morris, June 21, 1792, in Fitzpatrick, *GW*, 33:63.

6. Alexander DeConde, *Entangling Alliance: Politics and Diplomacy Under George Washington* (Durham, N.C.: Duke University Press, 1958), p. 59; John Spencer Bassett, *The Federalist System, 1789–1801*, vol. 11 of *The American Nation: A History*, ed. by A.B. Hart (New York: Harper and Brothers, 1906), p. 47; TJ to

the president of the United States, September 9, 1792, in Andrew A. Lipscomb and Albert Ellery Bergh, eds., *The Writings of Thomas Jefferson*, 10 vols. (Washington, D.C.: Thomas Jefferson Memorial Association, 1905), 8:406; Frank Luther Mott, *Jefferson and the Press* (Baton Rouge: Louisiana State University Press, 1943), pp. 20–21; John Bach McMaster, *A History of the People of the United States, From the Revolution to the Civil War*, 5 vols. (New York: D. Appleton, 1885), 2:53; George Gibbs, *Memoirs of the Administration of Washington and John Adams; Edited from the Papers of Oliver Wolcott, Secretary of the Treasury*, 2 vols. (New York: William Van Norden, 1846), 1:85, 107.

7. Douglas Southall Freeman, *George Washington, A Biography*, 7 vols. (New York: Charles Scribner's Sons, 1948–1957), 6:399; Page Smith, *John Adams*, 2 vols. (Garden City, N.Y.: Doubleday, 1962), 2:827; Stewart, *Opposition Press*, p. 520; GW to Gouverneur Morris, October 20, 1792, in Fitzpatrick, *GW*, 32:189.

8. DeConde, *Entangling Alliance*, pp. 60, 60n; Irving Brant, *James Madison, Father of the Constitution*, vol. 3 of *James Madison* (Indianapolis: Bobbs-Merrill, 1950), p. 356; AA to Mrs. Abigail Smith, February 10, 1793, in the microfilm edition of the Adams Papers, Adams Manuscript Trust, MHS.

9. JA to AA, January 24, 1793, in Charles Francis Adams, ed., *Letters of John Adams, Addressed to His Wife*, 2 vols. (Boston: Charles C. Little and James Brown, 1841), 2:121; *National Gazette*, May 21, 1793; JA to AA, January 31, 1793, in Adams, *JA-AA*, 2:123.

10. TJ to Madison, June 9, 1793, in Paul Leicester Ford, ed., *The Writings of Thomas Jefferson*, 10 vols. (New York: G.P. Putnam and Sons, 1894), 6:293; GW to Governor Henry Lee, July 21, 1793, in Fitzpatrick, *GW*, 33:23–24; Philip M. Marsh, *Philip Freneau: Poet and Journalist* (Minneapolis: Dillon, 1967), p. 199; GW to Richard Henry Lee, October 24, 1793, in Fitzpatrick, *GW*, 33:137–38; TJ's "Anas," November 8, 1798, in Ford, *Writings of TJ*, 1:266.

11. Harry Ammon, *The Genet Mission* (New York: Norton, 1973), p. 78; Flexner, *GW*, 4:74, 78.

12. GW to Edmund Pendleton, September 23, and GW to the secretary of state, October 7, 1793, in Fitzpatrick, *GW*, 33:95, 113; *Mirrour* (Concord), December 16, 1793.

13. Charles Francis Adams, *The Works of John Adams, Second President of the United States*, 10 vols. (Boston: Charles C. Little and James Brown, 1851), 1:456; JA to AA, January 2, 1794, in Adams, *Works of JA*, 1:460–61; JA to AA, January 9, 1794, in Adams, *JA-AA*, 2:137; *Aurora*, February 22, 1794; GW to the secretary of state, October 16, 1794, in Fitzpatrick, *GW*, 34:2–3; Smith, *JA*, 2:867.

14. DeConde, *Entangling Alliance*, p. 118; Charles A. Beard, *Economic Origins of Jeffersonian Democracy* (New York: Free Press, 1965), p. 296; Fay, *Franklins*, p. 315; Stewart, *Opposition Press*, p. 211ff note the classical pseudonyms and pp. 520–21 the poison-pen campaign.

15. William Jay, *The Life of John Jay*, 2 vols. (New York: J. & J. Harper, 1833), p. 365; F. Ames to Christopher Gore, January 10, 1795, in Seth Ames, *Works of Fisher Ames, With a Selection from His Speeches and Correspondence*, 2 vols. (Boston: Little, Brown, 1854), 1:161; repeats Callender's toast. Leonard Baker, *John Marshall: A Life in Law* (N.Y.: Macmillan, 1974), p. 203.

16. Stewart, *Opposition Press*, p. 534; Lewis Leary, *That Rascal Freneau: A Study in Literary Failure* (New Brunswick, N.J.: Rutgers University Press, 1941), p. 258; Charles Warren, *Jacobin and Junto; or Early American Politics as Viewed in*

the Diary of Dr. Nathaniel Ames, 1758–1822 (Cambridge: Harvard University Press, 1931), p. 65; *Aurora*, August 15, 1795.

17. DeConde, *Entangling Alliance*, p. 126; *Aurora*, August 22, 1795; "Valerius," September 9, 1795; "Belisarius," September 11, 1795; "Atticus," September 21, 1795; "Pittachus," September 23, 1795; *Aurora*, September 25, 1795; *Kentucky Gazette* (Lexington), September 26, 1795; *Aurora*, September 26 and October 23, 1795.

18. "Jasper Dwight, of Vermont" [William Duane], *A Letter to George Washington, President of the United States; Containing Strictures on His Address of the Seventeenth of September, 1796* (Philadelphia: n.p., 1796), p. 21; *Boston Independent Chronicle*, November 23, 1795; OW Sr. to OW Jr., November 23, 1795, in Gibbs, *Memoirs*, 1:269.

19. Jay, *John Jay*, 1:366; "Franklin" is cited in Woodbury, "Public Opinion," *Smith College* 5 (1919–20):82ff; F. Ames to Thomas Dwight, December 30, 1795, in Ames, *Fisher Ames*, 1:180; JA to AA, December 12, 1795, the Adams Papers.

20. *Aurora*, April 1, 1796.

21. JA to AA, March 1, 1796, in Adams, *JA-AA*, p. 206; OW to William Heth, June 19, 1796, in Gibbs, *Memoirs*, 1:362.

22. GW to AH, June 26, 1796, in Fitzpatrick, *GW*, 35:101; from the president, to OW, July 6, 1796, in Gibbs, *Memoirs*, 1:366; GW to TJ, July 6, and GW to the secretary of state, July 18, 1796, in Fitzpatrick, *GW*, 35:118–20, 144–45.

23. *Boston Independent Chronicle*, September 1, 1796; *Columbian Museum* (Savannah), September 27, 1796, cited in Stephen G. Kurtz, *The Presidency of John Adams: The Collapse of Federalism 1795–1800* (New York: A.S. Barnes, 1961), p. 87.

24. Samuel Flagg Bemis, "Washington's Farewell Address: A Foreign Policy of Independence," *AHR* 39 (1934):250, 263.

25. Henry Cabot Lodge, *The Works of Alexander Hamilton*, 12 vols. (New York: G.P. Putnam's Sons, 1904), 8:203; Flexner, *GW*, 4:293.

26. Duane, *Letter to GW*, respectively, pp. 6, 5, 47–48, 21, 10–11.

27. Gibbs, *Memoirs*, 1:377; abuse as a factor in GW's retirement is emphasized in John C. Miller, *Crisis in Freedom: The Alien and Sedition Acts* (Boston: Little, Brown, 1951), p. 27; DeConde, *Entangling Alliance*, pp. 64–65, 462; John C. Miller, *The Federalist Era, 1789–1801*, New American Nation Series (New York: Harper and Row, 1960), p. 196; Bassett, *Federalist System*, p. 142.

28. Samuel Eliot Morison, *By Land and by Sea: Essays and Addresses* (New York: Knopf, 1953), p. 175.

29. GW to David Humphreys, June 12, 1796, in Fitzpatrick, *GW*, 35:91–92; Rush to JA, June 4, 1812, in John A. Schutz and Douglass Adair, eds., *The Spur of Fame: Dialogues of . . . John Adams and Benjamin Rush, 1805–1813* (San Marino, Calif.: Huntington Library, 1966), p. 223.

30. Duane, *Letter to GW*, p. 34; *Aurora*, December 21, 1796.

31. Smith, *JA*, 2:909; Flexner, *GW*, 4:245; *Aurora*, October 17, 1796.

32. Thomas Paine, *Letter to George Washington, President of the United States of America, on Affairs Public and Private* (Philadelphia, 1796), pp. 63–64; GW to David Stuart, January 8, 1797, in Fitzpatrick, *GW*, 35:358–59; JA to AA, December 4, 1796, in Adams, *JA-AA*, 2:231.

33. *Minerva* (New York), March 3, 1797; *American Mercury* (Hartford), March 6 and 20, 1797; celebrations appeared, for example, in *Kline's Carlisle Weekly Gazette*, March 8, 1797.

34. Miller, *Crisis*, p. 29; *Aurora*, March 6 and 14, 1797.

35. GW was defended in, for example, *Connecticut Courant*, March 6, 1797, *Providence Gazette*, March 25, 1797, and *Gazette of the United States*, March 13, 1797; *American Mercury* (Hartford), March–June 5, 1797; *Federal Gazette* (Boston), January 6, 1798.

36. GW to the secretary of war, August 14, 1797, in Fitzpatrick, *GW*, 36:8; OW to GW, January 30, 1798, in Gibbs, *Memoirs*, 2:12; GW to John Nicholas, March 8, 1798, in Fitzpatrick, *GW*, 36:182–83; Flexner, *GW*, 4:387.

37. Marshall Smelser, "George Washington and the Alien and Sedition Acts," *AHR* 59 (1953–1954):327, 329, 334; Flexner, *GW*, respectively, 4:479, 423; the letter involved is from GW to Pickering, August 4, 1799, in Fitzpatrick, *GW*, 37:322–24.

38. James Thomson Callender, *The Prospect Before Us*, 2 vols. (Richmond: James Thomson Callender, 1800), 1:18; GW to the secretary of state, October 18, 1798, in Fitzpatrick, *GW*, 36:498; Smith, *JA*, 2:1024; Cobbett to E. Thornton, January 20, 1800, in G.D.H. Cole, ed., *Letters from William Cobbett to Edward Thornton Written in the Years 1797 to 1800* (London: Oxford University Press, 1937), p. 37; Stewart, *Opposition Press*, p. 509; Warren, *Jacobin*, p. 151.

39. Kurtz, *Presidency*, p. 9.

Chapter Five

1. John T. Morse, Jr., ed., *John Adams*, American Statesman Series (Boston: Houghton Mifflin, 1884), pp. 268–69.

2. Adams's political thought and scholarship are well treated in John R. Howe, Jr., *The Changing Political Thought of John Adams* (Princeton, N.J.: Princeton University Press, 1966); Edward Handler, *America and Europe in the Political Thought of John Adams* (Cambridge: Harvard University Press, 1964); Alfred Iacuzzi, *John Adams, Scholar* (New York: S.F. Vanni, 1952); Zoltan Haraszti, *John Adams and the Prophets of Progress* (New York: Grosset and Dunlap, 1952).

3. Page Smith, *John Adams*, 2 vols. (Garden City, N.Y.: Doubleday, 1962), 1:273; L.H. Butterfield, ed., *The Adams Papers; Diary and Autobiography of John Adams* (New York: Atheneum, 1964), 1:lxiii.

4. Stewart Mitchell, ed., *New Letters of Abigail Adams, 1788–1801* (Boston: Houghton Mifflin, 1947), xii; John Spencer Bassett, *The Federalist System, 1789–1801*, vol. 11 of *The American Nation: A History*, edited by A.B. Hart, 28 vols. (New York: Harper and Brothers, 1906), pp. 6–7; Morton Borden, *Parties and Politics in the Early Republic, 1789–1815* (New York: Thomas Y. Crowell, 1967), p. 42; Butterfield, *Diary and Autobiography*, 1:lxiii; Smith, *JA*, 1:558.

5. Gilbert Chinard, *Honest John Adams* (Boston: Little, Brown, 1964), p. 250.

6. Ben Franklin to Robert R. Livingston, July 22, 1783, in A.H. Smyth, ed., *The Writings of Benjamin Franlin* (New York: Macmillan, 1905–1907), 9:62.

7. James Thomas Flexner, *George Washington: Anguish and Farewell* (1793–1799), vol. 4 of *George Washington* (Boston: Little, Brown, 1969), p. 137.

8. Smith, *JA*, 1:70–71.

9. Butterfield, *Diary and Autobiography*, 3:316, 324, 360, 387; JA to John Trumbull, April 2, 1790, The Adams Papers, Adams Manuscript Trust, Massachusetts Historical Society.

10. John R. Howe, Jr., *The Changing Political Thought of John Adams* (Princeton, N.J.: Princeton University Press, 1966), p. 26; Diary, March 14, 1759, in *Butterfield, Diary and Autobiography*, 1:78; Butterfield, *Diary and Autobiography*, 3:335.

11. TJ to J. Madison, July 29, 1789, in Paul Leicester Ford, ed., *The Writings of Thomas Jefferson*, 10 vols. (New York: G.P. Putnam and Sons, 1894), 5:104.

12. Charles Francis Adams, *The Works of John Adams, Second President of the United States*, 10 vols. (Boston: Charles C. Little and James Brown, 1851), 5:488–89; comments on Turgot in Zoltan Haraszti, *John Adams and the Prophets of Progress* (New York: Grosset and Dunlap, 1952), p. 151.

13. Butterfield, *Diary and Autobiography*, 3:349; Samuel Eliot Morison, *The Life and Letters of Harrison Gray Otis, Federalist, 1765–1848*, 2 vols. (Boston: Houghton Mifflin, 1913), 1:104.

14. JA to AA, January 24, 1793, in Charles Francis Adams, ed., *Letters of John Adams, Addressed to His Wife*, 2 vols. (Boston: Charles C. Little and James Brown, 1841), 2:121.

15. See Haraszti, *JA and the Prophets*, p. 3; Flexner, *GW*, 4:332; James Truslow Adams, *The Adams Family* (Boston: Little, Brown, 1930), p. 55; JA to Rush, April 4, 1790, Adams Papers.

16. Butterfield, *Diary and Autobiography*, 3:336.

17. Butterfield, *Diary and Autobiography*, 2:44; Edmund S. Morgan, "John Adams and the Puritan Tradition," *New England Quarterly*, 34 (1961):520.

18. Morse, *JA*, p. 147; Butterfield, *Diary and Autobiography*, 4:5; Diary, November 13, 1782, in Butterfield, *Diary and Autobiography*, 3:54; JA to Mrs. Warren, December 12, 1785, Adams Papers.

19. JA to Justice Cushing, September 8, 1789, Adams Papers; JA to AA, March 12, 1796, in Adams, *JA-AA*, 2:211.

20. Clinton Rossiter, "The Legacy of John Adams," *Yale Review* 46 (1957):532.

21. Diary, August 20, 1770, in Butterfield, *Diary and Autobiography*, 1:363; JA to AA, August 8, 1776, in L.H. Butterfield, ed., *Adams Family Correspondence*, 2 vols. (Cambridge: Belknap Press of Harvard University Press, 1963), 2:100.

22. JA to AA, March 1, 1796, in Adams, *Works of JA*, 1:487; on Adams's dislike of Catholics, see, for example, Alfred Iacuzzi, *John Adams Scholar* (New York: S.F. Vanni, 1952), p. 233ff.

23. Alexander DeConde, *The Quasi-War: The Politics and Diplomacy of the Undeclared War with France, 1797–1801* (New York: C. Scribner's Sons, 1966), pp. 4–5; George Gibbs, *Memoirs of the Administration of Washington and John Adams; Edited from the Papers of Oliver Wolcott, Secretary of the Treasury*, 2 vols. (New York: William Van Norden, 1846), 1:457; Lester J. Cappon, ed., *The Adams-Jefferson Letters: The Complete Correspondence Between Thomas Jefferson and Abigail and John Adams*, 2 vols. (Chapel Hill: University of North Carolina Press, 1959), 2:287; "Essay on Self-Delusion," c. 1763, in Adams, *Works of JA*, 3:432; JA to Rush, February 17, 1790, Adams Papers.

24. Smith, *JA*, 1:35; Douglass Adair, ed., "James Madison's Autobiography," *WMQ*, 3d ser., 2 (1945):195.

25. Iacuzzi, *JA Scholar*, pp. 21–25; Claude G. Bowers, *Jefferson and Hamilton: The Struggle for Democracy in America* (Boston: Houghton Mifflin, 1966), p. 326; Adams, *Adams Family*, p. 20; for salty comment by JA, see for

example, Smith, *JA*, 2:1095 and 1108; on slavery see the Adams Papers, reel 123, *passim*.

26. Marshall Smelser, "The Federalist Period as an Age of Passion," *AQ* 10 (1958):392; Joseph Charles, *The Origins of the American Party System: Three Essays* (New York: Harper and Row, 1956), p. 54; Haraszti, *JA and the Prophets*, p. 46.

27. Smith, *JA*, 1:9, 12; Butterfield, *Diary and Autobiography*, 3:257ff; JA to B. Waterhouse, February 19,'1805, in Worthington Chauncey Ford, ed., *Statesman and Friend: Correspondence of John Adams with Benjamin Waterhouse, 1784–1822* (Boston: Little, Brown, 1927), pp. 11–13; Butterfield, *Diary and Autobiography*, 3:260–61; Smith, *JA*, 1:6.

28. Butterfield, *Diary and Autobiography*, 3:262–63; JA to Nathan Webb, October 12, 1755, in Adams, *Works of JA*, 1:23; Adams, *Works of JA*, 1:44; Butterfield, *Diary and Autobiography*, 3:272.

29. Chinard, *Honest JA*, p. 56; Weisberger, *Newspaperman*, p. 27; Butterfield, *Diary and Autobiography*, 1:215 and 217; Adams, *Works of JA*, 1:64ff; John Robert Irelan, *History of the Life, Administration, and Times of John Adams, Second President of the United States*, vol. 2 of *The Republic* (Chicago: Fairbank and Palmer, 1886), p. 86.

30. Adams, *Works of JA*, 1:61; Hiller B. Zobel, *The Boston Massacre* (New York: Norton, 1970); L. Kinvin Wroth and Hiller B. Zobel, eds., *Legal Papers of John Adams*, 3 vols. (Cambridge: Belknap Press of Harvard University Press, 1965), vol. 3.

31. JA to TJ, August 24, 1815, in Cappon, *Adams-Jefferson*, 2:455; "Novanglus #3," in Adams, *Works of JA*, 3:457.

32. JA to AA, c. 1774, in Adams, *Works of JA*, 1:150; Adams, *JA Works*, 179ff; Butterfield, *Diary and Autobiography*, 3:360.

33. Chinard, *Honest JA*, pp. 108–09; Diary, September 21, 1777, in Butterfield, *Diary and Autobiography*, 2:265; Leonard Baker, *John Marshall: A Life in Law*, (New York: Macmillan, 1974), p. 40.

34. Morse, *JA*, pp. 148–49; Butterfield, *Diary and Autobiography*, 4:10; Janet Whitney, *Abigail Adams* (Boston: Little, Brown, 1947), p. 147; Smith, *JA*, 1:543, 465–66.

35. Smith, *JA*, 1:466; JA to John Taylor, c. 1814, in Adams, *Works of JA*, 6:513; Diary, June 18, 1779, in Butterfield, *Diary and Autobiography*, 2:383.

36. Butterfield, *Diary and Autobiography*, 4:69, 118; Winslow C. Watson, *Men and Times of the Revolution: or Memoirs of Elkanah Watson* (New York: Dana, 1856), p. 287; JA to Rush, April 12, 1809, in Adams, *Works of JA*, 9:619.

37. Adams, *Works of JA*, 1:418; Smith, *JA*, 2:627, 647; Diary, July 20, 1786, in Butterfield, *Diary and Autobiography*, 3:195; AA to TJ, June 6, 1786, and TJ to AA, June 21, July 7, and September 25, 1785, in Cappon, *Adams-Jefferson*, 1:29–30, 34–37, 70.

38. Edward Handler, *America and Europe in the Political Thought of John Adams* (Cambridge: Harvard University Press, 1964), p. 109; Chinard, *Honest JA*, p. 159; Watson, *Watson*, p. 209.

39. "Thoughts on Government," in Adams, *Works of JA*, 4:195.

40. JA to TJ, March 1, 1787, in Cappon, *Adams-Jefferson*, 1:176; Adams, *Works of JA*, 4:227.

41. TJ to JA, August 30, and JA to TJ, December 6, 1787, in Cappon, *Adams-Jefferson*, 1:195ff, and 213.

42. Haraszti, *JA and the Prophets*, p. 15; Adams, *Works of JA*, respectively, 6:445, 1:439.

43. Smith, *JA*, 2:937; on integration, see 2:926; on nativism, see, for example, AA to Mary Cranch, January 9, 1791, in Mitchell, *Letters-AA*, p. 69.

44. GW to the secretary of war, January 1, and GW to Benjamin Lincoln, January 31, 1789, in John C. Fitzpatrick, ed., *The Writings of George Washington*, 39 vols. (Washington, D.C.: U.S. Government Printing Office, 1939), 30:174, 190; Flexner, *GW*, 3:161, 214.

45. Smith, *JA*, 2:739 and 752; Whitney, *AA*, p. 226.

46. JA to Arnold Welles, May 21, 1789, Adams Papers; JA to Rush, April 18, 1790, in Adams, *Works of JA*, 9:566–67; Adams, *Works of JA*, 1:444–45; JA to [?], May 17, 1789, Adams Papers.

47. *Gazette of the United States*, April 18–22, 1789, and April 28, 1790, to April 23, 1791; Adams, *Works of JA*, 6:272n; *Boston Independent Chronicle*, July 9, 1789.

48. On appointments, see, for example, JA to Wm. Kimman, May 22, 1789, Adams Papers; Adams, *Works of JA*, 1:449–50; AA to Mary Cranch, October 4 and August 9, 1789, in Mitchell, *Letters-AA*, respectively, pp. 28–29 and 20–21.

49. Clinton Rossiter, ed., *The Federalist Papers* (New York: New American Library, 1961), p. 511; JA to Rush, July 5 and 24, 1789, Adams Papers. Maclay is cited in Charles D. Hazen, *Contemporary American Opinion of the French Revolution*, vol. 16 of Johns Hopkins University Studies in History and Political Science, edited by Herbert Baxter Adams (Baltimore: Johns Hopkins University Press, 1897), pp. 143–44; *Massachusetts Centinel* (Boston), August 22, 1789.

50. JA to GW, May 17, 1789, in Adams, *Works of JA*, 8:491; JA to General Lincoln, June 19, 1789, Adams Papers.

51. JA to Roger Sherman, c. July 1789, in Adams, *Works of JA*, 6:434; JA to James Lovell, September 1, 1789, in Adams, *Works of JA*, 8:494; Manning J. Dauer, *The Adams Federalists* (Baltimore: Johns Hopkins University Press, 1968), p. 65; JA to John Trumbull, January 23, 1791, in Adams, *Works of JA*, 9:573; Smith, *JA*, 2:866.

52. Smith, *Pretensions*, pp. 22–23; Morse, *JA*, p. 254; Smith, *JA*, 2:822; John Gardner, *A Brief Consideration of the Important Services, and Distinguished Virtues and Talents Which Recommend Mr. Adams for the Presidency of the United States* (Boston: Manning and Loring, 1796), p. 13; JA to J. Trumbull, March 9, 1790, Adams Papers; H. Knox to JA, June 10, 1791, in Adams, *Works of JA*, 8:503.

53. Smith, *JA*, 2:815–16; JA to TJ, July 29, 1791, in Cappon, *Adams-Jefferson*, 1:247–49; TJ to the president of the United States, May 8, 1791, in Paul Leicester Ford, *The Writings of Thomas Jefferson*, 10 vols. (New York: G.P. Putnam and Sons, 1894), 5:329; *Boston Independent Chronicle*, August 26, 1791; JA to "A Recluse Man," January 19, 1792, in Adams, *Works of JA*, 8:512–13.

54. Gibbs, *Memoirs*, 1:79; *National Gazette*, July 7, 1792; "Valerius" in *National Gazette*, March 29, 1792; *Gazette of the United States*, September 26, 1792; Lisle A. Rose, *Prologue to Democracy: The Federalists in the South, 1789–1800* (Lexington: University of Kentucky Press, 1968), p. 35; JA to AA, January 14, 1793, in Adams, *JA-AA*, 2:119.

55. TJ to Thomas Pinckney, December 3, 1792, in Ford, *Writings of TJ*, 6:144; Malone, *TJ*, 2:367–68, 482; AH to JA, June 25 and September 9, 1792, in Adams, *Works of JA*, 8:514–15.

56. JA to AA, c. late 1792 or early 1793, in Adams, *Works of JA*, 1:494–95.

57. JA to AA, February 27, 1793, in Adams, *JA-AA*, 2:127; *National Gazette*, September 7, 1793; JA to AA, December 19, 1793, in Adams, *JA-AA*, 2:133; Adams's thinking on France is touched on in Hazen, *Opinion*, p. 152, and Haraszti, *JA and the Prophets*, p. 36.

58. JA to AA, January 2, March 12, March 15, and April 15, 1794, in Adams, *JA-AA*, 2:134–35, 146; Adams, *Works of JA*, 1:468, 471; JA to AA, November 26, 1794, Adams Papers.

59. Smith, *JA*, 2:883, 909; AA to JA, February 14, 1796, Adams Papers, cited in Smith, *JA*, 2:881.

60. Mitchell, *Letters-AA*, p. xxxv.

61. Adams, *Works of JA*, 4:284.

62. JA to AA, January 20 and February 10, 1796, in Adams, *JA-AA*, 2:191, 197.

63. JA to AA, January 23, 1796, in Adams, *JA-AA*, 2:192–93; Rose, *Prologue*, p. 123.

64. JA to TJ, April 6, 1796, in Cappon, *Adams-Jefferson*, 1:261; JA to AA, April 9, 1796, in Adams, *JA-AA*, 2:217.

65. "A Federalist," in *Gazette of the United States*, November 9, 1796; *Letter from Alexander Hamilton, Concerning the Public Conduct and Character of John Adams, Esq., President of the United States* (New York: George F. Hopkins, 1800), p. 12; Gibbs, *Memoirs*, 1:396–97; Robert Goodloe Harper to Ralph Izard, November 4, 1796, in U.B. Phillips, "South Carolina Federalist Correspondence, 1789–1797," *AHR*, 14 (1908–1909):783.

66. Gardner, *Brief Consideration*, p. 5.

67. Diary, August 11, 1796, in Butterfield, *Diary and Autobiography*, 3:240; *Aurora*, September 13 and October 17, 1796; Dumas Malone, *Jefferson and the Ordeal of Liberty*, vol. 3 of *Jefferson and His Time* (Boston: Little, Brown, 1962), p. 283; Smith, *JA*, 2:898; John Bach McMaster, *A History of the People of the United States, From the Revolution to the Civil War*, 5 vols. (New York: D. Appleton, 1885), 2:296; *Aurora*, November 4, 1796; Philadelphia *New World*, November 30, 1796; Smith, *Pretensions*, p. 17.

68. Henry William Elson, *History of the United States of America*, 5 vols. (New York: Macmillan, 1905), 2:202; JA to AA, November 27, 1796, in Adams, *JA-AA*, 2:229–30; John Wood, *The Suppressed History of the Administration of John Adams (from 1797–1801), As Printed and Suppressed in 1802* (Philadelphia: John H. Sherburne, 1846), pp. 32–33; TJ to JA, December 28, 1796, in Cappon, *Adams-Jefferson*, 1:262–63.

69. Stephen G. Kurtz, *The Presidency of John Adams: The Collapse of Federalism 1795–1800* (New York: A.S. Barnes, 1961), p. 283; OW to AH, June 14, 1796, in Gibbs, *Memoirs*, 1:359, shows Washington's willingness to consult AH during his terms; see also AH to OW, October 26 and 27, and OW to AH, October 29, 1795, in Gibbs, *Memoirs*, 1:261; JA to AA, January 1, 1796, in Adams, *Works of JA*, 1:483, shows Adams's understanding of the problems of cabinet replacements; JA to TJ, July 3, 1813, in Cappon, *Adams-Jefferson*, 2:349; Gibbs, *Memoirs*, 1:450, cites Wolcott's resignation.

70. *Aurora*, February 3, 1797; JA to Gerry, February 13, 1797, in Adams, *JA Works*, 8:523; Rossiter, "Legacy," p. 530, sees the cabinet retention as JA's greatest error; for a jaundiced view of Adams on patronage, see Gaillard Hunt,

"Office Seeking During the Administration of John Adams," *AHR* 2 (1896–97):241–42; AH to OW, April 5, 1797, in Gibbs, *Memoirs*, 1:490; Adams's thoughts on Hamilton, in addition to those cited earlier, can be found in Butterfield, *Diary and Autobiography*, 3:435; Dauer, *Federalists*, p. 122; Marshall Smelser, *Congress Founds the Navy, 1787–1798* (Notre Dame, Ind.: University of Notre Dame Press, 1959), p. 139.

71. Flexner, *GW*, 4:409–10, 428–29.

72. Bowers, *Jefferson*, p. 315, provides the Ali Baba allusion; Doris A. Graber, *Public Opinion, the President, and Foreign Policy: Four Case Studies from the Formative Years* (New York: Holt, Rinehart, and Winston, 1968), p. 85; Leonard D. White, *The Federalists: A Study in Administrative History, 1789–1801* (New York: Free Press, 1948), pp. 42, 42n, provides fairly concise dates of JA's absences.

73. Flexner, *GW*, 4:55; White, *Federalists*, p. 43; Chinard, *Honest JA*, p. 285; Iacuzzi, *JA Scholar*, p. 204.

74. Smith, *JA*, 1:313; Adams, *Works of JA*, 1:439; JA to Rush, February 17, 1790, Adams Papers; Bassett, *Federalist*, p. 156; JA to Gerry, February 20, 1797, in Worthington Chauncey Ford, *Warren-Adams Letters: Being Chiefly Correspondence Among John Adams, Samuel Adams, and James Warren*, 2 vols. (Boston: Massachusetts Historical Society, 1925), 2:330; JA to Joseph Ward, April 6, 1797, in Adams, *Works of JA*, 9:575; JA to Thomas Johnson, April 26, 1798, in Adams, *Works of JA*, 8:572; Howe, *Changing Political Thought*, p. 208.

Chapter Six

1. Bernard Fay, *The Two Franklins: Fathers of American Democracy* (Boston: Little, Brown, 1933), p. 307.

2. *Aurora*, December 21, 1796; TJ to Madison, January 1, and TJ to Archibald Stuart, January 4, 1797, in Paul Leicester Ford, ed., *The Writings of Thomas Jefferson*, 10 vols. (New York: G.P. Putnam and Sons, 1894), 7:99, 103.

3. *Aurora*, January 6, 7, 9, and 10, 1797; Chauncey Goodrich to OW Sr., January 9 and 18, 1797, in George Gibbs, *Memoirs of the Administration of Washington and John Adams; Edited from the Papers of Oliver Wolcott, Secretary of the Treasury*, 2 vols. (New York: William Van Norden, 1846), 1:417, 437.

4. *Aurora*, February 22, 1797.

5. Stephen G. Kurtz, *The Presidency of John Adams: The Collapse of Federalism, 1795–1800* (New York: A.S. Barnes, 1961), p. 239.

6. James D. Richardson, ed., *A Compilation of the Messages and Papers of the Presidents, 1789–1902*, 10 vols. (Washington: Bureau of National Literature and Art, 1904), 1:229, 231–32.

7. Gilbert Chinard, *Honest John Adams* (Boston: Little, Brown, 1964), p. 259; Page Smith, *John Adams*, 2 vols. (Garden City, N.Y.: Doubleday, 1962), 2:923.

8. Charles Francis Adams, *The Works of John Adams, Second President of the United States*, 10 vols. (Boston: Charles C. Little and James Brown, 1851), 1:507; JA to AA, March 5 and 9, 1797, in Charles Francis Adams, ed., *Letters of John Adams, Addressed to His Wife*, 2 vols. (Boston: Charles C. Little and James Brown, 1841), 2:2, 247–48.

9. Kurtz, *Presidency*, p. 222; Letter 13 to the *Boston Patriot*, in Adams, *JA Works*, 9:285; a more contemporary account of the incident is JA to Gerry, April 6, 1797, in Adams, *Works of JA*, 8:538.

10. Dumas Malone, *Jefferson and the Ordeal of Liberty*, vol. 3 of *Jefferson and His Time* (Boston: Little, Brown, 1962), p. 298.

11. *Minerva* (New York), March 7, 1797; *Farmer's Weekly Museum*, March 21, 1797; Hartford *American Mercury*, March 6 and 13, 1797.

12. *Readinger Adler*, March 14, 1797; *Minerva* (Philadelphia), March 4, 1797; *Claypoole's American Daily Advertiser*, March 3, 4, and 6, 1797.

13. *Boston Independent Chronicle*, March 6, 1797; *Boston Gazette*, March 6, 1797; *Connecticut Courant*, March 13, 1797.

14. *Gazette of the United States*, March 6, 7, 10, and 13, 1797; *Porcupine's Gazette*, March 4 and 7, 1797.

15. *Centinel of Freedom*, March 1, 8, 15, 1797; *Argus* (New York), March 1797, cited in John Bach McMaster, *A History of the People of the United States, from the Revolution to the Civil War*, 5 vols. (New York: D. Appleton, 1885), 2:310; *Aurora*, March 9 and 10, 1797.

16. *New Hampshire Gazette*, March 11, 1797; *Salem Gazette*, March 17, 1797; this was borrowed from some other source, as the same phrases appeared in *Kline's Carlisle Weekly Gazette*, March 15, 1797.

17. Adams's inaugural was printed without comment in the following Federalist-oriented sheets: *Columbian Centinel* (Boston), March 15, 1797; *United States Chronicle* (Providence), March 16, 1797; *Massachusetts Mercury*, March 17, 1797; *Middlesex Gazette*, March 24, 1797; *Courier of New Hampshire*, March 28, 1797.

18. *Aurora*, March 11 and 14, 1797; *Boston Independent Chronicle*, March 16, 1797.

19. JA to AA, March 17, 1797, in Adams, *JA-AA*, 2:252.

20. Knox to JA, March 19, and JA to Knox, March 30, 1797, in Adams, *Works of JA*, 8:532–33, 535.

21. *Aurora*, March 20, 1797; Lewis Leary, *That Rascal Freneau: A Study in Literary Failure* (New Brunswick, N.J.: Rutgers University Press, 1941), pp. 279–81; Alexander DeConde, *Entangling Alliance: Politics and Diplomacy Under George Washington* (Durham, N.C.: Duke University Press, 1958), p. 493.

22. See Lisle A. Rose, *A Prologue to Democracy: The Federalists in the South, 1789–1800* (Lexington: University of Kentucky Press, 1968), pp. 158–60, for the best treatment of North Carolina editors' volte-face.

23. *Aurora*, March 23, 1797; *Courier of New Hampshire*, March 23, 1797; *Boston Gazette*, April 3, 1797, contains examples of reprints from the *Aurora* before Bache became subdued; *Farmer's Weekly Museum*, April 4, 1797.

24. *Kline's Carlisle Weekly Gazette*, April 5, 1797.

25. Cited in Marshall Smelser, *Congress Founds the Navy, 1787–1798* (Notre Dame, Ind.: University of Notre Dame Press, 1959), p. 105.

26. Uriah Tracy to OW Sr., March 15, OW Sr. to OW Jr., March 20, and George Cabot to OW Jr., April 6, 1797, in Gibbs, *Memoirs*, 1:475, 476, 521.

27. E. Watson to JA, March 5, JA to E. Watson, March 17, and E. Watson to JA, April 1, 1797, in Winslow C. Watson, *Men and Times of the Revolution: or Memoirs of Elkanah Watson* (New York: Dana, 1856), pp. 345–47; Gibbs, *Memoirs*, 1:481; *Letter from Alexander Hamilton, Concerning the Public Conduct and Character of John Adams, Esq., President of the United States* (New York: George F. Hopkins, 1800), p. 20.

28. Alexander DeConde, *The Quasi-War: The Politics and Diplomacy of the*

Undeclared War with France, 1797–1801 (New York: C. Scribner's Sons, 1966), p. 23; JA to AA, April 24, 1797, in Adams, *JA-AA*, 2:254; *Aurora*, April 17 and 18, 1797.

29. G. Cabot to OW, May 1, 1797, in Gibbs, *Memoirs*, 1:250.

Chapter Seven

1. James D. Richardson, ed., *A Compilation of the Messages and Papers of the Presidents, 1789–1902*, 10 vols. (Washington, D.C.: Bureau of National Literature and Art, 1904), 1:233–39.

2. AA to Mary Cranch, May 16, 1797, in Stewart Mitchell, ed., *New Letters of Abigail Adams, 1788–1801* (Boston: Houghton Mifflin, 1947), p. 90.

3. Silence was adopted in the first issue of the Federalist *Columbian Centinel* (Boston), May 24, 1797, as well as the Republican *Claypoole's American Daily Advertiser*, May 16 and 17, 1797, and Freneau's New York *Time Piece*, May 19, 1797.

4. *Aurora*, May 18 to 23, 1797; *Time Piece*, May 24, 1797.

5. See TJ to Madison, May 17, 1797, *Jefferson Papers*, Library of Congress, cited in Marshall Smelser, *Congress Founds the Navy, 1787–1798* (Notre Dame, Ind.: University of Notre Dame Press, 1959), p. 108; Richardson, *Messages*, 1:241.

6. *Aurora*, May 24–27, June 6, 13, 19, 1797; the May 29, 1797, *Aurora* printed a column by an "Old American," who disagreed with JA, but the tone of the article is in strikingly dignified contrast to Bache's bile.

7. *Centinel of Freedom* (Newark), May 17 and 24, 1797; *Boston Independent Chronicle*, May 25 and June 1, 1797; see, for example, *Boston Gazette*, June 5, 1797.

8. *Porcupine's Gazette*, May 18, 1797; New York *Minerva*, May 19, 1797; *Columbian Centinel*, May 24, 1797; *Boston Price-Current and Marine Intelligencer*, May 25, 1797; *Massachusetts Mercury* (Boston), May 26 and 30, 1797.

9. *Providence Gazette*, May 27, 1797; *Farmer's Weekly Museum*, May 29 and June 12, 1797; *Norwich Packet*, June 8, 1797; *Connecticut Gazette*, June 11, 1797.

10. C. Goodrich to OW Sr., May 20, G. Cabot to OW, May 24 and 31, James Iredell to OW, June 5, 1797, in George Gibbs, *Memoirs of the Administration of Washington and John Adams; Edited from the Papers of Oliver Wolcott, Secretary of the Treasury*, 2 vols. (New York: William Van Norden, 1846), 1:535–36, 540, 542–543; GW to T. Pinckney, May 28, 1797, in John C. Fitzpatrick, ed., *The Writings of George Washington*, 39 vols. (Washington, D.C.: U.S. Government Printing Office, 1939), 35:453; GW to OW, May 29, 1797, in Gibbs, *Memoirs*, 1:539; W. Smith to Izard, June 2, 1797, in Ulrich Bonnell Phillips, ed., "South Carolina Federalist Correspondence, 1789–1797," *AHR* 14 (1908–1909):790.

11. Alexander DeConde, *The Quasi-War: The Politics and Diplomacy of the Undeclared War with France, 1797–1801* (New York: C. Scribner's Sons, 1966), p. 31; Smelser, *Congress*, p. 109; AA to Mary Cranch, May 24, June 8, and July 6, 1797, in Mitchell, *Letters-AA*, pp. 92, 96–97, 100.

12. Charles Francis Adams, *The Works of John Adams, Second President of the United States*, 10 vols. (Boston: Charles C. Little and James Brown, 1851), 1:510–11, and letter 13 to the *Boston Patriot*, in Adams, *JA Works*, 9:282; AA to Mary Cranch, June 3 and 23, 1797, in Mitchell, *Letters-AA*, pp. 94, 100.

13. Leonard D. White, *The Federalists: A Study in Administrative History*,

1789–1801 (New York: Free Press, 1948), 42n; *Aurora*, August 1797, *passim*, and November 10, 1797; see, for example, *Porcupine's Gazette*, September 9, 1797.

14. JA to Samuel B. Malcom, September 17, and JA to OW, September 15, 1797, Adams Papers, Adams Manuscript Trust, Massachusetts Historical Society.

15. *Time Piece* (New York), October 25, 1797; JA to Pickering, October 26, and JA to OW, October 27, 1797, in Adams, *Works of JA*, 8:557, 559.

16. AA to Mary Cranch, November 15 and December 12, 1797, in Mitchell, *Letters-AA*, pp. 112, 116–17; Richardson, *Messages*, 1:250–51, 256.

17. JA to the heads of departments, January 24, 1798, in Adams, *JA Works*, 8:561ff; AA to Mary Cranch, February 1–5, 1798, in Mitchell, *Letters-AA*, pp. 127–28; GW to the secretary of state, February 6, 1798, in Fitzpatrick, *GW*, 36:156; *Federal Gazette* (Boston), February 5, 1798.

18. AA to Mary Cranch, February 15 and 28, 1798, in Mitchell, *Letters-AA*, pp. 132–33, 135–36; TJ to Madison, March 2, 1798, *Jefferson Papers*, Library of Congress, cited in Page Smith, *John Adams*, 2 vols. (Garden City, N.Y.: Doubleday, 1962), 2:951; Samuel Eliot Morison, *Harrison Gray Otis, 1765–1848: The Urbane Federalist* (Boston: Houghton Mifflin, 1969), p. 128.

19. *Aurora*, February 27, 1798; GW to Alexander White, March 1, 1798, in Fitzpatrick, *GW*, 36:175–76; *Boston Independent Chronicle*, March 4, 1798.

20. JA to the heads of departments, March 13, 1798, in Mitchell, *Letters-AA*, pp. 143–44.

21. Richardson, *Messages*, 1:264.

22. TJ to Madison, March 21, 1798, in Paul Leicester Ford, ed., *The Writings of Thomas Jefferson*, 10 vols. (New York: G.P. Putnam and Sons, 1894), 7:219; *Boston Independent Chronicle*, March 15, 1798; *Aurora*, March 21 and 23, 1798; *Carey's United States Recorder*, March 29, 1798.

23. G. Cabot to OW, March 26, 1798, in Gibbs, *Memoirs*, 2:43; AA to Mary Cranch, March 27, 1798, in Mitchell, *Letters-AA*, p. 48.

24. Jonathan Mason, Jr., to Otis, March 30, 1798, in Samuel Eliot Morison, *The Life and Letters of Harrison Gray Otis, Federalist, 1765–1848*, 2 vols. (Boston: Houghton Mifflin, 1913), 1:93; *Boston Independent Chronicle*, April 2, 1798; *Aurora*, April 2, 1798; *Porcupine's Gazette*, April 3, 1798.

25. Lisle A. Rose, *Prologue to Democracy: The Federalists in the South, 1789–1800* (Lexington: University of Kentucky Press, 1968), p. 166.

26. Morison, *Life-Otis*, 1:83; see also Richard Hildreth, *The History of the United States of America*, 6 vols. (New York: Harper and Brothers, 1880), 5:207; DeConde, *Quasi-War*, p. 77; Bernard Fay, *The Two Franklins: Fathers of American Democracy* (Boston: Little, Brown, 1933), p. 340; Doris A. Graber, *Public Opinion, the President, and Foreign Policy: Four Case Studies from the Formative Years* (New York: Holt, Rinehart, and Winston, 1968), p. 70.

27. DeConde, *Quasi-War*, p. 79; Gibbs, *Memoirs*, 2:39; Adams, *Works of JA*, 2:541.

28. Timothy Pickering, *A Review of the Correspondence Between the Hon. John Adams, Late President of the United States, and the Late Wm. Cunningham, Esq., Beginning in 1803, and Ending in 1812* (Salem, Mass.: Cushing and Appleton, 1824), p. 105.

29. AA to Mary Cranch, April 13, 1798, in Mitchell, *Letters-AA*, p. 156.

30. *Gazette of the United States*, April 6, 1798; *New Hampshire Gazette*, May 15, 1798.

31. AA to Mary Cranch, April 28, 1798, in Mitchell, *Letters-AA*, p. 167; Bache was attacked in print for the remarks in, for example, *Massachusetts Mercury*, May 8, 1798, and *Columbian Centinel*, July 7, 1798.

32. *Providence Gazette*, April 28, 1798; *Porcupine's Gazette*, May 7, 1798.

33. Manning J. Dauer, *The Adams Federalists* (Baltimore: Johns Hopkins University Press, 1968), pp. xxii, 142; Dumas Malone, *Jefferson and the Ordeal of Liberty*, vol. 3 of *Jefferson and His Time* (Boston: Little, Brown, 1962), p. 375.

34. R. Troup to R. King, June 3, and William Bingham to R. King, September 30, 1798, in Charles P. King, *The Life and Correspondence of Rufus King*, 6 vols. (New York: G.P. Putnam's Sons, 1894), 2:329, 425.

35. JA to the students of New Jersey College, n.d., and JA to the inhabitants of Washington County, Maryland, n.d., in Adams, *Works of JA*, 9:207, 214.

36. JA to the mayor, aldermen, and citizens of the city of Philadelphia, April 1798; JA to the inhabitants of the county of Middlesex, Virginia, n.d.; JA to the students of Dickinson College, Pennsylvania, n.d.; JA to the inhabitants of Bridgeton, in the county of Cumberland, in the state of New Jersey, May 1, 1798; and JA to the inhabitants of the town of Hartford, Connecticut, May 10, 1798, in Adams, *JA Works*, respectively, 9:182, 214, 204, 186, and 192.

37. Reprinted in the *Salem Gazette*, June 8, 1798.

38. JA to TJ, June 30, 1813, in Lester J. Cappon, ed., *The Adams-Jefferson Letters: The Complete Correspondence Between Thomas Jefferson and Abigail and John Adams*, 2 vols. (Chapel Hill: University of North Carolina Press, 1959), 2:346; AA to Mary Cranch, May 21, 1798, in Mitchell, *Letters-AA*, p. 178.

39. George Cabot to OW, June 9, 1798, in Gibbs, *Memoirs*, 2:53; *Aurora*, July 14, 1798; *Salem Gazette*, July 20, 1798; *Kline's Carlisle Weekly Gazette*, May 2, 1798; *Connecticut Gazette*, May 23, 1798.

40. Boston *Columbian Centinel*, May 26, 1798; *Political Repository*, August 28, 1798; for the volume of petitions and replies, with occasional propaganda codas, see *Massachusetts Mercury*, beginning May 1, 1798; *Providence Gazette*, beginning May 5, 1798; *Kline's Carlisle Weekly Gazette*, beginning May 9, 1798; *Spectator* (New York), beginning May 9, 1798; *United States Chronicle*, beginning May 10, 1798; *Salem Gazette*, beginning May 15, 1798; *Farmer's Weekly Museum*, May 22, 1798; *Middlesex Gazette*, beginning June 1, 1798; *Green Mt. Patriot*, June 1, 1798; *Norwich Packet*, May 22, June 5, 1798; *Russell's Gazette*, beginning June 7, 1798; *Claypoole's American Daily Advertiser*, beginning July 4, 1798; *Courier of New Hampshire*, July 31, 1798.

41. *Connecticut Courant*, April 2 and 9, 1798; *American Mercury* (Hartford), April 12, 1798.

42. *Time Piece*, April 11, 13, 17, 23, and May 2, 1798.

43. *Carey's United States Recorder*, April 5, 1798.

44. GW to the secretary of state, April 6, 1798, in Fitzpatrick, *GW*, 36:249.

45. AA to Mercy Warren, April 25, 1798, in Worthington Chauncey Ford, *Warren-Adams Letters; Being Chiefly a Correspondence Among John Adams, Samuel Adams, and James Warren*, 2 vols. (Boston: Massachusetts Historical Society, 1925), 2:338.

46. Ames to OW, April 22, 1798, in Gibbs, *Memoirs*, 2:47.

47. For extras, see, for example, *New Hampshire Gazette*, April 19, 1798; *Norwich Packet*, May 1, 1798; poetic patriotism appeared in the *Boston Price-Current and Marine Intelligencer*, April 26, 1798.

48. TJ to Madison, April 26, and TJ to John Taylor, June 1, 1798, in Ford, *Writings of TJ*, 7:246ff, 265.

49. *Centinel of Freedom*, May 1, 8, 1798; *Connecticut Courant*, May 2, 1798; *The Spectator* (New York), May 5, 1798; *Porcupine's Gazette*, May 7, 1798.

50. *Kline's Carlisle Weekly Gazette*, May 15, 1798; *Boston Price-Current and Marine Intelligencer*, May 24, 1798; *American Mercury* (Hartford), May 10, 1798.

51. *Aurora*, May 9, 1798; Thomas Cooper, *Political Essays*, 2d ed. (Philadelphia: Robert Campbell, 1800), p. 1; *Carey's United States Recorder*, May 19, 1798; *Centinel of Freedom*, May 29, 1798.

52. An excellent treatment of Southern opinion is provided in Rose, *Prologue*, pp. 160–73; the conclusion that cautious Southern Federalism previewed the warhawks is mine.

53. GW to AH, May 27, 1798, in Fitzpatrick, *GW*, 36:271; Ames to Pickering, June 4, 1798, in Seth Ames, *Works of Fisher Ames, with a Selection from His Speeches and Correspondence*, 2 vols. (Boston: Little, Brown, 1854), 1:227–28; on Gerry, see AA to Mary Cranch, June 13, 1798, in Mitchell, *Letters-AA*, p. 192; DeConde, *Quasi-War*, p. 106, agrees with AA.

54. JA to the Senate and House of Representatives, June 21, 1798, in Richardson, *Messages*, 1:266.

55. J. Monroe to TJ, June 16, 1798, *Jefferson Papers*, Library of Congress, cited in Smelser, *Congress*, p. 169; *Aurora*, June 16, 1798; *Carey's United States Recorder*, June 21, 1798; *Aurora*, July 18, 19, 1798.

56. See *Russell's Gazette*, June 21, July 19, 1798; *Massachusetts Spy* (Worcester), August 1, 1798.

57. See *Middlesex Gazette*, July 6, 1798; *Massachusetts Spy*, July 11, 1798; *Kline's Carlisle Weekly Gazette*, July 11, 1798; and the Democratic *Claypoole's American Daily Advertiser*, July 14, 1798.

58. Stephen Higginson to OW, July 11, 1798, in Gibbs, *Memoirs*, 2:70–71; *Columbian Centinel*, July 14, 28, 1798; GW to the president of the United States, July 13, 1798, in Fitzpatrick, *GW*, 36:328; *New Hampshire Gazette*, June 12, 1798; *Massachusetts Spy*, July 4, 1798; and John C. Miller, *Crisis in Freedom: The Alien and Sedition Acts* (Boston: Little, Brown, 1951), pp. 8–9.

59. DeConde, *Quasi-War*, p. 94.

60. James Thomas Flexner, *George Washington: Anguish and Farewell* (1793–1799), vol. 4 of *George Washington* (Boston: Little, Brown, 1972), p. 421.

61. Gilbert Chinard, *Honest John Adams* (Boston: Little, Brown, 1964), p. 275.

62. Pollard, *President and the Press*, p. 41; Miller, *Crisis, passim*.

63. Leonard W. Levy, *Freedom of Speech and Press in Early American History: Legacy of Suppression* (New York: Harper and Row, 1963), p. 198; Edward Handler, *America and Europe in the Political Thought of John Adams* (Cambridge: Harvard University Press, 1964), pp. 179–80; Morton Borden, *Parties and Politics in the Early Republic, 1789–1815* (New York: Thomas Y. Crowell, 1967), p. 34; Irving Brant, *The Bill of Rights; Its Origin and Meanings* (Indianapolis: Bobbs-Merrill, 1965), p. 247.

64. Dauer, *Federalists*, pp. 242–43, xxii, respectively, shows Adams to be less extreme than the High-Federalists; Chinard, *Honest JA*, p. 297; Adams, *Works of JA*, 1:561–62, and 8:606.

65. *Columbian Centinel*, May 26, 1798.

66. James Morton Smith, *Freedom's Fetters: The Alien and Sedition Laws and American Civil Liberties* (Ithaca, N.Y.: Cornell University Press, 1966), p. 175; Dauer, *Federalists*, pp. 242–43; Brant, *Rights*, pp. 265, 309; TJ to AA, June 13, 1804, in Cappon, *Adams-Jefferson*, 1:270.

67. Adams, *Works of JA*, 9:291; JA to Rush, December 25, 1811, in John A. Schutz and Douglass Adair, eds., *The Spur of Fame: Dialogues of . . . John Adams and Benjamin Rush, 1805–1813* (San Marino, Calif.: Huntington Library, 1966), p. 201; JA to TJ, June 14, 1813, in Cappon, *Adams-Jefferson*, 2:329; JA to Pickering, August 13, 1799, in Adams, *Works of JA*, 9:13–14; Pickering to JA, July 24, JA to Pickering, August 1, and Pickering to JA, August 1, 1799, in Adams, *Works of JA*, 9:3–7; Chinard, *Honest JA*, p. 297, cites JA's approval of Chase's conduct; TJ to McKean, February 19, 1803, in Ford, *Writings of TJ*, 8:218–19.

68. AA to Mary Cranch, April 21, 26, May 10, 26, June 1, 23, and July 9, 1798, in Mitchell, *Letters-AA*, pp. 159, 164–65, 171–72, 179, 193, 196, and 200.

69. Smith, *Fetters*, p. 151; Miller, *Crisis*, p. 75; Morison, *Otis*, p. 119; Harper to Izard, November 4, 1796, in Phillips, "S.C. Federalist Correspondence," p. 783; Claude G. Bowers, *Jefferson and Hamilton: The Struggle for Democracy in America* (Boston: Houghton Mifflin, 1966), pp. 433–34; Morison, *Otis*, pp. 162, 173.

70. See Goodrich to OW Sr., January 9 and 18, 1797, in Gibbs, *Memoirs*, 1:417, 437; GW to Pickering, February 6, 1798, in Fitzpatrick, *GW*, 36:156; Ames to Pickering, June 4, 1798, in Ames, *Fisher Ames*, 1:227–28; Cabot to OW, March 26, and Higginson to OW, July 11, 1798, in Gibbs, *Memoirs*, 2:43, 70–71; R. Troup to Rufus King, June 3, 1798, in King, *Rufus King*, 2:329; for the volte-face, see OW to Goodrich, July 20, 1800, Cabot to OW, May 2, 1799, Ames to OW, August 3, 1800, Higginson to OW, February 14, 1799, and March 29, 1799, Ames to Goodrich, June 12, 1800, Cabot to OW, June 14, OW to Cabot, June 16, 1800, B. Goodhue to OW, July 10, OW to McHenry, July 18, 1800, and OW to AH, September 3, 1800, in Gibbs, *Memoirs*, respectively, 2:383, 239, 393–96, 179–80, 229–30, 367, 370–71, 379, 381, 416–17; on Pickering and enforcement, see Brant, *Rights*, p. 272; Frank M. Anderson, "The Enforcement of the Alien and Sedition Acts," *AHA Annual Report for the Year 1912* (1914): 119; Levy, *Legacy*, p. 300; Miller, *Crisis*, p. 73; on Adams's mistrust of Pickering, see JA to JQA, June 2, 1797, in Adams, *Works of JA*, 8:545; on Pickering's attempted control of Adams, see Gibbs, *Memoirs*, 2:212–14; Pickering, *Review*, pp. 110, 137; on Marshall, see Miller, *Crisis*, pp. 182–85, and Brant, *Rights*, p. 285ff.

71. Smith, *Fetters*, p. 177; *Porcupine's Gazette*, February 20, 1799; John Ward Fenno, *Desultory Reflections on the New Political Aspects of Public Affairs in the United States of America Since the Commencement of the Year 1799* (New York: John Ward Fenno, 1800), *passim*; Noah Webster to OW, June 23, 1800, in Gibbs, *Memoirs*, 2:373–74.

72. Smith, *Fetters*, pp. 185–87; Brant, *Rights*, p. 279ff; Morison, *Life-Otis*, 1:195; JA to AA, February 22, 1799, in Adams, *Works of JA*, 1:545; John C. Miller, *The Federalist Era, 1789–1801*, New American Nation Series (New York: Harper and Row, 1960), p. 263.

73. See Morison, *Life-Otis*, 1:106; Clarence L. Brigham, *Journals and Journeymen: A Contribution to the History of Early American Newspapers* (Philadelphia: University of Pennsylvania Press, 1950), p. 66; John Bach McMaster, *A History of the People of the United States, from the Revolution to the Civil War*, 5 vols. (New

York: D. Appleton, 1885), 2:389, 397; Frank Luther Mott, *American Journalism; A History: 1690–1960* (New York: Macmillan, 1962), p. 152; Robert W. Jones, *Journalism in the United States* (New York: Dutton, 1947), p. 170; Edwin Emery, *The Press and America: An Interpretive History of Journalism*, 2d ed. (Englewood Cliffs, N.J.: Prentice-Hall, 1962), p. 162; Noble E. Cunningham, Jr., *The Jeffersonian—Republicans: The Formation of Party Organization, 1789–1809* (Chapel Hill: University of North Carolina Press, 1957), p. 126; and others.

74. Levy, *Legacy*, p. xiii.

75. Miller, *Crisis*, pp. 221–22.

76. John Hopkins to OW, in Gibbs, *Memoirs*, 2:108; GW to William Vans Murray, in Fitzpatrick, *GW*, 37:71–72; Rose, *Prologue*, p. 213.

77. JA to Otis, n.d. (1798), in Morison, *Life-Otis*, 1:162; DeConde, *Quasi-War*, p. 77; Morison, *Life-Otis*, 1:99.

78. Adams, *Works of JA*, 1:531; G. Cabot to OW, October 10, 1798, in Gibbs, *Memoirs*, 2:110.

79. AA to Mary Cranch, July 3, 1798, in Mitchell, *Letters-AA*, p. 199; GW to the secretary of war, July 4, 1798, in Fitzpatrick, *GW*, 36:306.

80. See JA to GW, June 22 and July 7, 1798, in Adams, *Works of JA*, 8:573, 575.

81. Federalist support was universal. Most Republican sheets reported the appointment, with the likes of *Readinger Adler*, July 24, 1798, providing mild praise.

82. *The Spectator* (New York), July 28, 1798.

83. *State Gazette of North Carolina* (Edenton), July 18, 1798; Flexner, *GW*, 4:400ff, especially 403, 411.

84. JA to McHenry, August 29, 1798, in Adams, *Works of JA*, 8:588.

85. Flexner, *GW*, 4:397; Stephen G. Kurtz, *The Presidency of John Adams: The Collapse of Federalism, 1795–1800* (New York: A.S. Barnes, 1961), p. 327.

86. Adams, *Works of JA*, 1:530; Gibbs, *Memoirs*, 2:104; Kurtz, *Presidency*, pp. 324–25; DeConde, *Quasi-War*, pp. 98, 112; Chinard, *Honest JA*, pp. 278–79.

87. Rose, *Prologue*, pp. 194–203.

88. Janet Whitney, *Abigail Adams* (Boston: Little, Brown, 1947), p. 283ff; Kurtz, *Presidency*, p. 321; Joseph Charles, *The Origins of the American Party System: Three Essays* (New York: Harper and Row, 1956), p. 71.

89. JA to Pickering, October 20, and JA to McHenry, October 22, 1798, in Adams, *Works of JA*, 8:609, 613.

90. DeConde, *Quasi-War*, pp. 163–65.

91. OW to JA, November 1798, in Gibbs, *Memoirs*, 2:172; F. Ames to Pickering, November 22, 1798, in Ames, *Fisher Ames*, 1:241–42; Webster pushed the navy in, for example, the *Commercial Advertiser* (New York), July 27, 1798.

92. DeConde, *Quasi-War*, pp. 177, 191; Kurtz, *Presidency*, p. 327; DeConde, *Quasi-War*, p. 111.

93. Chinard, *Honest JA*, pp. 297–98; Smith, *JA*, 2:998; Adams, *Works of JA*, 1:538; DeConde, *Quasi-War*, p. 169; Dauer, *Federalists*, p. 226; *Aurora*, December 10, 1798; Boston *Independent Chronicle*, December 24, 1798.

94. Smith, *JA*, 2:971; James Alton James, "French Opinion as a Factor in Preventing War Between France and the United States, 1795–1800," *AHR* 30 (1924):52–53; GW to the president of the United States, July 4, 1798, in Fitzpatrick, *GW*, 36:313–14; see, for example, *New Hampshire Gazette*, June 5, 1798; DeConde, *Quasi-War*, p. 143.

95. DeConde, *Quasi-War*, pp. 157, 160–61.

96. JA to JQA, June 2, 1797, in Adams, *Works of JA*, 8:545; JA to Pickering, October 26, 1798, in Adams, *Works of JA*, 8:614.

97. Richardson, *Messages*, 1:272–73; John Spencer Bassett, *The Federalist System, 1789–1801*, vol. 11 of *The American Nation: A History*, edited by A.B. Hart, 28 vols. (New York: Harper and Brothers, 1906), p. 236; Richardson, *Messages*, 1:275–77.

98. JA to Pickering, January 15, 1799, in Adams, *Works of JA*, 8:621.

99. Flexner, *GW*, 4:426–28; Kurtz, *Presidency*, p. 347; DeConde, *Quasi-War*, p. 173; Smith, *JA*, 2:996; S. Higginson to OW, February 14, 1799, in Gibbs, *Memoirs*, 2:179–80; Richardson, *Messages*, 1:282.

Chapter Eight

1. James D. Richardson, ed., *A Compilation of the Messages and Papers of the Presidents, 1789–1902*, 10 vols. (Washington, D.C.: Bureau of National Literature and Art, 1904), pp. 282–83; Alexander DeConde, *The Quasi-War: The Politics and Diplomacy of the Undeclared War with France, 1797–1801* (New York: C. Scribner's Sons, 1966), p. 179, notes TJ's amazement.

2. JA to GW, February 19, and JA to AA, February 22, 1799, in Charles Francis Adams, *The Works of John Adams, Second President of the United States*, 10 vols. (Boston: Charles C. Little and James Brown, 1851), respectively, 8:626, 1:544–45.

3. Letter 5 to the *Boston Patriot*, in Adams, *Works of JA*, 9:250–79; Alexander DeConde, *The Quasi-War: The Politics and Diplomacy of the Undeclared War with France, 1797–1801* (New York: C. Scribner's Sons, 1966), p. 185, discusses Ellsworth's intervention; Richardson, *Messages*, 1:284.

4. Letter 4 to the *Boston Patriot*, in Adams, *Works of JA*, 9:248; JA to AA, February 22 and 25, 1799, in Adams, *Works of JA*, 1:545, 547.

5. GW to Major General AH, February 25, 1799, in John C. Fitzpatrick, ed., *The Writings of George Washington*, 39 vols. (Washington, D.C.: U.S. Government Printing Office, 1939), 37:137; TJ to James Madison, February 26, 1799, in Paul Leicester Ford, ed., *The Writings of Thomas Jefferson*, 10 vols. (New York: G.P. Putnam's Sons, 1894), 7:370.

6. John Ward Fenno, *Desultory Reflections on the New Political Aspects of Public Affairs in the United States of America Since the Commencement of the Year 1799* (New York: John Ward Fenno, 1800), pp. 6–8, 8n, 21–22, 31; Timothy Pickering, *A Review of the Correspondence Between the Hon. John Adams, Late President of the United States, and the Late Wm. Cunningham, Esq., Beginning in 1803, and Ending in 1812* (Salem, Mass.: Cushing and Appleton, 1824), pp. 110, 137; George Gibbs, *Memoirs of the Administration of Washington and John Adams; Edited from the Papers of Oliver Wolcott, Secretary of the Treasury*, 2 vols. (New York: William Van Norden, 1846), 2:184–85; see also Richard Hildreth, *The History of the United States of America*, 6 vols. (New York: Harper and Brothers, 1880), 5:290.

7. DeConde, *Quasi-War*, pp. 181–82; Samuel Eliot Morison, *Harrison Gray Otis, 1765–1848: The Urbane Federalist* (Boston: Houghton Mifflin, 1969), p. 161.

8. DeConde, *Quasi-War*, p. 179; James Thomson Callender, *The Prospect Before Us*, 2 vols. (Richmond: James Thomson Callender, 1800), 1:85; Thomas

Woodrow Wilson, *A History of the American People*, 5 vols. (New York: William H. Wise, 1931), 3:160; Hildreth, *History*, 5:288; Page Smith, *John Adams*, 2 vols. (Garden City, N.Y.: Doubleday, 1962), 2:1002.

9. Marshall Smelser, "The Federalist Period as an Age of Passion," *AQ* 10 (1958): 414; Samuel Eliot Morison, *The Life and Letters of Harrison Gray Otis, Federalist, 1765–1848*, 2 vols. (Boston: Houghton Mifflin, 1913), 1:182; R. Troup to Rufus King, April 19, 1799, in Charles R. King, *The Life and Correspondence of Rufus King*, 6 vols. (New York: G.P. Putnam's Sons, 1894), 2:596–97.

10. Letters 1, 2, and 10 to the *Boston Patriot*, in Adams, *Works of JA*, 9:241–44, 270–72.

11. H. Knox to JA (Secret and Confidential), March 5, 1799, in Adams, *Works of JA*, 8:626–27; Smith, *JA*, 2:1000–01; DeConde, *Quasi-War*, p. 183; JA to Charles Lee, March 29, 1799, in Adams, *Works of JA*, 8:629.

12. Donald H. Stewart, *The Opposition Press of the Federalist Period* (Albany: State University of New York Press, 1969), p. 335.

13. *Aurora*, February 19-21, 1799.

14. *Centinel of Freedom*, February 26, March 5, 1799; *Claypoole's American Daily Advertiser*, February 19, 1799; *Kline's Carlisle Weekly Gazette*, February 27, 1799.

15. *Gazette of the United States*, February 22, 28, and March 4, 1799.

16. *Porcupine's Gazette*, February 20, 1799; William Cobbett, *Porcupine's Works*, 12 vols. (London: Cobbett and Morgan, 1801), 10:151–53; *Porcupine's Gazette*, February 27, 1799.

17. Doris A. Graber, *Public Opinion, the President, and Foreign Policy: Four Case Studies from the Formative Years* (New York: Holt, Rinehart, and Winston, 1968), pp. 77–78; Manning J. Dauer, *The Adams Federalists* (Baltimore: Johns Hopkins University Press, 1968), p. 232; Claude G. Bowers, *Jefferson and Hamilton: The Struggle for Democracy in America* (Boston: Houghton Mifflin, 1966), p. 465.

18. *Columbian Centinel*, February 27 and March 6, 1799; *Russell's Gazette*, February 28, March 4 and 11, and April 1, 1799; Adams was credited for trying one more time, although specific objections to the mission were cited.

19. *Massachusetts Mercury*, March 8, 1799; *New Hampshire Gazette*, March 13, 1799; *Providence Gazette*, March 9, 1799.

20. See *Massachusetts Mercury*, March 5, 1799; *American Mercury*, February 28, 1799; *Middlesex Gazette*, March 1, 1799; *Norwich Packet*, March 20, 1799; *Courier of New Hampshire*, March 2, 1799, and *Connecticut Gazette* (New London), February 27, 1799.

21. *New Hampshire Gazette*, March 6, 1799; *American Mercury*, March 14, 1799; *Spectator* (New York), February 27, 1799; *Norwich Packet*, March 6, 1799; *Green Mt. Patriot*, March 14, 1799; and *Massachusetts Spy* (Worcester), March 20, 1799.

22. Zoltan Haraszti, *John Adams and the Prophets of Progress* (New York: Grosset and Dunlap, 1952), pp. 101, 109.

23. DeConde, *Quasi-War*, pp. 186–87, 216; Bowers, *Jefferson and Hamilton*, pp. 433–34; *Argus* (New York), April 8, 1799; S. Higginson to OW, March 29, 1799, in Gibbs, *Memoirs*, 2:229–30.

24. Uriah Forrest to JA, April 28, 1799, in Adams, *Works of JA*, 8:637–38; George Cabot to OW, May 2, 1799, in Gibbs, *Memoirs*, 2:239.

25. JA to OW, May 17, 1799, in Gibbs, *Memoirs*, 2:241.

26. *Sunbury and Northumberland Gazette*, June 29, 1799, reprinted in, for example, *Aurora*, July 12, 1799; JA to Pickering, August 13, 1799, in Adams, *Works of JA*, 9:13–14.

27. *Aurora*, July 24, 1799; Pickering to JA, July 24, JA to Pickering, August 1, and Pickering to JA, August 1, 1799, in Adams, *Works of JA*, 9:3–7; GW to the secretary of state, August 4, 1799, in Fitzpatrick, *GW*, 37:323; JA to the attorney general and the district attorney of Pennsylvania, May 16, 1800, in Adams, *Works of JA*, 9:56; James Morton Smith, *Freedom's Fetters: The Alien and Sedition Laws and American Civil Liberties* (Ithaca, N.Y.: Cornell University Press, 1966), p. 287.

28. GW to the secretary of war, August 11, and GW to Governor Jonathan Trumbull, August 30, 1799, in Fitzpatrick, *GW*, 37:328, 349.

29. B. Stoddert to JA, August 29 and September 13, 1799; JA to Stoddert, September 21, and JA to Pickering, September 21, 1799, in Adams, *Works of JA*, 9:18–19, 25–28, 33–34.

30. Gilbert Chinard, *Honest John Adams* (Boston: Little, Brown, 1964), pp. 290–91; JA to Pickering, October 16, 1799, in Adams, *Works of JA*, 9:39; Gibbs, *Memoirs*, 2:263ff, especially 269 and 276.

31. JA to William Cunningham, November 7, 1808, in *Correspondence Between the Hon. John Adams, Late President of the United States, and the Late Wm. Cunningham, Esq.; Beginning in 1803, and Ending in 1812* (Boston: E.M. Cunningham, 1823), pp. 48–50; AA to Mary Cranch, November 1–3, and December 11, 1799, in Stewart Mitchell, ed., *New Letters of Abigail Adams, 1788–1801* (Boston: Houghton Mifflin, 1947), pp. 212–13, 221.

32. E. Wilson Lyon, "The Directory and the United States," *AHR* 43 (1938):532; Stephen G. Kurtz, *The Presidency of John Adams: The Collapse of Federalism, 1795–1800* (New York: A.S. Barnes, 1961), p. 389; Edward Channing, *A History of the United States*, 6 vols. (New York: Macmillan, 1917), 4:205; John T. Morse, Jr., ed., *John Adams*, American Statesman Series (Boston: Houghton Mifflin, 1884), p. 308; James Truslow Adams, *The Adams Family* (Boston: Little, Brown, 1930), p. 110; JA to AA, October 25, 1799, in Charles Francis Adams, *Letters of John Adams, Addressed to His Wife*, 2 vols. (Boston: Charles C. Little and James Brown, 1841), 2:263.

33. Smith, *JA*, 2:1009; *Constitutional Telegraph* (Boston), October 16, 1799; Stewart, *Opposition Press*, p. 242, sees Robbins as a "synthetic" martyr; *Aurora*, September 3, 1799; DeConde, *Quasi-War*, p. 205; *Constitutional Telegraph*, October 26, 1799; *Argus* (New York), October 15, 1799.

34. DeConde, *Quasi-War*, p. 205; TJ to Charles Pinckney, October 29, 1799, in Ford, *Writings of TJ*, 7:397.

35. See McHenry to GW, November 10, Jedediah Morse to OW, November 8, George Cabot to OW, November 17, and Chauncey Goodrich to OW, November 18, 1799, in Gibbs, *Memoirs*, 2:281–82, 286–88.

36. AA to Mary Cranch, November 26, 1799, in Mitchell, *Letters-AA*, p. 216; Gibbs, *Memoirs*, 2:309.

37. Richardson, *Messages*, 1:290–96; Smith, *JA*, 2:1020; *Constitutional Diary* (Philadelphia), December 7, 1799.

38. Gibbs, *Memoirs*, 2:310; Adams, *Works of JA*, 1:132–33; Rose, *Prologue*, p. 235; *Constitutional Diary* (Philadelphia), December 20, 1799; Frank M. Anderson, "Contemporary Opinion of the Virginia and Kentucky Resolutions," *AHR* 5 (October, 1899): 242–43.

39. JA, "Reply to the Address of the Senate, on the Death of George Washington," December 23, 1799, in Adams, *Works of JA*, 9:142; for Republican displeasure, see above; see also AA to Mary Cranch, January 28, 1800, in Mitchell, *Letters-AA*, pp. 228–29.

40. OW to Fisher Ames, December 29, 1799, in Gibbs, *Memoirs*, 2:313–15; Joseph Charles, *The Origins of the American Party System: Three Essays* (New York: Harper and Row, 1956), p. 50.

41. JA to Benjamin Lincoln, March 10, 1800, in Adams, *Works of JA*, 9:46–47; William Duane to ----, April 17, 1800, in Worthington Chauncey Ford, ed., "Letters of William Duane," *MHS Proceedings* 20 (1906–1907):260.

42. Smith, *JA*, 2:1028–29; J. McHenry to JA, May 6, JA to Pickering, May 10, Pickering to JA, May 12, JA to Pickering, May 12, 1800, in Adams, *Works of JA*, 9:51–55.

43. Gibbs, *Memoirs*, 2:212–14.

44. Morison, *Life-Otis*, 1:189.

45. *Aurora*, May 9 and 15, 1800; Salem *Impartial Register*, May 19, 1800.

46. See *Providence Gazette*, May 24, 1800; *Farmer's Weekly Museum*, May 26, 1800; *Green Mt. Patriot* (Peacham, Vt.), May 28, 1800.

47. Rose, *Prologue*, p. 241.

48. *Letter from Alexander Hamilton, Concerning the Public Conduct and Character of John Adams, Esq., President of the United States* (New York: George F. Hopkins, 1800), pp. 37–38.

49. *Aurora*, June 7, 1800; Boston *Columbian Centinel*, June 11, 1800, is the Adams sheet; Trenton *Federalist*, June 2, 1800, seems High-Federalist; Gibbs, *Memoirs*, 2:352–53; John C. Miller, *The Federalist Era, 1789–1801*, New American Nation Series (New York: Harper and Row, 1960), p. 261; James McHenry to John McHenry, May 20, 1800, in Gibbs, *Memoirs*, 2:347.

50. *Aurora*, June 7 and 18, 1800; Abraham Bishop, *An Oration on the Extent and Power of Political Delusion* (Newark, N.J.: Pennington and Gould, 1800), pp. 40–41; Morton Borden, *Parties and Politics in the Early Republic, 1789–1815* (New York: Thomas Y. Crowell, 1967), p. 55.

51. Gibbs, *Memoirs*, 2:356–58; OW, "Notice to the Public," in Gibbs, *Memoirs*, 2:359.

52. JA to Barnabas Bidwell, August 27, 1800, and letter 10 to the *Boston Patriot*, in Adams, *Works of JA*, 9:79, 273; JA to William Cunningham, October 15, 1808, in *Adams-Cunningham*, pp. 38–40.

53. JA to Charles Lee, secretary of state, pro tem, May 21, 1800, in Adams, *Works of JA*, 9:60–61; Gibbs, *Memoirs*, 2:360; *Aurora*, May 22, 1800; *Farmer's Museum, or Literary Gazette*, June 2, 1800; Miller, *Federalist Era*, p. 248.

54. OW to Chauncey Goodrich, July 20, 1800, in Gibbs, *Memoirs*, 2:383.

Chapter Nine

1. John C. Miller, *The Federalist Era, 1789–1801*, New American Nation Series (New York: Harper and Row, 1960), p. 255; Frank M. Anderson, "Contemporary Opinion of the Virginia and Kentucky Resolutions," *AHR* 5 (October, 1899):244; Donald H. Stewart, *The Opposition Press of the Federalist Period* (Albany: State University of New York Press, 1969), p. 340.

2. Henry William Elson, *History of the United States of America,* 5 vols. (New York: Macmillan, 1905), 2:214; AA to Mary Cranch, March 5, 1800, in Stewart Mitchell, ed., *New Letters of Abigail Adams, 1788–1801* (Boston: Houghton Mifflin, 1947), p. 237; John C. Miller, *Crisis in Freedom: The Alien and Sedition Acts* (Boston: Little, Brown, 1951), p. 223.

3. Noble E. Cunningham, Jr., *The Jeffersonian-Republicans: The Formation of Party Organization, 1789–1809* (Chapel Hill: University of North Carolina Press, 1957); *The Jeffersonian Republicans in Power: Party Operations, 1801–1809* (Chapel Hill: University of North Carolina Press, 1963).

4. Stephen G. Kurtz, *The Presidency of John Adams: The Collapse of Federalism, 1795–1800* (New York: A.S. Barnes, 1961), p. 141; Page Smith, *John Adams,* 2 vols. (Garden City, N.Y.: Doubleday, 1962), 2:1024.

5. OW to William Bingham, July 28, and Fisher Ames to OW, August 3, 1800, in George Gibbs, *Memoirs of the Administration of Washington and John Adams; Edited from the Papers of Oliver Wolcott, Secretary of the Treasury,* 2 vols. (New York: William Van Norden, 1846), 2:393, 396.

6. Edwin Emery, *The Press and America: An Interpretive History of Journalism,* 2d ed. (Englewood Cliffs, N.J.: Prentice-Hall, 1962), pp. 140, 163; Frank Luther Mott, *American Journalism: A History, 1690–1960* (New York: Macmillan, 1962), pp. 121–22.

7. Uriah Tracy to OW, August 7, 1800, in Gibbs, *Memoirs,* 2:399.

8. Charles Pinckney to Madison, October 26, 1800, in "South Carolina in the Presidential Election of 1800," *AHR* 4 (1898):116; "Americanus" [John Beckley], *Address to the People of the United States: With an Epitome and Vindication of the Public Life and Character of Thomas Jefferson* (Newport, R.I.: Oliver Farnsworth, 1800), pp. 7ff and 23ff.

9. *Centinel of Freedom,* April 22 and May 13, 1800; *Kline's Carlisle Weekly Gazette,* August 27, September 24, and October 8, 1800; *American Mercury* (Hartford), September 4 and 18, 1800.

10. See James Morton Smith, "The Sedition Law, Free Speech, and the American Political Process," *WMQ,* 3d ser., 9 (1952):504; see also Dumas Malone, *Jefferson and the Ordeal of Liberty,* vol. 3 of *Jefferson and His Time* (Boston: Little, Brown, 1962), p. 466; Stewart, *Opposition Press,* p. 486; Leonard W. Levy, *Freedom of Speech and Press in Early American History: A Legacy of Suppression* (New York: Harper and Row, 1963), p. 153; Noah Webster to OW, June 23, 1800, in Gibbs, *Memoirs,* 2:373–74.

11. *Constitutional Telegraph* (Boston), March 12, 1800; *Aurora,* May 17, 1800; James Thomson Callender, *The Prospect Before Us,* 2 vols. (Richmond: James Thomson Callender, 1800), vol. 2, cited in James Morton Smith, *Freedom's Fetters: The Alien and Sedition Laws and American Civil Liberties* (Ithaca, N.Y.: Cornell University Press, 1966), p. 358.

12. Joseph Charles, *The Origins of the American Party System: Three Essays* (New York: Harper and Row, 1956), p. 135; Miller, *Federalist Era,* p. 158.

13. B. Stoddert to JA, October 27, 1811, in Charles Francis Adams, ed., *The Works of John Adams, Second President of the United States,* 10 vols. (Boston: Charles C. Little and James Brown, 1851), 10:5; see TJ to Madison, January 1, 1797, in Paul Leicester Ford, ed., *The Writings of Thomas Jefferson,* 10 vols. (New York: G.P. Putnam and Sons, 1894), 7:99.

14. Miller, *Federalist Era,* p. 256; Kurtz, *Presidency,* p. 395.

15. *Aurora*, February 17 and May 19, 1800.

16. Fisher Ames to OW, June 12, 1800, in Gibbs, *Memoirs*, 2:370; Smith, *JA*, 2:1038.

17. Lisle A. Rose, *Prologue to Democracy: The Federalists in the South, 1789–1800* (Lexington: University of Kentucky Press, 1968), pp. 243–65.

18. See Salem, *Impartial Register*, June 26, 1800; Smith, *JA*, 2:1048.

19. Samuel Eliot Morison, *The Life and Letters of Harrison Gray Otis, Federalist, 1765–1848*, 2 vols. (Boston: Houghton Mifflin, 1913), 1:185.

20. Gibbs, *Memoirs*, 2:364.

21. See Fisher Ames to Chauncey Goodrich, June 12, George Cabot to OW, June 14, OW to Cabot, June 16, Benjamin Goodhue to OW, July 10, OW to J. McHenry, July 18, Cabot to OW, July 20, Thomas Fitzsimmons to OW, July 24, OW to Ames, August 10, OW to McHenry, August 26, OW to AH, September 3, Timothy Phelps to OW, September 18, and McHenry to OW, November 9, 1800, in Gibbs, *Memoirs*, 2:367, 370–71, 379, 381, 384, 388, 401–02, 410, 417–19, 445.

22. Cobbett to E. Thornton, October 1, 1800, in G.D.H. Cole, ed., *Letters from William Cobbett to Edward Thornton Written in the Years 1797 to 1800* (London: Oxford University Press, 1937), p. 117; F. Ames to Pickering, October 19, 1799, in Charles Warren, *Jacobin and Junto; or Early American Politics as Viewed in the Diary of Dr. Nathaniel Ames, 1758–1822* (Cambridge: Harvard University Press, 1931), p. 149.

23. John Ward Fenno, *Desultory Reflections on the New Political Aspects of Public Affairs in the United States of America Since the Commencement of the Year 1799* (New York: John Ward Fenno, 1800), pp. 33ff, 52ff.

24. Cobbett to E. Thornton, February 2, 1800, in Cole, *Cobbett-Thornton*, p. 43.

25. *Gazette of the United States*, October 4, 8, and 14, 1800; *Salem Gazette*, October 3, 1800; *Middlesex Gazette*, October 10, 1800; *Norwich Packet*, October 28, 1800; Salem *Impartial Register*, October 27, 1800; *American Citizen*, September 24, 1800.

26. Smith, *JA*, 2:1042; Adrienne Koch, "Hamilton, Adams, and the Pursuit of Power," *RP*, 16 (1954):54–55; Margaret Woodbury, "Public Opinion in Philadelphia, 1789–1801," *Smith College Studies in History* 5 (1919–20), 5:128; Miller, *Crisis*, p. 224; Morison, *Life-Otis*, 1:157; Marshall Smelser, "The Federalist Period as an Age of Passion," *AQ* 10 (1958):417–18.

27. AH to OW, July 1 and August 3, OW to AH, September 3, AH to OW, September 26, 1800, in Gibbs, *Memoirs*, 2:376, 397, 416–17, 421–22.

28. Richard Hildreth, *The History of the United States of America*, 6 vols. (New York: Harper and Brothers, 1880), 5:386; *AH Letter*, pp. 4, 50.

29. "A Federalist" [Noah Webster], *A Letter to General Hamilton, Occasioned by His Letter to President Adams* (New York: E. Selder, 1800), pp. 3, 12, 14; see also Uzal Ogden, *A Letter to Major General Alexander Hamilton* (New York: Hopkins, 1800); and William Pinckney, *A Few Remarks on Mr. Hamilton's Late Letter* (Baltimore: Warner and Hanna, 1800).

30. Salem *Impartial Register*, October 27 and November 13, 1800; Philip M. Marsh, *Philip Freneau: Poet and Journalist* (Minneapolis: Dillon, 1967), p. 276; *Gazette of the United States*, October 25, 1800; *National Intelligencer*, October 31 and November 7, 1800; *American Citizen*, October 25, 1800; *Courier of New*

Hampshire, December 5, 1800; *Boston Independent Chronicle*, November 24, 1800; *Farmer's Museum, or Literary Gazette*, November 24, 1800.

31. Duane is cited in Adams, *JA Works*, 1:588; AA to Mary Cranch, November 21, 1800, in Mitchell, *Letters-AA*, p. 258; Letter 12 to the *Boston Patriot*, in Adams, *Works of JA*, 9:273; L.H. Butterfield, ed., *The Adams Papers: Diary and Autobiography of John Adams*, 4 vols. (New York: Atheneum, 1964), 3:387; JA to John Jay, November 24, 1800, JA to James Lloyd, February 17, 1815, JA to Dr. Ogden, December 3, 1800, in Adams, *Works of JA*, respectively, 9:90–91, 10:123ff, 9:576; JA to Benjamin Rush, January 25, 1806, in John A. Schutz and Douglass Adair, eds., *The Spur of Fame: Dialogues of . . . John Adams and Benjamin Rush, 1805–1813* (San Marino, Calif.: Huntington Library, 1966), p. 48.

32. See Salem *Impartial Register*, May 22, 1800; *Connecticut Courant*, September 29 and October 5, 1800, which serialized "Burleigh"; *Middlesex Gazette*, October 3, 1800; *Norwich Packet*, November 25, 1800; *Farmer's Museum, or Literary Gazette*, October 17, 1800; *Massachusetts Spy*, November 26, 1800; *U.S. Chronicle* (Providence), November 21, 1800; *Green Mt. Patriot*, October 29 and November 20, 1800; *Providence Gazette*, November 15, 1800; *Spectator* (New York), November 5, 8, and 15, 1800; *Russell's Gazette*, October 2 and 6, 1800; for anti–TJ polemics, see, for example, Fenno, *Desultory Reflections*, p. 15; *Courier of New Hampshire*, October 4, 1800, and following issues; *Salem Gazette*, August–September, 1800; *Farmer's Museum, or Literary Gazette*, October 13, 1800; *Massachusetts Mercury*, October 7, 1800; Boston *Columbian Centinel*, June-August, 1800; and Burleigh, cited above.

33. *Aurora*, June 17, August 8 and 11, 1800; *Virginia Argus* (Richmond), July 11, 1800.

34. *Aurora*, August 28 and 29, 1800; J. McHenry to OW, September 1, and OW to B. Goodhue, July 30, 1800, in Gibbs, *Memoirs*, 2:414–15, 395; *Aurora*, September 12, 1800; *American Citizen*, September 15, 1800; *Constitutional Telegraph*, October 18, 1800.

35. *Gazette of the United States*, October 1, 30, and November 12, 1800; *Aurora*, October 4, 1800.

36. See, for example, *Green Mt. Patriot*, November 20, 1800.

37. *Virginia Argus* (Richmond), September 16, 1800; AA is cited in Janet Whitney, *Abigail Adams* (Boston: Little, Brown, 1947), p. 303.

38. See *Aurora*, October 4, 1800; Callender, *Prospect*, 1:167; *Gazette of the United States*, October 7, 1800; *Temple of Reason*, November 8 and 15, 1800; *American Citizen*, October 8, 1800; Callender, *Prospect*, respectively, 1:3, 143, 112; 2:50.

39. Rose, *Prologue*, p. 273; *National Intelligencer*, November 12, 1800; *City Gazette* (Charleston), October 3, 1800; Cunningham, *Jeffersonians*, p. 235.

40. Salem *Impartial Register*, October 9, 1800; *New Hampshire Gazette*, November 11, 1800; *Courier of New Hampshire*, November 22, 1800; *Middlesex Gazette*, December 5, 1800; *Gazette of the United States*, November 24, 1800.

41. *National Intelligencer*, December 15, 1800; *Centinel of Freedom*, December 16, 1800.

42. F. Ames to C. Gore, December 29, 1800, in Seth Ames, *Works of Fisher Ames, with a Selection from His Speeches and Correspondence*, 2 vols. (Boston: Little, Brown, 1854), 1:286–87; JA to Gerry, February 7, 1801, in Adams, *JA Works*, 9:98; *Aurora*, March 3, 1801.

43. See Manning J. Dauer, *The Adams Federalists* (Baltimore: Johns Hopkins University Press, 1968), pp. 272–74, 282–85.

44. Leonard D. White, *The Federalists: A Study in Administrative History, 1789–1801* (New York: Free Press, 1948); and *The Jeffersonians; A Study in Administrative History, 1801–1829* (New York: Free Press, 1951); Levy, *Legacy*, p. 247; Smith, *JA*, 2:1058; Edward Channing, *A History of the United States*, 6 vols. (New York: Macmillan, 1917), respectively, 4:291, 235–36; Kurtz, *Presidency*, pp. 353, 407; Alexander DeConde, *The Quasi-War: The Politics and Diplomacy of the Undeclared War with France, 1797–1801* (New York: C. Scribner's Sons, 1966), p. 285; Marshall Smelser, "The Jacobin Phrenzy: Federalism and the Menace of Liberty, Equality, and Fraternity," *RP* 13 (1951):481; Miller, *Federalist Era*, p. 266ff; DeConde, *Quasi-War*, p. 267; Adams, *Works of JA*, 1:589; Samuel Eliot Morison, *Harrison Gray Otis, 1765–1848: The Urbane Federalist* (Boston: Houghton Mifflin, 1969), p. 175.

45. F. Ames to Theodore Dwight, March 19, 1801, in Ames, *Fisher Ames*, 1:294.

46. JA to John Trumbull, September 10, 1800, in Adams, *Works of JA*, 9:83–84.

Chapter Ten

1. Gilbert Chinard, *Honest John Adams* (Boston: Little, Brown, 1964), p. 314; Charles Francis Adams, *The Works of John Adams, Second President of the United States*, 10 vols. (Boston: Charles C. Little and James Brown, 1851), 1:599–600; Samuel Eliot Morison, *By Land and by Sea: Essays and Addresses* (New York: Knopf, 1953), p. 228; Page Smith, *John Adams*, 2 vols. (Garden City, N.Y.: Doubleday, 1962), 2:1065; John T. Morse, Jr., ed., *John Adams*, American Statesman Series (Boston: Houghton Mifflin, 1884), p. 322.

2. Franking privilege is cited in Richard Hildreth, *The History of the United States of America*, 6 vols. (New York: Harper and Brothers, 1880), 5:412.

3. Smith, *JA*, 2:1067; George Gibbs, *Memoirs of the Administration of Washington and John Adams; Edited from the Papers of Oliver Wolcott, Secretary of the Treasury*, 2 vols. (New York: William Van Norden, 1846), 1:454; L.H. Butterfield, *The Adams Papers: Diary and Autobiography of John Adams* (New York: Atheneum, 1964), 1:v, xv.

4. *Massachusetts Spy*, March 18, 1801; *Constitutional Telegraph*, March 14 and 18, 1801; *American Citizen*, March 13, 1801.

5. *Middlesex Gazette*, March 13 and 20, 1801; *Norwich Packet*, March 17, 1801; *Political Repository* (Brookfield, Mass.), March 24, 1801; *Massachusetts Spy*, March 18, 1801; *Connecticut Courant*, March 23, 1801.

6. JA to John Trumbull, September 10, 1800, in Adams, *Works of JA*, 9:83–84; Zoltan Haraszti, *John Adams and the Prophets of Progress* (New York: Grosset and Dunlap, 1952), p. 55; Smith, *JA*, 2:1088; JA to William Cunningham, November 7, 1808, in *Correspondence Between the Hon. John Adams, Late President of the United States, and the Late Wm. Cunningham, Esq.; Beginning in 1803, and Ending in 1812* (Boston: E.M. Cunningham, 1823), p. 43; JA to Joseph Lyman, April 20, 1809, and letter 9 to the *Boston Patriot*, in Adams, *Works of JA*, 9:620–621, 267.

7. JA to B. Waterhouse, March 29, 1811, in Worthington Chauncey Ford,

ed., *Statesman and Friend: Correspondence of John Adams with Benjamin Waterhouse, 1784–1822* (Boston: Little, Brown, 1927), p. 54; JA to TJ, February 3, 1812, in Lester J. Cappon, ed., *The Adams-Jefferson Letters: The Complete Correspondence Between Thomas Jefferson and Abigail and John Adams*, 2 vols. (Chapel Hill: University of North Carolina Press, 1959), 2:295; JA to James Lloyd, February 6, 1815, and Rufus King to JQA, February 9, 1825, in Adams, *Works of JA*, respectively, 10:115, 1:632.

   8. Manning J. Dauer, *The Adams Federalists* (Baltimore: Johns Hopkins University Press, 1968), pp. 264–65; Irving Brant, *James Madison, Father of the Constitution*, vol. 3 of *James Madison* (Indianapolis: Bobbs-Merrill, 1950), p. 450; Lisle A. Rose, *Prologue to Democracy: The Federalists in the South, 1789–1800* (Lexington: University of Kentucky Press, 1968), pp. 244–45; Adams, *Works of JA*, 1:575–76; Stephen G. Kurtz, *The Presidency of John Adams: The Collapse of Federalism, 1795–1800* (New York: A.S. Barnes, 1961), p. 347; Gibbs, *Memoirs*, 2:507.

   9. JA to William Cunningham, November 7, 1808, and February 22, 1809, in *Adams-Cunningham*, pp. 43–50, 95.

   10. Letter 10 to the *Boston Patriot*, in Adams, *Works of JA*, 9:273; JA to Rush, March 4, 1809, in John A. Schutz and Douglass Adair, eds., *The Spur of Fame: Dialogues of . . . John Adams and Benjamin Rush, 1805–1813* (San Marino, Calif.: Huntington Library, 1966), p. 132; JA to William Cunningham, March 20, 1809, in *Adams-Cunningham*, p. 107; JA to William Keteltas, November 25, 1812, in Adams, *Works of JA*, 10:23; JA to TJ, June 30, 1813, in Cappon, *Adams-Jefferson*, 2:346.

   11. OW to Pickering, December 28, 1800, in Gibbs, *Memoirs*, 2:461.

   12. Timothy Pickering, *A Review of the Correspondence Between the Hon. John Adams, Late President of the United States, and the Late Wm. Cunningham, Esq., Beginning in 1803, and Ending in 1812* (Salem, Mass.: Cushing and Appleton, 1824), pp. 1, 3, 12n, 21–22, 70, 73, 86, 89–97.

   13. Bernard Fay, *The Two Franklins: Fathers of American Democracy* (Boston: Little, Brown, 1933), p. 359; Smith, *JA*, 2:1068; Stewart Mitchell, ed., *New Letters of Abigail Adams, 1788–1801* (Boston: Houghton Mifflin, 1947), xl; Joseph Charles, *The Origins of the American Party System: Three Essays* (New York: Harper and Row, 1956), pp. 35, 128.

   14. Adams, *Works of JA*, 9:239–40; JA to Cunningham, September 27, October 15, 1808, in *Adams-Cunningham*, pp. 28, 40.

   15. Letters 9, 10, 12, and 13 to the *Boston Patriot*, in Adams, *Works of JA*, 9:268, 270–71, 278, 281, 289–90.

   16. Letter 13 to the *Boston Patriot*, in Adams, *Works of JA*, 9:285; JA to James Lloyd, April 21, 1815, and John Taylor to JA, April 8, 1824, in Adams, *Works of JA*, 10:127–28, 412.

   17. John Bach McMaster, *A History of the People of the United States, from the Revolution to the Civil War*, 5 vols. (New York: D. Appleton, 1885), 2:439; Margaret Woodbury, "Public Opinion in Philadelphia, 1789–1801," *Smith College Studies in History* 5 (1919–1920):27; TJ to Monroe, October 19, 1823, in Paul Leicester Ford, *The Writings of Thomas Jefferson*, 10 vols. (New York: G.P. Putnam's Sons, 1894), 10:275.

   18. JA to B. Stoddert, March 31, and JA to Christopher Gadsden, April 16, 1801, in Adams, *Works of JA*, 9:582, 584–85; *Adams-Cunningham*, p. 10; AA to TJ,

July 1, 1804, in Cappon, *Adams-Jefferson*, 1:272; Butterfield, *Diary and Autobiography*, 3:280.

19. JA to Rush, April 11, 1805, in Schutz and Adair, *JA-Rush*, p. 26; JA to Cunningham, February 22, 1809, in *Adams-Cunningham*, p. 93; JA to Rush, April 12, 1809, and January 21, 1810, in Adams, *Works of JA*, 9:619, 626; JA to TJ, July 15, 1813, in Cappon, *Adams-Jefferson*, 2:358; JA to John Taylor, n.d., and JA to James Lloyd, February 6, 1815, in Adams, *Works of JA*, 6:482–83, 10:116; JA to Charles Holt, March 22, 1825, in The Adams Papers, Adams Manuscript Trust, MHS; Holt to JA, March 4, 1825, in Adams, *Works of JA*, 1:631.

20. TJ to Mazzei, December 30, 1801, in Howard R. Marraro, "Unpublished Correspondence of Jefferson and Adams to Mazzei," *VaMHB*, 51 (1943):124; Leonard W. Levy, *Freedom of Speech and Press in Early American History: Legacy of Suppression* (New York: Harper and Row, 1963), pp. 297–98.

21. TJ to AA, July 22, and AA to TJ, August 18, 1804, in Cappon, *Adams-Jefferson*, 1:275–76; letter 13 to the *Boston Patriot*, in Adams, *Works of JA*, 9:291; JA to Rush, December 25, 1811, in Schutz and Adair, *JA-Rush*, p. 201; TA to TJ, June 14, 1813, in Cappon, *Adams-Jefferson*, 2:329; Pickering, *Review*, p. 15; House Report 218, January 20, 1832, 22nd Cong., 1st sess., cited in Frank Luther Mott, *Jefferson and the Press* (Baton Rouge: Louisiana State University Press, 1943), p. 37.

22. "Novanglus #3," in Adams, *Works of JA*, 4:31–32; JA to AA, March 9, 1797, in Adams, *JA-AA*, 2:247–48.

23. Butterfield, *Diary and Autobiography*, 3:253.

24. Haraszti, *JA and the Prophets*, pp. 135, 221, 251.

25. JA to Mercy Warren, August 30, 1803, in Worthington Chauncey Ford, *Warren-Adams Letters: Being Chiefly a Correspondence Among John Adams, Samuel Adams, and James Warren*, 2 vols. (Boston: Massachusetts Historical Society, 1925), 2:345; Rush to JA, June 10, 1806, JA to Rush, June 22, 1806, May 1, 1807, April 18, 1808, March 23, September 27, and October 25, 1809, in Schutz and Adair, *JA-Rush*, pp. 53, 55, 83, 107, 138–39, 155–59.

26. JA to William Cunningham, February 11, March 20, June 7, and July 31, 1809, in *Adams-Cunningham*, pp. 83, 101, 123, 151.

27. JA to Thomas Adams, September 15, 1801, Adams Papers; JA to Benjamin Waterhouse, September 17, 1810, in Ford, *Statesman*, p. 49; JA to Josiah Quincy, February 9, 1811, in Adams, *Works of JA*, 9:631; JA to Rush, August 28, 1811, in Schutz and Adair, *JA-Rush*, p. 192.

28. JA to Benjamin Waterhouse, March 11 and August 19, 1812, in Ford, *Statesman*, pp. 76–77, 86; JA to Rush, January 4, 1813, in Schutz and Adair, *JA-Rush*, p. 192.

29. See JA to TJ, June 25 and 30, July 12 and 13, 1813, in Cappon, *Adams-Jefferson*, 2:333, 348, 354, 356.

30. JA to John Taylor, n.d. (c. 1814–15), in Adams, *Works of JA*, 6:482, 500–01, 515–16, 518.

31. JA to James Lloyd, January 1815, and March 31, 1815, in Adams, *Works of JA*, 10:12–13, 154–55.

32. JA to Dr. Jedediah Morse, March 4, 1815, in Adams, *Works of JA*, 10:133; JA to Gerry, April 17, 1813, in Ford, *Warren-Adams*, 2:380.

33. JA to TJ, February 10, 1823, in Cappon, *Adams-Jefferson*, 2:587; JA to TJ, February 25 and December 1, 1825, and JA to Charles Francis Adams, December

19, 1825, in Adams Papers; JA to TJ, April 17, 1826, in Cappon, *Adams-Jefferson,* 2:614.

34. Marcus Cunliffe, *The Nation Takes Shape, 1789–1837,* History of American Civilization Series, edited by Daniel Boorstin (Chicago: University of Chicago Press, 1959), p. 5.

35. See Donald H. Stewart, *The Opposition Press of the Federalist Period* (Albany: State University of New York Press, 1969), pp. 3, 537, 605, 632.

36. Edward Channing, *A History of the United States,* 6 vols. (New York: Macmillan, 1917), 4:211.

37. Fisher Ames to OW, April 22, 1798, in Gibbs, *Memoirs,* 2:47; Fisher Ames to Theodore Dwight, March 19, 1801, in Seth Ames, *Works of Fisher Ames, with a Selection from His Speeches and Correspondence,* 2 vols. (Boston: Little, Brown, 1854), 1:294.

Bibliography

MANUSCRIPTS

The Adams Papers; Adams Manuscript Trust; Massachusetts Historical Society.

BOOKS

Primary Sources

Adams, Charles Francis, ed. *Letters of John Adams, Addressed to His Wife*. 2 vols. Boston: Charles C. Little and James Brown, 1841.

————. *The Memoirs of John Quincy Adams*. 12 vols. Philadelphia: J.B. Lippincott, 1874–1877.

————. *The Works of John Adams, Second President of the United States*. 10 vols. Boston: Charles C. Little and James Brown, 1851.

Ames, Seth. *Works of Fisher Ames, with a Selection from His Speeches and Correspondence*. 2 vols. Boston: Little, Brown, 1854.

Boyd, Julian P., ed. *Papers of Thomas Jefferson*. Multivol. Princeton, N.J.: Princeton University Press, 1950–.

Butterfield, L.H., ed. *Adams Family Correspondence*. 2 vols. Cambridge: Belknap Press of Harvard University Press, 1963.

————. *The Adams Papers: Diary and Autobiography of John Adams*. 4 vols. New York: Atheneum, 1964.

————. *Letters of Benjamin Rush*. 2 vols. Princeton, N.J.: Princeton University Press, 1951.

Cappon, Lester J., ed. *The Adams-Jefferson Letters: The Complete Correspondence Between Thomas Jefferson and Abigail and John Adams*. 2 vols. Chapel Hill: University of North Carolina Press, 1959.

Cobbett, William. *Porcupine's Works*. 12 vols. London: Cobbett and Morgan, 1801.

Cole, G.D.H., ed. *Letters from William Cobbett to Edward Thornton Written in the Years 1797 to 1800*. London: Oxford University Press, 1937.

Correspondence Between the Hon. John Adams, Late President of the United States, and the Late Wm. Cunningham, Esq., Beginning in 1803, and Ending in 1812. Boston: E.M. Cunningham, 1823.

Debates and Proceedings in the Congress of the United States. Multivol. First through Sixth Congresses. Washington, D.C.: Gales and Seaton, 1849.

Fitzpatrick, John C., ed. *The Writings of George Washington.* 39 vols. Washington, D.C.: U.S. Government Printing Office, 1939.

Foner, Philip S., ed. *The Complete Writings of Thomas Paine.* 2 vols. New York: Citadel, 1945.

Ford, Paul Leicester, ed. *The Writings of Thomas Jefferson.* 10 vols. New York: G.P. Putnam's Sons, 1894.

Ford, Worthington Chauncey, ed. *Statesman and Friend: Correspondence of John Adams with Benjamin Waterhouse, 1784–1822.* Boston: Little, Brown, 1927.

_____. *Warren-Adams Letters; Being Chiefly a Correspondence Among John Adams, Samuel Adams, and James Warren.* 2 vols. Boston: Massachusetts Historical Society, 1925.

_____. *The Writings of John Quincy Adams.* 7 vols. New York: Macmillan, 1913–1917.

Gibbs, George. *Memoirs of the Administration of Washington and John Adams; Edited from the Papers of Oliver Wolcott, Secretary of the Treasury.* 2 vols. New York: William Van Norden, 1846.

Hamilton, John C., ed. *The Works of Alexander Hamilton.* 7 vols. New York: J.F. Trow, 1850–1851.

Hamilton, Stanislaus M., ed. *The Writings of James Monroe.* 9 vols. New York: G.P. Putnam's Sons, 1898–1903.

Hunt, Gaillard, ed. *The Writings of James Madison.* 9 vols. New York: G.P. Putnam's Sons, 1900–1910.

Johnston, Henry P., ed. *The Correspondence and Public Papers of John Jay.* 4 vols. New York: G.P. Putnam's Sons, 1890–1893.

King, Charles R. *The Life and Correspondence of Rufus King.* 6 vols. New York: G.P. Putnam's Sons, 1894.

Lipscomb, Andrew A., and Albert Ellery Bergh, eds. *The Writings of Thomas Jefferson.* 10 vols. Washington, D.C.: Thomas Jefferson Memorial Association, 1905.

Lodge, Henry Cabot, ed. *The Works of Alexander Hamilton.* 12 vols. New York: G.P. Putnam's Sons, 1904.

Maclay, William. *The Journal of William Maclay.* New York: Frederick Unger, 1965.

Mitchell, Stewart, ed. *New Letters of Abigail Adams, 1788–1801.* Boston: Houghton-Mifflin, 1947.

Morison, Samuel Eliot. *The Life and Letters of Harrison Gray Otis, Federalist, 1765–1848.* 2 vols. Boston: Houghton Mifflin, 1913.

Morris, Anne C., ed. *Diary and Letters of Gouverneur Morris.* 2 vols. New York: Charles Scribner, 1888.

Morris, Richard B., ed. *Alexander Hamilton and the Founding of the Nation.* New York: Harper and Row, 1957.

Pickering, Octavius, and Charles W. Upham. *The Life of Timothy Pickering.* 4 vols. Boston: Little, Brown, 1867–1873.

Pickering, Timothy. *A Review of the Correspondence Between the Hon. John Adams, Late President of the United States, and the Late Wm. Cunningham, Esq., Beginning in 1803, and Ending in 1812.* Salem, Mass.: Cushing and Appleton, 1824.

Richardson, James D., ed. *A Compilation of the Messages and Papers of the Presidents,*

1789–1902. 10 vols. Washington, D.C.: Bureau of National Literature and Art, 1904.

Rossiter, Clinton, ed. *The Federalist Papers.* New York: New American Library, 1961.

Schutz, John A., and Douglass Adair, eds. *The Spur of Fame: Dialogues of . . . John Adams and Benjamin Rush, 1805–1813.* San Marino, Calif.: Huntington Library, 1966.

Smyth, Albert Henry, ed. *The Writings of Benjamin Franklin.* 10 vols. New York: Macmillan, 1905–1907.

Steiner, Bernard C. *The Life and Correspondence of James McHenry.* Cleveland: Burroughs, 1907.

Warren, Charles. *Jacobin and Junto; or Early American Politics as Viewed in the Diary of Dr. Nathaniel Ames, 1758–1822.* Cambridge: Harvard University Press, 1931.

Watson, Winslow C. *Men and Times of the Revolution; or Memoirs of Elkanah Watson.* New York: Dana, 1856.

Wood, John. *The Suppressed History of the Administration of John Adams (from 1797 to 1801), as Printed and Suppressed in 1802.* Philadelphia: John H. Sherburne, 1846.

Wroth, L. Kinvin, and Hiller B. Zobel, eds. *Legal Papers of John Adams.* 3 vols. Cambridge: Belknap Press of Harvard University Press, 1965.

Secondary Sources

Adams, James Truslow. *The Adams Family.* Boston: Little, Brown, 1930.
————. *The Living Jefferson.* New York: Charles Scribner's Sons, 1936.

Allen, Gardiner W. *Our Naval War with France.* Boston: Houghton Mifflin, 1909.

Ammon, Harry. *The Genet Mission.* New York: Norton, 1973.

Anderson, Dice R. *William Branch Giles: A Study in the Politics of Virginia and the Nation from 1790 to 1830.* Menasha, Wis.: George Banta, 1914.

Andrews, J. Cutler. *Pittsburgh's Post Gazette.* Boston: Chapman and Grimes, 1936.

Austin, James T. *The Life of Elbridge Gerry.* 2 vols. Boston: Wells and Lilly, 1827–1829.

Austin, Mary C. *Philip Freneau, Poet of the Revolution.* New York: A. Wessells, 1901.

Axelrod, Jacob. *Philip Freneau.* Austin: University of Texas Press, 1967.

Baker, Leonard. *John Marshall: A Life in Law.* New York: Macmillan, 1974.

Baldwin, Leland D. *Whiskey Rebels: The Story of a Frontier Uprising.* Pittsburgh: University of Pittsburgh Press, 1939.

Banner, James M., Jr. *To the Hartford Convention: The Federalists and the Origins of Party Politics in Massachusetts.* New York: Knopf, 1970.

Bassett, John Spencer. *The Federalist System, 1789–1801.* Vol. 11 of *The American Nation: A History.* Edited by A.B. Hart. 28 vols. New York: Harper and Brothers, 1906.

Baumgartner, Apollinaris W. *Catholic Journalism: A Study of Its Development in the United States, 1789–1930.* New York: Columbia University Press, 1931.

Beard, Charles A. *Economic Origins of Jeffersonian Democracy.* New York: Free Press, 1965.

BIBLIOGRAPHY

Bemis, Samuel Flagg, ed. *The American Secretaries of State*. 10 vols. New York: Knopf, 1927–1929.

————. *Jay's Treaty: A Study in Commerce and Diplomacy*. New Haven: Yale University Press, 1962.

————. *Pinckney's Treaty: A Study of America's Advantage from Europe's Distress*. Baltimore: Johns Hopkins University Press, 1926.

Bernhard, Winfred E.A. *Fisher Ames: Federalist and Statesman, 1758–1808*. Chapel Hill: University of North Carolina Press, 1965.

Beveridge, Albert J. *The Life of John Marshall*. 4 vols. Boston: Houghton Mifflin, 1916–1919.

Binckley, Wilfred E. *American Political Parties*. 3d ed. New York: Knopf, 1958.

Bleyer, Willard Grosvenor. *Main Currents in the History of American Journalism*. Boston: Houghton Mifflin, 1927.

Borden, Morton. *Parties and Politics in the Early Republic, 1789–1815*. New York: Thomas Y. Crowell, 1967.

Bowers, Claude G. *Jefferson and Hamilton: The Struggle for Democracy in America*. Boston: Houghton Mifflin, 1966.

Boyd, Julian P. *Number 7: Alexander Hamilton's Secret Attempts to Control American Foreign Policy*. Princeton, N.J.: Princeton University Press, 1964.

Brant, Irving. *The Bill of Rights; Its Origins and Meanings*. Indianapolis: Bobbs-Merrill, 1965.

————. *James Madison, Father of the Constitution*. Vol. 3 of *James Madison*. Indianapolis: Bobbs-Merrill, 1950.

Brigham, Clarence L. *History and Bibliography of American Newspapers, 1690–1820*. 2 vols. Worcester, Mass.: American Antiquarian Society, 1947.

————. *Journals and Journeymen; A Contribution to the History of Early American Newspapers*. Philadelphia: University of Pennsylvania Press, 1950.

Brown, Charles R. *The Northern Confederacy: New England and the "Essex Junto," 1795–1800*. Princeton, N.J.: Princeton University Press, 1916.

Brown, Stuart Gerry. *The First Republicans*. Syracuse, N.Y.: Syracuse University Press, 1954.

Bryan, W.B. *A History of the National Capital*. Multivol. New York: Macmillan, 1914–1916.

Buckingham, Joseph T. *Specimens of Newspaper Literature*. Boston: Reading, 1852.

Burt, Alfred R. *The United States, Great Britain, and British North America, 1783–1812*. New York: Russell and Russell, 1961.

Caldwell, Langton Keith. *The Administrative Theories of Hamilton and Jefferson*. Chicago: University of Chicago Press, 1944.

Callahan, North. *Henry Knox: George Washington's General*. New York: Rinehart, 1958.

Chambers, William Nisbet. *Political Parties in a New Nation: The American Experience, 1776–1809*. New York: Oxford University Press, 1963.

Channing, Edward. *A History of the United States*. 6 vols. New York: Macmillan, 1917.

Charles, Joseph. *The Origins of the American Party System: Three Essays*. New York: Harper and Row, 1956.

Chinard, Gilbert. *Honest John Adams*. Boston: Little, Brown, 1964.

————. *Thomas Jefferson: Apostle of Americanism*. Boston: Little, Brown, 1929.

Clancy, Herbert J. *The Democratic Party: Jefferson to Jackson*. New York: Fordham University Press, 1962.

Clark, Allen Cullen. *William Duane*. Washington, D.C.: n.p., 1905.

Clark, Mary E. *Peter Porcupine in America: The Career of William Cobbett, 1792–1800*. Philadelphia: University of Pennsylvania Press, 1939.

Cunliffe, Marcus. *George Washington: Man and Monument*. New York: Mentor Books, 1958.

————. *The Nation Takes Shape, 1789–1837*. A volume in the Chicago History of American Civilization Series. Edited by Daniel Boorstin. Chicago: University of Chicago Press, 1959.

Cunningham, Noble E., Jr. *The Jeffersonian-Republicans: The Formation of Party Organization, 1789–1809*. Chapel Hill: University of North Carolina Press, 1957.

————. *The Jeffersonian Republicans in Power: Party Operations, 1801–1809*. Chapel Hill: University of North Carolina Press, 1963.

Curti, Merle. *The Growth of American Thought*. New York: Harper and Row, 1943.

Dauer, Manning J. *The Adams Federalists*. Baltimore: Johns Hopkins University Press, 1968.

DeConde, Alexander. *Entangling Alliance: Politics and Diplomacy Under George Washington*. Durham, N.C.: Duke University Press, 1958.

————. *The Quasi-War: The Politics and Diplomacy of the Undeclared War with France, 1797–1801*. New York: C. Scribner's Sons, 1966.

Elson, Henry William. *History of the United States of America*. 5 vols. New York: Macmillan, 1905.

Emery, Edwin. *The Press and America: An Interpretive History of Journalism*. 2d ed. Englewood Cliffs, N.J.: Prentice-Hall, 1962.

Fay, Bernard. *Notes on the American Press at the End of the Eighteenth Century*. New York: Grolier Club, 1927.

————. *The Two Franklins: Fathers of American Democracy*. Boston: Little, Brown, 1933.

Fee, Walter R. *The Transition from Aristocracy to Democracy in New Jersey, 1789–1829*. Somerville, N.J.: Somerset Press, 1933.

Flexner, James Thomas. *George Washington and the New Nation (1783–1793)*. Volume 3 of *George Washington*. Boston: Little, Brown, 1969.

————. *George Washington: Anguish and Farewell (1793–1799)*. Volume 4 of *George Washington*. Boston: Little, Brown, 1972.

Ford, Worthington Chauncey. *Thomas Jefferson and James Thomson Callender*. Brooklyn, N.Y.: Historical Printing Club, 1897.

Freeman, Douglas Southall. *George Washington*. 7 vols. New York: Charles Scribner's Sons, 1948–1954.

Gilpatrick, Delbert H. *Jeffersonian Democracy in North Carolina, 1789–1816*. New York: Columbia University Press, 1931.

Goddard, Delano A. *Newspapers and Newspaper Writers in New England, 1787–1815*. Boston: A. Williams, 1880.

Graber, Doris A. *Public Opinion, the President, and Foreign Policy: Four Case Studies from the Formative Years*. New York: Holt, Rinehart, and Winston, 1968.

Hamilton, Milton W. *The Country Printer in New York State, 1785–1930*. New York: Columbia University Press, 1936.

Hammond, Bray. *Banks and Politics in America from the Revolution to the Civil War*. Princeton, N.J.: Princeton University Press, 1957.

Hammond, Jabez D. *The History of Political Parties in the State of New York; From the Ratification of the Federal Constitution to December, 1840.* 2 vols. Cooperstown, N.Y.: H and E. Phinney, 1846.

Handler, Edward. *America and Europe in the Political Thought of John Adams.* Cambridge: Harvard University Press, 1964.

Haraszti, Zoltan. *John Adams and the Prophets of Progress.* New York: Grosset and Dunlap, 1952.

Hazen, Charles D. *Contemporary American Opinion of the French Revolution.* Vol. 16 of Johns Hopkins University Studies in History and Political Science. Edited by Herbert Baxter Adams. 16 vols. Baltimore: Johns Hopkins University Press, 1897.

Hildreth, Richard. *The History of the United States of America.* 6 vols. New York: Harper and Brothers, 1880.

Hofstadter, Richard. *American Political Tradition and the Men Who Made It.* New York: Vintage Books, 1948.

Howe, John R., Jr. *The Changing Political Thought of John Adams.* Princeton, N.J.: Princeton University Press, 1966.

Iacuzzi, Alfred. *John Adams Scholar.* New York: S.F. Vanni, 1952.

Irelan, John Robert. *History of the Life, Administration, and Times of John Adams, Second President of the United States.* Vol. 2 of *The Republic.* Chicago: Fairbank and Palmer, 1886.

Jay, William. *The Life of John Jay.* 2 vols. New York: J.&J. Harper, 1833.

Jones, Robert W. *Journalism in the United States.* New York: Dutton, 1947.

Koch, Adrienne. *Jefferson and Madison.* New York: Oxford University Press, 1964.

Krout, John A., and Dixon Ryan Fox. *The Completion of Independence, 1790–1830.* Volume 5 of *A History of American Life.* Edited by Arthur M. Schlesinger and Dixon Ryan Fox. 13 vols. New York: Macmillan, 1944.

Kurtz, Stephen G. *The Presidency of John Adams: The Collapse of Federalism, 1795–1800.* New York: A.S. Barnes, 1961.

Leary, Lewis. *That Rascal Freneau: A Study in Literary Failure.* New Brunswick, N.J.: Rutgers University Press, 1941.

Levy, Leonard W. *Freedom of Speech and Press in Early American History: Legacy of Suppression.* New York: Harper and Row, 1963.

_____. *Jefferson and Civil Liberties: The Darker Side.* Cambridge: Belknap Press of Harvard University, 1963.

Link, Eugene Perry. *Democratic-Republican Societies, 1790–1800.* New York: Columbia University Press, 1942.

Livermore, Shaw, Jr. *The Twilight of Federalism.* Princeton, N.J.: Princeton University Press, 1962.

McMaster, John Bach. *A History of the People of the United States, from the Revolution to the Civil War.* 5 vols. New York: D. Appleton, 1885.

Malone, Dumas. *Jefferson and the Ordeal of Liberty.* Volume 3 of *Jefferson and His Time.* Boston: Little, Brown, 1962.

_____. *Jefferson and the Rights of Man.* Vol. 2 of *Jefferson and His Time.* Boston: Little, Brown, 1951.

Marsh, Philip M. *Philip Freneau: Poet and Journalist.* Minneapolis: Dillon, 1967.

Miller, John C. *Alexander Hamilton: Portrait in Paradox.* New York: Harper and Bros., 1959.

_____. *Crisis in Freedom: The Alien and Sedition Acts.* Boston: Little, Brown, 1951.

_____. *The Federalist Era, 1789–1801.* New American Nation Series. New York: Harper and Row, 1960.

Mitchell, Broadus. *Alexander Hamilton.* 2 vols. New York: Macmillan, 1957–1962.

Monaghan, Frank. *John Jay: Defender of Liberty.* New York: Bobbs-Merrill, 1935.

Morison, Samuel Eliot. *By Land and by Sea: Essays and Addresses.* New York: Knopf, 1953.

_____. *Harrison Gray Otis, 1765–1848: The Urbane Federalist.* Boston: Houghton Mifflin, 1969.

Morse, Anson E. *The Federalist Party in Massachusetts to the Year 1800.* Princeton, N.J.: University Library, 1909.

Morse, John T., Jr. *John Adams.* American Statesman Series. Boston: Houghton Mifflin, 1884.

Mott, Frank Luther. *American Journalism: A History, 1690–1960.* New York: Macmillan, 1962.

_____. *A History of American Magazines, 1741–1850.* 3 vols. New York: D. Appleton, 1930.

_____. *Jefferson and the Press.* Baton Rouge: Louisiana State University Press, 1943.

Nevins, Allan. *American Press Opinion, Washington to Coolidge.* Boston: D.C. Heath, 1928.

Perkins, Bradford. *The First Rapproachment: England and the United States, 1795–1805.* Philadelphia: University of Pennsylvania Press, 1953.

Pollard, James E. *The President and the Press.* New York: Macmillan, 1947.

Robinson, William A. *Jeffersonian Democracy in New England.* New Haven: Yale University Press, 1916.

Rogers, George C., Jr. *Evolution of a Federalist: William Loughton Smith of Charleston (1758–1812).* Columbia: University of South Carolina Press, 1962.

Rose, Lisle A. *Prologue to Democracy: The Federalists in the South, 1789–1800.* Lexington: University of Kentucky Press, 1968.

Schachner, Nathan. *Alexander Hamilton.* New York: D. Appleton, 1946.

Smelser, Marshall. *Congress Founds the Navy, 1787–1798.* Notre Dame, Ind.: University of Notre Dame Press, 1959.

Smith, J. Eugene. *One Hundred Years of Hartford's Courant; From Colonial Times Through the Civil War.* New Haven: Yale University Press, 1949.

Smith, James Morton. *Freedom's Fetters: The Alien and Sedition Laws and American Civil Liberties.* Ithaca, N.Y.: Cornell University Press, 1966.

Smith, Page. *John Adams.* 2 vols. Garden City, N.Y.: Doubleday, 1962.

Stewart, Donald H. *The Opposition Press of the Federalist Period.* Albany: State University of New York Press, 1969.

Thomas, Isaiah. *The History of Printing in America.* 2 vols. Albany, N.Y.: Joel Munsell, 1874.

Tinkcom, Harry M. *The Republicans and Federalists in Pennsylvania, 1790–1801: A Study in National Stimulus and Local Response.* Harrisburg: Pennsylvania Historical and Museum Commission, 1950.

Tolles, Frederick B. *George Logan of Philadelphia.* New York: Oxford University Press, 1953.

Weisberger, Bernard A. *The American Newspaperman.* Chicago History of American Civilization Series. Chicago: University of Chicago Press, 1961.

White, Leonard D. *The Federalists: A Study in Administrative History, 1789–1801.* New York: Free Press, 1948.

————. *The Jeffersonians: A Study in Administrative History, 1801–1829.* New York: Free Press, 1951.

Whitney, Janet. *Abigail Adams.* Boston: Little, Brown, 1947.

Wilson, Thomas Woodrow. *A History of the American People.* 5 vols. New York: William H. Wise, 1931.

Wolfe, John Harold. *Jeffersonian Democracy in South Carolina.* Chapel Hill: University of North Carolina Press, 1940.

Zobel, Hiller. *The Boston Massacre.* New York: Norton, 1970.

PAMPHLETS

"Americanus" [Beckley, John]. *Address to the People of the United States: With an Epitome and Vindication of the Public Life and Character of Thomas Jefferson.* Newport, R.I.: Oliver Farnsworth, 1800.

Aufrere, Anthony. *Cannibal's Progress; or, the Dreadful Horrors of French Invasion!* Savannah, Ga.: N. Johnston, 1798.

Bache, Benjamin Franklin. *Remarks Occasioned by the Late Conduct of Mr. Washington, as President of the United States.* Philadelphia: Benjamin Franklin Bache, 1797.

Bishop, Abraham. *An Oration on the Extent and Power of Political Delusion.* Newark, N.J.: Pennington and Gould, 1800.

Callender, James Thomson. *The American Annual Register; or, Historical Memoirs of the United States, for the Year 1796.* Philadelphia: Bioren and Madan, 1796.

————. *The History of the United States for 1796.* Philadelphia: Snowden and M'Corkle, 1797.

————. *The Prospect Before Us.* 2 vols. Richmond: James Thomson Callender, 1800.

————. *Sedgewick and Company; or a Key to a Six Per Cent Cabinet.* Philadelphia: James Thomson Callender, 1798.

Clinton, George. *An Oration, Delivered on the Fourth of July, 1798.* New York: M. L. Davis and W. A. Davis, 1798.

Cobbett, William. *History of the American Jacobins, Commonly Denominated Democrats.* Philadelphia: William Cobbett, 1796.

————. *A Little Plain English.* Philadelphia: Free and Independent Political and Literary Press of Thomas Bradford, 1797.

Cooper, Thomas. *Political Essays.* 2d ed. Philadelphia: Robert Campbell, 1800.

"Dwight, Jasper" [Duane, William]. *A Letter to George Washington, President of the United States; Containing Strictures on His Address of the Seventeenth of September, 1796.* Philadelphia: n.p., 1796.

Erskine, Thomas. *A View of the Causes and Consequences of the Present War with France.* Philadelphia: William Cobbett, 1797.

"A Federalist" [Webster, Noah]. *A Letter to General Hamilton, Occasioned by His Letter to President Adams.* New York: E. Selder, 1800.

Fenno, John Ward. *Desultory Reflections on the New Political Aspects of Public Affairs in the United States of America Since the Commencement of the Year 1799.* New York: John Ward Fenno, 1800.

Freneau, Philip N. "Robert Slender." In *Letters on Various Interesting and Important Subjects.* Philadelphia: D. Hogan, 1799.

Gardner, John. *A Brief Consideration of the Important Services, and Distinguished Virtues and Talents Which Recommend Mr. Adams for the Presidency of the United States.* Boston: Manning and Loring, 1796.

Harper, Robert Goodloe. *Observations on the Dispute Between the United States and France.* Philadelphia: William Cobbett, 1798.

Haswell, Anthony. *An Oration Delivered at Bennington, Vermont, August 16, 1799.* Bennington, Vt.: Anthony Haswell, 1799.

_____. *Patriotic Exultation on Mathew Lyon's Release from the Federal Bastile in Vergennes, State of Vermont . . . No Thanks to Power.* Bennington, Vt.: Anthony Haswell, 1799.

Hopkinson, Joseph. *What Is Our Situation? And What Our Prospects? A Few Pages for Americans, by an American.* Philadelphia: n.p., 1798.

Letter From Alexander Hamilton, Concerning the Public Conduct and Character of John Adams, Esq., President of the United States. New York: George F. Hopkins, 1800.

Lowell, John. *An Oration, Pronounced July 4, 1799.* Boston: Manning and Loring, 1799.

Ogden, Uzal. *A Letter to Major General Alexander Hamilton.* New York: George F. Hopkins, 1800.

Osgood, David. *Some Facts Evincive of the Atheistical, Anarchical, and in Other Respects, Immoral Principles of the French Republicans, Stated in a Sermon, Delivered on the 9th of May, 1798.* Boston: Samuel Hall, 1798.

Pinckney, William. *A Few Remarks on Mr. Hamilton's Late Letter.* Baltimore: Warner and Hanna, 1800.

"Slender, Robert" [Freneau, Philip N.]. *Letters on Various Interesting and Important Subjects.* Philadelphia: D. Hogan, 1799.

Smith, William Loughton. *The Pretensions of Thomas Jefferson to the Presidency Examined; And the Charges Against John Adams Refuted.* Philadelphia: n.p., 1796.

Swanwick, John. *A Rub from Snub.* Philadelphia: n.p., 1795.

Warner, George James. *Means for the Preservation of Public Liberty.* New York: Printed at the *Argus* office, 1797.

NEWSPAPERS

Connecticut
American Mercury (Hartford), 1793–1798

Bee (New London), 1797–1801

Connecticut Courant (Hartford), 1797–1801

Connecticut Gazette (New London), 1797–1798

Connecticut Journal (New Haven), 1797–1800

Middlesex Gazette (Middletown), 1797–1801

Norwich Packet, 1797–1801

District of Columbia
National Intelligencer, 1800

Georgia
Columbian Museum (Savannah), 1796

Southern Centinel (Augusta), 1797–1799

Kentucky
Kentucky Gazette (Lexington), 1795–1799

Palladium (Frankfort), 1798–1800

Maryland

American (Baltimore), 1800
Baltimore Intelligencer, 1798–1799
Maryland Gazette (Annapolis), 1795–1799
Republican Star (Easton), 1800

Massachusetts

Boston Gazette, 1791–1797
Boston Price-Current and Marine Intelligencer, 1797–1798
Columbian Centinel (Boston), 1792–1800
Constitutional Telegraph (Boston), 1799–1801
Federal Gazette (Boston), 1798
Impartial Register (Salem), 1800
Independent Chronicle (Boston), 1789–1800
Massachusetts Centinel (Boston), 1789
Massachusetts Mercury (Boston), 1797–1800
Massachusetts Spy (Worcester), 1798–1801
Political Repository (Brookfield), 1798–1801
Russell's Gazette (Boston), 1798–1800
Salem Gazette, 1797–1800

New Hampshire

Courier of New Hampshire (Concord), 1797–1800
Farmer's Weekly Museum, later the *Farmer's Museum, or Literary Gazette* (Walpole), 1797–1800
Mirrour (Concord), 1793
New Hampshire Gazette (Portsmouth), 1797–1800

New Jersey

Centinel of Freedom (Newark), 1797–1800
Federalist; New Jersey Gazette (Trenton), 1800
Genius of Liberty (Morristown), 1798–1801
Jersey Chronicle (Mt. Pleasant), 1795–1796
State Gazette (Trenton), 1797–1798

New York

American Citizen and General Advertiser (New York), 1797–1798
Argus (New York), 1797–1801
Commercial Advertiser (New York), 1798–1801
Minerva (New York), 1797
New York Journal, 1790
Spectator (New York), 1798
Temple of Reason (New York), 1800
Time Piece (New York), 1797–1798

North Carolina

North Carolina Gazette (New Bern), 1795–1797
North Carolina Minerva (Raleigh), 1797–1800
State Gazette of North Carolina (Edenton), 1798–1799
Wilmington Gazette, 1798–1800

Pennsylvania

Aurora (Philadelphia), 1790–1801; actually named the *General Advertiser* in the years 1790–1794
Carey's United States Recorder (Philadelphia), 1798
Carlisle Gazette and the Western Repository of Knowledge, 1792
Claypoole's American Daily Advertiser (Philadelphia), 1797–1798
Constitutional Diary (Philadelphia), 1799
Courier Français (Philadelphia), 1797–1798
Deutsche Porcupein (Lancaster), 1797
Gazette of the United States (Philadelphia), 1789–1800
Independent Gazeteer (Philadelphia), 1791–1796
Kline's Carlisle Weekly Gazette, 1797–1798
Minerva (Philadelphia), 1797
National Gazette (Philadelphia), 1791–1793
New World (Philadelphia), 1796–1797
Pennsylvania Packet (Philadelphia), 1789–1790
Pittsburgh Gazette, 1796–1801

Porcupine's Gazette, 1797–1799
Readinger Adler, 1797–1798
Sunbury and Northumberland Gazette, 1799–1800

Rhode Island
Newport Mercury, 1797–1800
Providence Gazette and Country Journal, 1797–1800
United States Chronicle (Providence), 1797–1800

South Carolina
City Gazette (Charleston), 1798–1800
Federal Carolina Gazette (Charleston), 1800

State Gazette (Columbia), 1797–1800
The Times (Charleston), 1800–1801

Vermont
Green Mt. Patriot (Peacham), 1798–1800
Vermont Gazette (Bennington), 1797–1798

Virginia
Alexandria Times, 1797–1800
Epitome of the Times (Norfolk), 1798–1800
Examiner (Richmond), 1799–1801
Virginia Argus (Richmond), 1800
Virginia Federalist (Richmond), 1799–1800

ARTICLES

Adair, Douglass, ed. "James Madison's Autobiography." *William and Mary Quarterly*, 3d ser., 2 (April, 1945): 191–210.
Anderson, Frank M. "Contemporary Opinion of the Virginia and Kentucky Resolutions." *American Historical Review* 5 (October, 1899): 45–63, 225–52.
_____. "The Enforcement of the Alien and Sedition Acts." *American Historical Association Annual Report for the Year 1912* (1914): 113–26.
Bailyn, Bernard. "Butterfield's Adams: Notes for a Sketch." *William and Mary Quarterly*, 3d ser., 19 (1962): 238–56.
Bemis, Samuel Flagg. "Jay's Treaty and the Northwest Boundary Gap." *American Historical Review* 27 (1922): 465–84.
_____. "Washington's Farewell Address: A Foreign Policy of Independence." *American Historical Review* 39 (1934): 250–68.
Benjamin, S.G.W. "Notable Editors Between 1776 and 1800." *Magazine of American History* 17 (1887): 97–127.
Berns, Walter. "Freedom of the Press and the Alien and Sedition Laws: A Reappraisal." *Supreme Court Review* (1970).
Brant, Irving. "Edmund Randolph, Not Guilty!" *William and Mary Quarterly*, 3d ser., 7 (1950): 179–98.
Bridenbaugh, Carl. "The Press and the Book in Eighteenth Century Philadelphia." *Pennsylvania Magazine of History and Biography* 65 (1941): 1–30.
Brinton, Clarence G. "The Membership of the Jacobin Clubs." *American Historical Review* 34 (1929): 740–56.
_____. "Political Ideas in the Jacobin Clubs." *Political Science Quarterly* 43 (1928): 249–62.
Butterfield, L.H. "The Dream of Benjamin Rush: The Reconciliation of John Adams and Thomas Jefferson." *Yale Review* 40 (1950–1951): 297–319.
Chambers, William Nisbet. "Partly Development and Party Action: The American Origins." *History and Theory* 3 (1963): 91–120.
Channing, Edward. "Washington and Parties, 1789–1797." *Massachusetts Historical Society Proceedings* 47 (1914): 35–44.

Chinard, Gilbert. "Correspondence of Jefferson and DuPont de Nemours." *American Historical Review* 37 (1932): 358–91.

Cunningham, Noble E., Jr. "John Beckley: An Early American Party Manager." *William and Mary Quarterly*, 3d ser., 13 (1956): 40–52.

Davidson, Philip G. "Virginia and the Alien and Sedition Laws." *American Historical Review* 36 (1931): 336–42.

Dumbauld, Edward. "Thomas Jefferson and Pennsylvania." *Pennsylvania History* 5 (1938): 157–65.

Dunbar, Louise B. "A Study of 'Monarchical Tendencies' in the United States from 1776 to 1801." *University of Illinois Studies in the Social Sciences* 10 (1922): 2–164.

Eastman, Frank M. "The Fries Rebellion." *Americana* 16 (1922): 71–82.

Farrand, Max. "The Judiciary Act of 1801." *American Historical Review* 5 (1899–1900): 682–86.

Fay, Bernard. "Benjamin Franklin Bache, a Democratic Leader of the Eighteenth Century." *Proceedings of the American Antiquarian Society* 40 (1930): 277–304.

Ford, Worthington Chauncey, ed. "Letters of William Duane." *Massachusetts Historical Society Proceedings* 20 (1906–1907): 257–394.

Grinnell, Frank W., ed. "Hitherto Unpublished Correspondence between Chief Justice Cushing and John Adams in 1789." *Massachusetts Law Quarterly* 27 (1942): 12–16.

Hunt, Gaillard. "Office Seeking During the Administration of John Adams." *American Historical Review* 2 (1896–1897): 241–61.

James, James Alton. "French Opinion as a Factor in Preventing War Between France and the United States, 1795–1800." *American Historical Review* 30 (1924): 44–55.

Koch, Adrienne. "Hamilton, Adams, and the Pursuit of Power." *Review of Politics* 16 (1954): 37–66.

Levy, Leonard W. "Liberty and the First Amendment: 1790–1800." *American Historical Review* 68 (1962): 22–37.

Libby, Orin G. "Political Factions in Washington's Administrations." *Quarterly Journal of the University of North Dakota* 3 (1912): 293–303.

Lyon, E. Wilson. "The Directory and the United States." *American Historical Review* 43 (1938): 514–32.

Marraro, Howard R. "Unpublished Correspondence of Jefferson and Adams to Mazzei." *Virginia Magazine of History and Biography* 51 (1943): 111–33.

Marsh, Philip M. "John Beckley; Mystery Man of the Early Jeffersonians." *Pennsylvania Magazine of History and Biography* 72 (1948): 54–69.

Morgan, Edmund S. "John Adams and the Puritan Tradition." *New England Quarterly* 34 (1961): 518–29.

Morison, Samuel Eliot. "DuPont, Talleyrand, and the French Spoliations." *Massachusetts Historical Society Proceedings* 49 (1916): 63–79.

————. "Squire Ames and Doctor Ames." *New England Quarterly* 1 (1928): 5–31.

Mott, Frank Luther. "Newspapers in Presidential Campaigns." *Public Opinion Quarterly* 8 (1944): 348–67.

Padover, Saul K. "Wave of the Past." *New Republic* 116 (1947): 14–18.

Phillips, Ulrich Bonnell, ed. "South Carolina Federalist Correspondence, 1789–1797." *American Historical Review* 14 (1908–1909): 779–96.

Reitzen, William. "William Cobbett and Philadelphia Journalism, 1794–1800." *Pennsylvania Magazine of History and Biography* 59 (1935): 223–44.

Rossiter, Clinton. "The Legacy of John Adams." *Yale Review* 46 (1957): 528–50.

Smelser, Marshall. "The Federalist Period as an Age of Passion." *American Quarterly* 10 (1958): 391–419.

————. "George Washington and the Alien and Sedition Acts." *American Historical Review* 59 (1953–1954): 322–34.

————. "George Washington Declines the Part of El Libertador." *William and Mary Quarterly*, 3d ser., 11 (1954): 42–51.

————. "The Jacobin Phrenzy: Federalism and the Menace of Liberty, Equality, and Fraternity." *Review of Politics* 13 (1951): 457–82.

Smith, James Morton. "The Sedition Law, Free Speech, and the American Political Process." *William and Mary Quarterly*, 3d ser., 9 (1952): 497–511.

Tolles, Frederick B. "Unofficial Ambassador: George Logan's Mission to France, 1798." *William and Mary Quarterly*, 3d ser., 7 (1950): 3–25.

Turner, Frederick Jackson. "The Policy of France Toward the Mississippi Valley in the Period of Washington and Adams." *American Historical Review* 10 (1905): 249–79.

Werner, Raymond C. "War Scare and Politics, 1794." *New York Historical Association Quarterly Journal* 11 (1930): 324–34.

Woodbury, Margaret. "Public Opinion in Philadelphia, 1789–1801." *Smith College Studies in History* 5 (1919–1920): 5–138.

UNPUBLISHED MATERIALS

Carroll, Warren H. "John Adams, Puritan Revolutionist: A Study in His Part in the Making of the American Revolution, 1764–1776." Ph.D. dissertation, Columbia University, 1959.

Dauer, Manning F. "The Basis of Support for John Adams in the Federalist Party." Ph.D. dissertation, University of Illinois, 1933.

Miller, William. "The Democratic Clubs of the Federalist Period, 1793–1795." Master's thesis, New York University, 1937.

Woodfin, Maude H. "Citizen Genet and His Mission." Ph.D. dissertation, University of Chicago, 1928.

Index